Praise

MW00862345

Iraq, Its Neighbors, and the United States

"While the Middle East is in a state of flux, this book tries to capture the picture of present complexities and future possibilities for Iraq, both in relationship to its neighbors and the United States. The result is an incisive, precise, and highly informative piece of work, which I highly recommend to students of the region and to policymakers."
—**Ghassan Atiyyah,** Iraq Foundation for Development and Democracy

"Ten seasoned experts take their turn in describing first a changed and still changing Iraq now eight years into its post-Saddam era and thereafter in separate chapters the diplomacy of Turkey, Iran, Saudi Arabia, the Gulf states, Syria, and Jordan vis-à-vis Iraq. Concluding chapters address Iraq in the context of Arab political reform and the American role. Abandon all jibes about collected works and committees. This is scholarship at its best."
—**L. Carl Brown,** Garrett Professor in Foreign Affairs Emeritus, Princeton University

"*Iraq, Its Neighbors, and the United States* paints a comprehensive picture of a nation and region in the balance. This collection of case studies, ably edited by Henri Barkey, Scott Lasensky, and Phebe Marr, skillfully traces the continuities and ruptures—political, economic, ethnic, and religious—that characterize Iraq's own internal dynamics as well as the external relationships between Iraq and its neighbors, with whom it is deeply enmeshed. The editors couch the question of Iraq within an effective analytical framework: through examining the interests, insecurities, threat perceptions, and strategic objectives of Iraq's neighbors and of the United States, we arrive at a clearer awareness of Iraq itself, and the many and varied challenges to its stability, prosperity, and democracy. This is an integrated, holistic approach to understanding Iraq's internal dynamics, and its new posture vis-à-vis the broader Middle East. Considering Iraq from the outside in and the inside out, a perception emerges of a country that, despite its powerful democratic aspirations and developing political and economic capacity, is still very much in thrall to sectarian contests and competing interests from both within and beyond its borders."
—**Wendy Chamberlin,** president of the Middle East Institute

"A timely and important book featuring the preeminent specialists on the region."
—**Haleh Esfandiari,** director Middle East Program, Woodrow Wilson International Center for Scholars

"This volume is the most up-to-date collection on what will be a major issue in the international politics of the Middle East for years to come— how Iraq reintegrates itself into regional politics. The authors of the chapters are among the best people writing about the topic. This is a very useful and timely contribution to the debate about Iraq as the deadline for complete American military withdrawal from the country approaches."
—**F. Gregory Gause,** III, University of Vermont

"Since the American intervention in Iraq in 2003, Baghdad's relations with all of its neighbors have been heavily influenced by the American presence. That is bound to change as the American presence in Iraq is reduced. A "new Iraq" is going to find itself navigating some very tricky waters in a "new Middle East". For those who want a reliable guide to the kinds of challenges that will face Iraq—and the United States—as a new balance of power unfolds, this is a particularly timely and informative book."
—**William B. Quandt,** University of Virginia

Iraq, Its Neighbors, and the United States

Iraq, Its Neighbors, and the United States

Competition, Crisis, and the Reordering of Power

Henri J. Barkey, Scott B. Lasensky, and Phebe Marr, editors

Foreword by James A. Baker III and Lee H. Hamilton

UNITED STATES INSTITUTE OF PEACE

WASHINGTON, D.C.

UNITED STATES INSTITUTE OF PEACE
2301 Constitution Avenue, NW
Washington, D.C. 20037
www.usip.org

First published 2011

Printed in the United States of America

The paper used in this publication meets the minimum requirements of American National Standards for Information Science—Permanence of Paper for Printed Library Materials, ANSI Z39.48-1984.

Library of Congress Cataloging-in-Publication Data

Iraq, its neighbors, and the United States : competition, crisis, and the reordering of power / edited by Henri J. Barkey, Scott B. Lasensky, and Phebe Marr.
     p. cm.
  Includes index.
  ISBN 978-1-60127-077-1 (alk. paper)
  eISBN 978-1-60127-119-8
  1. Iraq—Politics and government—2003- 2. Iraq—Foreign relations—2003- 3. United States—Foreign relations—Iraq.
4. Iraq—Foreign relations—United States. I. Barkey, Henri J.
II. Lasensky, Scott. III. Marr, Phebe.
  DS79.769.I734 2011
  327.567—dc23
                                2011031917

Contents

Foreword

On December 6, 2006, the Iraq Study Group released a report that flatly stated: "The situation in Iraq is grave and deteriorating. There is no path that can guarantee success, but the prospects can be improved."

Those simple declarative statements came after the study group—which the two of us chaired with able assistance from the U.S. Institute of Peace—had spent most of that year examining Iraq, a country that was, and remains, critical to regional stability in the Middle East. In our report, study group members made the first bipartisan assessments of the problems facing the war-torn country. We were candid. At the time, three years after Saddam Hussein had been removed from power, violence fueled by a Sunni Arab insurgency, death squads, and al Qaeda was flourishing. Widespread corruption and criminality were rampant. Sectarian conflict was tearing the country apart, making it difficult for its fledgling democracy to advance reconciliation, provide security, or promote basic services. At the same time, the domestic political debate in the United States had reached a high boil.

Although the study group recognized that there was no guarantee for success, it provided seventy-nine recommendations as a way forward in Iraq. The central focus of the recommendations called for new and enhanced diplomatic and political efforts in Iraq and the region as well as a change in the primary mission of U.S. forces in Iraq so that the country's military could begin to take control of security. If implemented, study group members believed that this approach could lead to a drawdown of U.S. troops in the 2008 time frame that the Bush administration military commanders had proposed. We also said we could support a short-term surge of troops as a way to stabilize Baghdad.

Most of the Iraq Study Group's recommendations were ultimately followed. Three years later, U.S. military forces began a drawdown. Nevertheless, eight years after the United States led an international coalition that removed Saddam Hussein from power, America is still engaged in Iraq. At every key juncture, whether it was the height of Iraq's civil strife from 2005 to 2007, or the more recent effort to transition from an American military to a civilian presence, relations with Iraq's neighbors have remained pivotal—as they will for years to come.

It is for these and other reasons that we believe it is important that Henri J. Barkey, Scott B. Lasensky, and Phebe Marr have written *Iraq, Its Neighbors, and the United States: Competition, Crisis, and the Reordering of Power.* This volume offers rich and sophisticated historical perspectives on complex relationships and issues that have shaped events on the ground in Iraq. Such understanding can help policymakers advance stability in Iraq.

Early on, according to the authors, Washington paid too little attention to Iraq's regional relations and missed opportunities to engage other countries in a shared effort to secure Iraq's borders and stabilize its politics. In the first years following the fall of Saddam Hussein, some neighboring countries worked with the United States and the new Iraq leadership. But most either sat on the sidelines or actively sought to undermine efforts.

In early 2007, following the Iraq Study Group report, the authors explain, the Bush administration began to reach out to Iraq's neighbors—working in tandem with Prime Minister Nouri al-Maliki and his government. President Obama later intensified that effort. The U.S. role has changed dramatically with the signing in 2008 of a Status of Forces Agreement with Iraq, which included a timetable for drawing down American military forces. By the end of 2011, all American troops are scheduled to depart although some uniformed personnel will probably remain for some time as trainers and to reassure both Iraq and its neighbors.

As the authors explain, Iraq is not out of the woods yet. Violence, albeit much diminished from the peak days during Iraq's greatest civil strife, continues to exact a terrible toll on the daily lives of Iraqis. The government has yet to resolve some critical issues such as the delivery of basic services including electricity, gasoline, and water. Corruption continues to breed and the economy remains too dependent on oil. Politically, stalemate has become all too common. Iraqis had to endure the fruitless spectacle of a political class incapable of agreeing upon who should govern following the 2010 elections. This paralysis, which continues to this day despite the formation of a government, does not augur well for the future.

Still, as the authors point out, one can take heart at the fact that Iraqis are beginning to embrace democratic participation. A free press, for example, is developing and activists of many stripes are beginning to have their voices heard. The road ahead remains difficult and authoritarianism remains. But those and other problems are not insurmountable. How Iraq's allies and others in the region respond is of critical importance.

This timely volume about Iraq and its neighbors, written by leading analysts and scholars, will be an important resource to anyone interested in Iraq and the Middle East. It explores new directions in Iraqi foreign policy and offers detailed portraits of each neighbor—examining their interests and influence in Iraq, and their relations with the United States. The authors also look at how post-Saddam Iraq has impacted politics in the neighboring countries and in the region as a whole. This is particularly relevant given the sweeping changes brought about by the "Arab Spring" and the ongoing transformation of Arab politics.

Understanding the impact Iraq has had on the broader strategic environment, as well as the region's impact on Iraq, is critical to the foreign policy decision-making process. Too often policies are crafted in a vacuum or with incomplete understanding of potential consequences. Events move fast and decision makers have little time to fully contemplate the broad aftereffects of their actions. This volume takes a step back and allows the reader to understand and evaluate a broad set of strategically vital relationships. The authors, as well as the U.S. Institute of Peace, should be commended for this work.

—James A. Baker III and Lee H. Hamilton

Acknowledgments

We are pleased to acknowledge the support of the United States Institute of Peace throughout the development and creation of this book and the Institute's past work to promote improved relations between Iraq, its neighbors, and the United States. As is often the case, the Institute embarks on work that is vital, necessary, and urgent—but not always politically popular. This was the case with the Institute's early efforts on Iraq's regional relations, as the Institute faced myriad challenges and political sensitivities.

Many past and present members of the Institute's staff, including Abiodun Williams, William Taylor, Daniel Serwer, Paul Hughes, Rusty Barber, Paul Stares, A. Heather Coyne, Sean Kane, Sheldon Himelfarb, Rend al-Rahim Francke, Manal Omar, and Britt Manzo, have offered their support, advice, and time at various points in the development of this book. In particular, we owe a debt of gratitude to Hesham Sallam, Robert Grace, Kerem Levitas, Sajjad Talib, Sam Parker, and Leslie Thompson, all of whom worked "above and beyond" in arranging a series of track II conferences and visits to the region in support of the project.

We also wish to acknowledge the United States Institute of Peace Press and its entire staff for their strong support of this book. Valerie Norville, Michelle Slavin, Marie Marr, and Kay Hechler have made important and lasting contributions. Kurt Volkan is a terrific and tireless editor.

When the book was in its concept phase, we received valuable insights and feedback from L. Carl Brown, Fred Hof, Steve Simon, Joseph McMillan, Adam Wasserman, Laith Kubba, and Malik Mufti. We are also grateful to the many colleagues from Iraq who have advised the Institute on its work and us as we developed this project. We are particularly grateful to Ali Dabbagh, Safeen Dizayee, Fareed Yaseen, Ghassan Atiyyah, and Saifaldin Abdul-Rahman for sharing their views with us. We are also appreciative of the involvement and advice of numerous colleagues—too many to name here—from Iraq's neighboring countries.

Two of the book's coeditors, Phebe Marr and Henri J. Barkey, have been involved in the Institute's work in the Middle East for many years—and to such a degree that might lead outside observers to confuse them with the Institute's full-time staff. Their vital contributions to this book and to USIP's work more broadly have left a lasting impression.

Last, but certainly not least, a debt of gratitude is owed to the contributors, whose patience and hard work have made this book possible. They have all been strongly supportive of and active in the Institute's Middle East program, and several of them are current or former Institute staff members. Collectively, we share the common goals of a more peaceful Iraq and a more stable and prosperous Middle East.

The editors and contributors take sole responsibility for the views expressed herein.

MIDDLE EAST

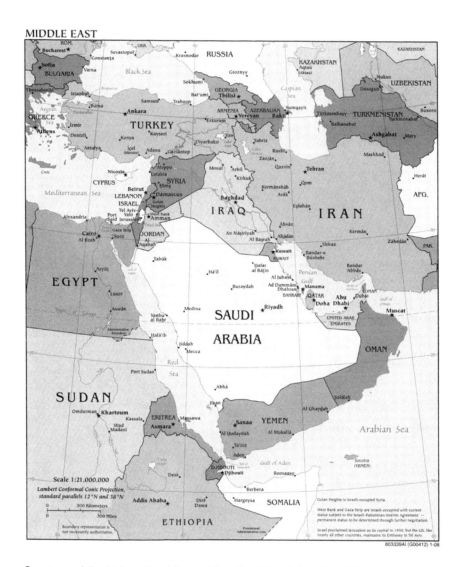

Courtesy of the University of Texas Libraries, The University of Texas at Austin

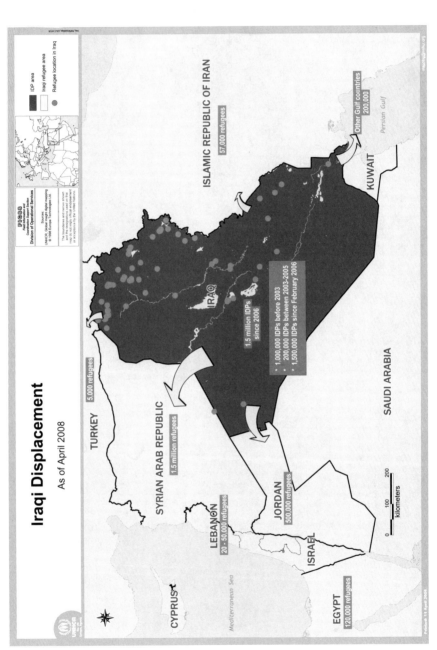

Iraqi Displacement

As of April 2008

Courtesy of UN Office for the Coordination of Humanitarian Affairs (OCHA)

TURKEY
5,000 refugees

SYRIAN ARAB REPUBLIC
1.5 million refugees

LEBANON
20 - 50,000 refugees

JORDAN
500,000 refugees

ISRAEL

EGYPT
120,000 refugees

ISLAMIC REPUBLIC OF IRAN
57,000 refugees

IRAQ

1.5 million IDPs
since 2006

* 1,000,000 IDPs before 2003
* 200,000 IDPs between 2003-2005
* 1,500,000 IDPs since February 2006

KUWAIT

Other Gulf countries
200,000

SAUDI ARABIA

Persian Gulf

Mediterranean Sea

CYPRUS

IDP area
Iraqi refugee area
Refugee location in Iraq

0 100 200
kilometers

Introduction

Henri J. Barkey, Scott B. Lasensky,
and Phebe Marr

For a quarter century, Saddam Hussein's regime in Iraq was a source of tension and uncertainty in the Middle East. Its demise has served to change the nature and focus of instability in the region as Iraq's neighbors confront a situation that is new and unprecedented. In many respects, instability has increased with unprecedented refugee flows, cross-border terror ties, heightened sectarian tensions, and a new, dangerous competition by Iraq's neighbors for influence in the former regional powerhouse, now humbled by years of sanctions, occupation, civil strife, and political gridlock. The U.S.-led overthrow of the Hussein regime, and the instability that followed, upended Iraq's relations with its neighbors, profoundly altered both the regional balance of power and America's role in the region, and fundamentally changed assumptions about Iraq's future. As destabilizing as the Ba'th regime was, fundamental power dynamics in the region are even more uncertain in the post-Saddam period, perhaps greater than at any time since the Iranian Revolution.

This uncertainty has been magnified by the tumultuous political upheavals throughout the Arab world that began in early 2011. Authoritarian leaders have been challenged by popular protests and opposition movements in a wave of unrest that has shaken the entire Arab political order. The quick ouster of autocratic leaders in Tunisia and Egypt had a powerful demonstration effect, reversing the numbing effect on regional reform and democratization brought about by the U.S. invasion of Iraq and the subsequent civil war. George W. Bush promised that U.S. action in Iraq would spark democratic reform across the greater Middle East, yet this design was deferred for nearly a decade. When the "Arab Spring" did arrive, it upended politics throughout the region. Coupled with Iraq's still emerging political order, these two transformations leave the strategic environment in flux, particularly as the United States draws down its military. Iraq and its neighbors face a new, still largely undefined regional order, complicated by divergent agendas, long histories of mistrust and conflict, and political upheavals across the region.

As the case studies in this volume demonstrate, alongside the dramatic changes brought about by the U.S. invasion and the post-Saddam political order, there is also a remarkable degree of continuity across this set of relationships. Even in the case of Iran, whose bilateral relationship with Iraq—compared with other neighbors—has been most transformed, old tensions involving boundaries, natural resources, and political identity still simmer just below the surface.

The challenge for Washington—as well as for Iraq—is to foster greater cooperation among a disparate set of actors whose narrow interests just as easily point to competition and confrontation absent a refashioned regional order. "None of Iraq's neighbors . . . see it in their interest for the situation in Iraq to lead to aggrandized regional influence by Iran," wrote the James A. Baker and Lee H. Hamilton–led Iraq Study Group in its late 2006 report that called for greater American engagement with Iraq's neighbors, including Syria and Iran. "Indeed, [the neighbors] may take active steps to limit Iran's influence, steps that could lead to an intraregional conflict. . . . Left to their own devices, these governments will tend to reinforce ethnic, sectarian, and political divisions within Iraqi society."[1]

The dominant theme of this book—that of a region unbalanced, shaped by both new and old tensions, struggling with a classic collective-action dilemma and anxiety about Iraq's political future and America's role in the region—suggests trouble ahead absent more concerted efforts to promote regional cooperation. Different neighbors will continue to have different responses to developments in Iraq, based on their individual interests, their influence, and their relationships with Washington. America's role in determining the course of these relationships is profound, and under most scenarios it will continue to be so for some years to come. But Washington is not central. Neither are any of Iraq's neighbors, on their own. There is a tendency in the United States to overemphasize America's own role in determining outcomes, just as there is a tendency to conflate attempts by

---

1. James A. Baker III and Lee H. Hamilton, et al., *The Iraq Study Group Report* (New York: Vintage Books, 2006), 48.

neighboring countries to intervene (through political manipulation, military assistance, business dealings, or economic aid) with actual impact. The reality of how Iraqi domestic politics develops, and the outcome of the popular protest movements sweeping the region, will remain decisive in shaping regional relations. Internal dynamics remain primary, not the implementation of any outside scheme or model.

Under the sponsorship of the United States Institute of Peace, a diverse team of country and area experts was assembled and charged with mapping out these complex, multidimensional relationships. Individual case studies have been published as part of a research series that began with Henri Barkey's 2005 study of Turkey and Iraq. Out of this series emerged a much broader effort to assess the full measure of Iraq's regional relations and their impact on the strategic environment—an effort that produced this book. The comprehensive survey of regional relationships that forms the basis of this book begins and ends with Iraq. Iraq's own political development is and will remain the key variable in the region's strategic environment. It will have an overriding impact on how this set of regional relationships develops over time.

New Tensions

Despite a long-standing set of core interests and threat perceptions that have shaped Iraq's relations with its neighbors throughout the modern era, post-Saddam Iraq presents new challenges and new sources of tension. Prior to 1991, Iraq's strength, ambition, and aggressiveness were the source of instability in the region. Saddam invaded two neighbors—Iran and Kuwait— terrorized his own population, and threatened and intimidated other neighbors. The Iraqi threat, conventional wisdom used to hold, was itself a product of Iraq's military and political strength and Saddam's ambitions. This assumption is no longer valid. The Iraqi threat for some time will be weakness, not strength—specifically, its inability to act as a counterbalance to Iran's regional ambitions and to contain the spillover effects of its fragile domestic situation. This fragility has generated new tensions, as has Iraq's new political order.

The new Iraq, as unfinished as it may appear to be, is very different than its preceding incarnations. It is a federal entity where the Kurds have an important say in both domestic and foreign policy. Neither is it a "Sunni" state, as the Shiite majority has not only secured the right to vote in competitive elections but has also repeatedly demonstrated a baseline of cohesion that defies its many intrasectarian rifts. As Turkey and Iran gain influence in the region, Middle Eastern politics may become more fractured and decidedly less "Arab." Iraq in the future will remain part of this new order, even if the nature and degree of its participation is not certain. It is also likely to be quite unconstrained by the traditional dogmas of Arab politics, given its close ties with Iran, Turkey, and the United States. This has left Iraq's Arab neighbors uneasy, and it could be a generation or more before they are fully reconciled with Iraq's new political order.

Moreover, having been the source of regional grievance for decades, Iraq is now ruled by an aggrieved political elite, some with their own scores to settle with Iraq's neighbors, the United States, and opposing groups at home.[2] Out of the upheaval and violence that has characterized Iraqi politics, a new political elite has arisen that is willing to wield sectarian identity in order to prevail over its rivals, particularly over former Ba'thists and Sunnis—a trend that creates concern among many of Iraq's neighbors. Grievance and victimhood are not the defining elements of Iraqi foreign policy—interests certainly prevail—but they are unmistakable features and ones that regional players are unaccustomed to dealing with, given the Iraqi state's long history of bullying its neighbors and internal opponents.

As a result, Iraq's neighbors are faced with a complicated set of factors. They face the prospect of political instability and the ever-present threat of civil war, whether sectarian or ethnic in nature. Understandably, in a region where ethnic, sectarian, and cultural affiliations straddle boundaries, the likelihood of a regional contamination effect is of primary importance for Iraq's neighbors. The chapters on Turkey, Syria, Jordan, and Saudi Arabia certainly reflect this heightened anxiety about the implications of Iraq's new identities. As Toby Jones points out in his chapter on Saudi Arabia, almost a decade has passed since Saddam's regime was ousted, and yet Riyadh is still not reconciled to Iraq's new politics and its altered regional posture. On the opposite side of the ledger stands Iran, where the post-Saddam order has been energetically embraced. Tehran has cultivated Iraq's new political elite and has built extensive networks of influence across Iraq, as Mohsen Milani lays out in his chapter.

Other neighbors, like Turkey, faced new challenges with the fall of Saddam and the rise of Kurdish power in Iraq. But unlike Riyadh, Ankara has managed to adapt and refashion its approach to Iraq. This shift by Turkey, from containment to engagement, is deeply intertwined with domestic political developments and the ruling Justice and Development Party's (AKP's) emphasis on renewing the country's regional role. As Henri Barkey argues in his chapter, Turkey's position on Iraq has moved 180 degrees over a relatively brief period.

---

2. For profiles of Iraq's new political class, see Phebe Marr, *Who Are Iraq's New Leaders? What Do They Want?* Special Report no. 160 (Washington, DC: United States Institute of Peace Press, March 2006).

There is also tension concerning the United States' long-term influence and presence in Iraq, concomitant with a military relationship that will invariably include arms sales, a novel development given the long-term enmity that had characterized relations between Baghdad and Washington. The nature of America's role in Iraq is still an open question, but one that poses a variety of dilemmas for Iraq's neighbors—whether adversaries, like Iran and Syria, or allies, like Jordan, Kuwait, Turkey, and Saudi Arabia. It also poses a major dilemma for Iraq itself, perhaps the greatest foreign policy test for Iraq's post-Saddam leadership. Balancing Iraq's reliance on U.S. security assistance with the country's own homegrown nationalist sentiments—not to mention Iraq's newfound and strong ties with Iran—will be no easy feat. Reconciling Iraq's domestic politics with these two pivotal relationships—Washington and Tehran—would go a long way toward reducing regional tensions.

Continuities

Iraq's fragility, its altered political landscape, and the U.S. intervention may have led to new tensions, but these coexist with a high degree of continuity in Iraq's regional relations. Iraq's unresolved boundary and natural resource and financial disputes with its neighbors are no less prominent than in years past. As Phebe Marr and Sam Parker argue in their chapter on Iraq, the traditional cross-border tensions Saddam so eagerly exploited have not disappeared and are likely to plague regional relations for years to come. Political rivalries have also not faded, as with Iraq's uneasy relations with Syria. "Hostility and rivalry then are the norm," Mona Yacoubian writes in her chapter.

Iraq's hydrocarbon wealth and the ways in which it shapes regional relations represent another point of continuity. Iraq's oil infrastructure suffered terribly from Saddam's wars and the panoply of sanctions imposed by the international community. A rejuvenated Iraqi oil industry may once again return Iraq to a position of regional power broker. Moreover, Iraq will reemerge as an oil and gas exporter. Given the devastation caused by successive wars, oil and gas provide the fastest means to marshalling the resources Iraq will need to rebuild its infrastructure and improve its citizens' standard of living. As of 2010, Iraqi oil exports were not very significant for world consumption. However, the expansion of its oil production capacity—especially considering that very little in the form of modern-day exploration has taken place since 1980—will make Iraq a formidable power in oil markets, and potentially a competitor once again with Saudi Arabia, given differing outlooks on price and production levels. While increasing its capacity may be desirable for Iraq, neighbors may not be as keen. In this context it is worth remembering that Iraq is an almost land-locked country; it will be in need of its neighbors for commerce and trade, especially the export of oil and gas.[3] For the foreseeable future, oil could continue to shape ties with other neighbors, like Turkey and Syria—which seek to be outlets for Iraqi exports—and with Jordan, which hopes to perpetuate its Saddam-era oil perks, as Scott Lasensky explores in his chapter. Environmental challenges plaguing Iraq and its neighbors have also been long in the making, but the pace of change has accelerated them. Water may be the most prominent among these, and is certain to complicate Iraq's ties with Iran, Syria, and Turkey for the foreseeable future.

Some of the continuity is regionwide, as with the case of Arab po-litical reform. Despite the expressed intentions and hopes of the Bush administration—not to mention Arab reformers themselves—the net im-pact of the post-Saddam political order has been to stunt political devel-opment, as authoritarian regimes have used Iraq's instability to tighten their grip on power. As Hesham Sallam argues in his chapter, disparate reform-ist camps initially united in opposition to the U.S. occupation, but as Iraq began to come apart at the seams the ruling Arab regimes regained the upper hand. Iraq's demonstration effect may very well be the opposite of what George W. Bush had hoped for.

Collective-Action Dilemma

Iraq, the United States, and Iraq's neighbors share a common interest in a cohesive, stable Iraq. But nearly a decade after the fall of Saddam there's no consensus on how to achieve stability. It is a classic collective-action dilemma that is exacerbated by metaconflicts between Arabs and Iran, and between the United States and Iran. As Ken Pollack argues in his chapter, the need for collective action is two-fold. Most urgently, it is needed to prevent another civil war. But over time, there is also a shared interest in preventing Iraq's reemergence as a powerhouse that could again threaten its neighbors. The Bush administration, following recommendations of the Iraq Study Group, reluctantly initiated a regional diplomacy process in 2007, but its commitment to engage with adversaries like Syria and Iran was half-hearted at best. Moreover, Iraqis soon grew to resent this multilateral process. They felt like the region's charity case and instead opted to deal with the neighbors and the United States in a more ad hoc, direct way.

---

3. See Joseph McMillan, *Saudi Arabia and Iraq: Oil, Religion, and an Enduring Rivalry*, Special Report no. 157 (Washington, DC: United States Institute of Peace Press, January 2006).

President Barack Obama, despite a stronger commitment to regional diplomacy, did not fare much better in his first two years—an attempt to cooperate with Syria vis-à-vis Iraq was vetoed by Baghdad; outreach to Iran stalled early; and entreaties to Saudi Arabia to engage Iraq appear to have fallen on deaf ears. With the United States drawing down, Iraq still too weak to lead, none of Iraq's neighbors positioned to drive a regional process, and revolutionary contagion sweeping the region, the collective-action dilemma appears likely to persist.

Uncertainty

Fourth, and last, the case studies in this volume highlight a common theme of uncertainty. As Marr and Parker lay out, there are radically divergent futures for Iraq, each of which would suggest a different set of regional relationships. The uncertainty reigning over Iraq's future creates myriad temptations for the neighbors to intervene. In the pursuit of greater influence in Baghdad and around the country, the neighbors intercede not just to shape future events and policies so as to better align them with their own interests, but also to deny others, be they other neighbors or the United States, from achieving any gains at their own expense. The temptation to intervene is not always malevolent in intent but predicated by concerns over self-preservation, as may be the case with preventing ethnic or sectarian spillover effects, or even spurred by benign intentions designed to help a struggling neighbor. Nonetheless, what is important is how these interventions are perceived by neighbors and other interested parties.

As the neighbors plan and execute their policies on Iraq, they will not just be influencing events in that country; their actions will have regional implications, including the possibility for triggering chain reactions that could contribute to furthering instability in the region. The unintended consequences of their behavior loom large over the future of Iraq and the region. Were they to engage in an intense round of competition among themselves for influence, they stand the possibility of undermining their own relations with each other. Moreover, given the wide diversity of interests among the neighbors and the high probability of miscalculation and error, understanding how they view Iraq and interact with it is of critical importance to the United States, not only to fully understand the threat, but also to appreciate the opportunities that lay ahead. As the Iraq Study Group said in 2006,

> The United States must build a new international consensus for stability in Iraq and the region. In order to foster such consensus, [it] should embark on a robust

diplomatic effort to establish an international support structure intended to stabilize Iraq and ease tensions in other countries in the region. This support structure should include every country that has an interest in averting a chaotic Iraq, including all of Iraq's neighbors—Iran and Syria among them. Despite the well-known differences between many of these countries, they all share an interest in avoiding the horrific consequences that would flow from a chaotic Iraq, particularly a humanitarian catastrophe and regional destabilization.[4]

President Obama echoed these ideas in a major Iraq policy address early in his administration:

> The future of Iraq is inseparable from the future of the broader Middle East, so we must work with our friends and partners to establish a new framework that advances Iraq's security and the region's. It is time for Iraq to be a full partner in a regional dialogue, and for Iraq's neighbors to establish productive and normalized relations with Iraq. And going forward, the United States will pursue principled and sustained engagement with all of the nations in the region, and that will include Iran and Syria.[5]

The U.S. decision to disengage from Iraq is in principle not contingent solely on developments in Iraq; the fact remains that the pace of the withdrawal and nature of U.S. involvement will be determined by progress in Iraq, actions of neighbors, and America's ability to promote the kind of international support structure first outlined by the Iraq Study Group.[6]

Methodology

The bulk of this book is devoted to analyses of Iraq's immediate neighbors. These case studies adhere to a common analytical framework. First, they are designed to probe various interests and threat perceptions of the neighbors. How have threat perceptions developed/changed throughout various historical eras? What is the impact of domestic politics, and the neighbors' broader foreign policy objectives—specifically, are there political divides that impact Iraq policy? Second, they focus on each neighbor's vectors of influence in Iraq—economic, political, etc. How does each neighbor use its influence? What are the limiting or enabling factors to the country's influence in Iraq? How do they perceive their influence, both on its own, and also in relation to the influence of other regional actors? Lastly, the book looks at how the neighbors' interests and influence intersect with those of the United States. Are they compatible or problematic? How can differences be reconciled?

---

4. Baker and Hamilton, et al., *Iraq Study Group Report*, 32.
5. President Barack Obama, "Responsibly Ending the War in Iraq" (speech, Camp Lejeune, North Carolina, February 27, 2009).
6. Baker and Hamilton, et al., *Iraq Study Group Report*, 32–36.

In addition, a centerpiece of the book is a chapter on Iraq's threat perceptions and expectations vis-à-vis its neighbors—a treatment that captures the range of Iraqi views, and sets forth a variety of alternative futures (Marr and Parker). Individual snapshots of Iraqi views on particular neighbors are woven into each case study. In an attempt to widen the lens, the book also includes two broadly defined thematic chapters. The first explores how post-Saddam Iraq has affected political contestation in the Arab world and what impact it has had on relations between regimes and the opposition (Sallam). The second addresses the American role in Iraq and how Iraq's regional relations have affected long-term U.S. strategic interests and the regional order as a whole. This chapeau essay draws upon the individual chapters and assesses the broader impact of these relationships and Iraq's radically changed position in the regional order (Pollack).[7]

Collectively, these chapters focus on the differing interests and motivations of the neighbors and Iraq and aim at providing context and understanding to future policy choices. The book does not aim at predicting future courses of action. It does, however, factor in both Iraqi and American views in that it tries to also answer how Iraqis perceive their neighbors. Iraq, needless to say, is also an actor in the drama unfolding in the region. The policies and the positions taken by its constituent groups and parties are shaping the country's future.

Finally, the United States does not face easy choices in Iraq. Washington will continue to maintain its large diplomatic and assistance missions in Iraq, not to mention its military assets that are deployed close to Iraq's borders. That said, there is a process of drawdown under way, and it will inevitably lessen America's ability to assert itself as

- an arbiter of Iraqi domestic political disputes;
- the principal provider of external assistance to the new Iraqi state;
- a defender of Iraq's interests and sovereignty in regional and international fora.

America also confronts a paradox. Reassuring Iraqis (and the neighbors) about the lasting nature of U.S. involvement may undermine steps Iraqis and the neighbors need to take to reconcile. But the opposite message that Washington intends to pull out lock, stock, and barrel could set off a

---

7. Two case studies—Israel and Egypt—were not included in this volume. Historically, Israeli-Iraqi tension has been an important factor shaping Arab politics and the Arab-Israeli conflict. But with the fall of Saddam and Iraq's increasing preoccupation with its new participatory politics, the Israel factor has receded. While not unimportant, Israel falls outside the framework of this study, as does Egypt. Cairo and Baghdad have a long, often troubled history as competitors for Arab leadership. There is also a post-Saddam story involving Iraqi refugees, Arab opposition to the U.S. occupation, and halting attempts at regional and Iraqi reconciliation. Still, the organizing principle for this book from the outset has been Iraq's immediate neighbors.

regional rush to exploit the power vacuum and set off domestic power plays. In this respect, the current approach of a measured drawdown, combined with increased engagement with Iraq's neighbors, strikes a good balance. It is effectively the policy Bush handed off to Obama, though rarely cast that way for political reasons. If anything, the Obama administration learned in its first two years the merits of the policy it was handed, even if the larger Iraq issue was infused with deep-seated political acrimony.

The likelihood for complex challenges emerging at a moment's notice will necessitate deeper diplomatic engagement between the United States, Iraq, and Iraq's neighbors. With this in mind, we believe that the book has unique value in the breadth of its findings and in the common framework of analysis employed by the research team and hope that it will provide the policy community, scholars, and students with a comprehensive picture of the role that Iraq's neighbors could play in advancing the country's transition to security and stability.

I
The View from Iraq

1

The New Iraq

The Post-2003 Upheavals and Regional Aftershocks

Phebe Marr and Sam Parker

Since the U.S. invasion in March 2003, Iraq has undergone unprecedented civil violence and fundamental political and social change. The Saddam Hussein regime was driven out, the country's military disintegrated and was disbanded by the United States, and the ruling elite fled the country or went underground. Exiled political leaders of all kinds (secularists and Islamists, those living in the West and the Middle East), including an emboldened Kurdish leadership already ensconced in the north, moved in to fill the political vacuum. As postwar politics evolved, indigenous voices—the Shiite Sadrist movement and the nationalist, predominantly Sunni resistance—challenged both the exiles and the U.S. occupation. Over time, these actors gradually shifted from armed struggle and violence to participation in the new political order, but the process has been halting and tentative.

Despite these vectors toward state consolidation, the process remains fragile and incomplete. Violent conflict has largely given way to a political struggle for power within accepted contours. However, a clearly defined, coherent polity has not yet emerged. The most prominent divisions are sectarian and ethnic, with a Shi'a-dominated government that has only reluctantly included Sunnis, particularly those connected to the former regime, and with efforts by the Kurdish Regional Government (KRG) to maximize its autonomy and expand its territory. Even within the political blocs of Sunni and Shi'a, Arab and Kurd, profound divisions remain, both political and tribal. In addition, there are ideological disputes over fundamental issues such as state structure, the relationship between religion and state, and Iraq's engagement with foreign powers, both in the region and throughout the world.

Despite these changes, enduring features of Iraqi history, political culture, and geography—as well as the realities of Iraq's strategic position in the region—are reasserting themselves. The Iraqi state is slowly reemerging and, with it, so too are its long-established traditions of statecraft and power maintenance. These include a proclivity for a strong central government, personal control by political leaders over the instruments of power, a sense of nationalism and a desire for unity (at least among Arabs), dislike of foreign interference, and a recognition of Iraq's potential economic and political power. These trends are already in evidence. Recent history—the Saddam era—has also produced a legacy not only of Iraqi strength but of a desire for regional hegemony, often at the expense of neighbors, that lingers in certain quarters. Given this recent history, neighbors understandably fear the return of a nationalistic Iraq with aspirations of regional dominance. As Iraq's government consolidates, its military rearms, and its society recovers, the concern over a strong Iraqi state will increase, both domestically and regionally. This concern is already evident internally among the Kurdish community, which would like to keep Iraq a highly decentralized state.

However, Iraq is not yet on the verge of becoming a strong state. The primary problem is the legacy of societal distrust left not only by the post-2003 civil conflict but also by the decades-long oppression of Saddam and the effort to remove him. This lack of trust, combined with Iraq's nascent and weak political institutions and lack of a tradition of sharing power, means that Iraq's progress toward democracy and inclusivity will come at the direct cost of state functioning. The 2010 national elections illustrated this trend. They were largely free and fair and marked a major step forward in Iraq's democratic development, particularly by regional standards. However, the inconclusive result and the long, fractious period of government formation highlighted the divisions within the Iraqi polity and the zero-sum attitude that dominates so many Iraqis' approach to politics. These systemic problems will not be solved quickly.

But the election also showed that it is Iraqi domestic forces and personalities that will determine the outcome, not regional actors, however much they may wish to. The electorate itself may play an increasing role. In 2010, it sent a message that political actors cannot ignore—its desire for the return of an Iraqi state and a government that can deliver normalcy and services and a preference for economic development over political bickering. While all of Iraq's neighbors were involved to some degree in an effort to influence the election, the results were a lesson on the limits of their ability to control the outcome.

Iran, presumably the leading regional player in Iraq, attempted to get a unified Shiite coalition together that would maintain Shiite dominance under its sway. It failed. Incumbent prime minister Nuri al-Maliki, a key Shiite player, split the coalition, ran independently on an Iraqi national-ist platform, and almost came in first; the rump Shiite ticket came in a poor third, largely because it was seen as too sectarian and pro-Iranian. The Turks and the Arab states, most notably Saudi Arabia, opposed a Shi'a-dominated government in Baghdad and supported the Sunni-backed secular ticket led by Ayad Allawi. He had surprising success in reversing his previous poor electoral showings, with a two-vote edge over his rival, Maliki, but failed to achieve a dominant position in the new government. While the neighbors will continue to interfere in a weakened Iraq, it is Iraqis who will determine these issues—bargaining domestically and balancing outside powers (including the United States) to achieve their goals, one of which is to regain their sovereignty. They already show every sign of doing so.

Nonetheless, given events since 2003, the return of a unified Iraqi state, in full control of its territory and its policy, is still a work in progress and, in any case, is a considerable distance away. In the short term (three to five years), it is the recent changes, rather than the continuities, that will most define the relationship between Iraq and its neighbors. The most important of these changes are a weak Iraqi state, the dominance of new political groups in power (with new alignments with neighbors), and Iraq's new strategic relationship with the United States.

Changes in Post-2003 Iraq

A Weak Iraqi State

Under Saddam Hussein, the Iraqi state reached its apogee as a unified, strong state with a central government capable of extending its power throughout its territory and controlling its borders. Since its founding by the British, the growth of the Iraqi state has been episodic and troubled, but constant. A key element in this state formation has been the military, which steadily grew in size and domestic importance. The 1958 revolt (which ended the monarchy) put the military in power in Iraq, and in the decades between 1960 and 1990, Iraq and its military came to play an increasingly assertive role in the region, often with disastrous consequences.

In 1961, Prime Minister Abd al-Karim Qasim laid claim to Kuwait, resulting in his regional isolation and contributing to his eventual overthrow.

In the mid-1960s, at the height of a pan-Arab trend in the region, Iraq was constantly drawn into Arab politics to the detriment of its internal stability, and in 1967 it participated in the Arab war with Israel. The Arab rout in that venture again contributed to the fall of the military-based regime in Baghdad. When the Ba'th came to power in 1968, Saddam, a civilian, asserted control over the military, but used it to expand Iraq's influence in the region, helped by growing oil revenues in the 1970s. As Iraq's military and economic resources grew, especially after Saddam became president in 1979, it became a threat to its neighbors. In 1980, after provocations from the new Islamic regime in Tehran, Saddam attacked Iran, a much larger neighbor but one gravely weakened by the turmoil accompanying its revolution. Despite a calamitous eight-year war with that country, which ended with no gains in 1990, Saddam once again resorted to military means to solve a diplomatic problem by attacking and occupying Kuwait, a small, vulnerable neighbor. This action was only reversed by an international military action, followed by a decade of severe sanctions that weakened both Saddam and the Iraqi state. Iraq, as a strong state, with aggressive leadership and a growing military capacity, had proved to be a destabilizing influence in the region.

This situation is now reversed. Iraq is viewed as a potential threat by its neighbors because it is weak and fragmented, with a government that cannot control all of its territory. In the post-2003 era, Iraq's most significant interactions with its neighbors have been the result of a range of social ills that have spilled across its borders. These include militancy—that is, cells of active, violent extremists who operate in Iraqi territory and can cross its borders (al-Qaida, Kurdistan Workers' Party [PKK])—crime (smuggling, gangs, and violence associated with illegal activity), and, above all, refugees.[1] Syria and Jordan alone are host to as many as 1.6 million Iraqis who have fled Iraq's violence and who constitute a long-term financial and social burden on Damascus and Amman.[2] Lastly, the rise of ethnic and sectarian identity in Iraq has caused anxiety in neighbors who fear its impact on their own populations. Turkey fears the spread of Kurdish

---

1. International Crisis Group (ICG), *Failed Responsibility: Iraqi Refugees in Syria, Jordan and Lebanon* (Brussels: ICG, July 10, 2008). For a good study of these refugees, see Joseph Sassoon, *The Iraqi Refugees* (London: I.B. Taurus, 2009).

2. Numbers are current as of February 2010: see Office of the United Nations High Commissioner for Refugees (UNHCR), "2010 UNHCR Country Operations Profile—Iraq," www.unhcr.org/cgi -bin/texis/vtx/page?page=49e486426. Estimates vary widely due to lack of reliable reporting data. The 1.6 million figure is based on Jordanian (500,000) and Syrian government (1.1 million) estimates. These numbers constitute the upper limit of the estimates, as regime figures are based on cross-border movements and thus may count persons more than once. See United States Government Accountability Office (GAO), *Iraqi Refugee Assistance* (Washington, DC: GAO, April 2009).

separatism, and Saudi Arabia and Bahrain fear the impact of rising Shiite power on their own Shiite populations, especially in the wake of the antiregime demonstrations that swept much of the Arab world early in 2011.

The weakness of the Iraqi state and Iraq's highly contested politics have also resulted in the country becoming a forum for regional competition. The Arab states, Iran, and Turkey all have an interest in influencing the shape and direction of the Iraqi state and the composition of its leadership, as well as in pursuing material advantages. While each state has different policy orientations and priorities and supports different groups, all neighbors have an interest in an Iraq that is strong enough to prevent massive spillover like that seen at the peak of the conflict, but not so strong that it could again pose a threat to their stability.

The neighbors' interference in Iraq takes various forms. It includes active support to mainstream political actors, such as Iran's support for the Islamic Supreme Council of Iraq (ISCI).[3] The neighbors also provide support to militants to destabilize Iraq, either directly, as in the case of Iranian support to Sadrist factions, such as the "special groups" (splinter factions from the Sadrist Mahdi Army),[4] or indirectly, as in the case of Syrian acquiescence to foreign fighters entering Iraq and the support by individual Saudis (as opposed to the government) to Salafi-jihadi insurgents.[5] Turkey has been active in increasing its economic interests in the KRG, not only for economic gain but to achieve some leverage over local politics. As Mohsen Milani indicates in his chapter, Iran is active on a broader front (including political, cultural, religious, and economic) than the other neighbors, working to shore up a popular basis for pro-Iranian sentiment in Iraq.

New Political Groups in Power (with New Alignments with Neighbors)

Iraq is a country of striking demographic diversity, with a variety of ethnic, sectarian, tribal, and socioeconomic components. This demography straddles borders. The Shiite population, roughly 60 percent of Iraq's population,

---

3. ICG, *Shiite Politics in Iraq: The Role of the Supreme Council* (Brussels: ICG, November 15, 2007).

4. For an excellent, detailed analysis of Iranian support for militants in Iraq, see Marisa Cochrane, *The Fragmentation of the Sadrist Movement* (Washington, DC: Institute for the Study of War, January 2009).

5. For more on Syrian acquiescence, see James A. Baker III and Lee H. Hamilton, et al., *The Iraq Study Group Report* (New York: Vintage Books, 2006), 29; Brian Fishman, ed., *Bombers, Bank Accounts and Bleedout: Al-Qa'ida's Road in and out of Iraq* (West Point, NY: Combating Terrorism Center, 2008), especially chapters 2 and 4. For more on individual Saudi support, see Christopher M. Blanchard and Alfred B. Prados, *Saudi Arabia: Terrorist Financing Issues* (Washington, DC: Congressional Research Service, September 14, 2007), 7–9.

has religious and cultural links of varying degrees of strength with the Shi'a of Iran. The Arabic-speaking population, some 80 percent, have linguistic and in some cases strong cultural ties to neighboring Arab states, especially Syria and Jordan. These ties are particularly strong among the Arab Sunni population, a minority of about 20 percent, which has often affiliated politically with Arab Sunnis across the borders in Syria, Jordan, Palestine, and Egypt, mainly on the basis of various iterations of Arab nationalist ideology. The Kurdish population, 17–20 percent, has strong linguistic and political links to Kurds in Turkey, Iran, and Syria. There are tribal links between tribes in western Iraq and Arab neighbors and shared family ties between the Arab populations of Basra and Kuwait, as well as other crosscutting linkages.

These linkages have always affected Iraq's foreign policy and its attitude toward neighbors, but the new Iraqi political order has produced a major shift. From the monarchy through the Saddam era, Arab Sunnis dominated political decision making (although they did so in the name of other ideologies) and their rule was buttressed by the support of a relatively secular middle class. From the mid-1960s on, Iraq, led by Arab Sunnis influenced by Arab nationalism, was increasingly drawn into pan-Arab politics.[6] A growing Kurdish national movement in the north, which intermittently challenged the government militarily between 1961 and 1975, was repressed by the government. The same was true for a budding Shiite Islamist movement in the south. Both of these movements had support from Iran, although under different circumstances.[7] Suspicion and distrust of Iran reached its apogee after the onset of the Iranian Revolution in 1979–80 and open Iranian calls for the overthrow of the Iraqi regime. When Saddam initiated the Iran-Iraq War (1980–88), both Kurdish and Shiite opposition movements, headquartered in Iran, fought with Iranians to unseat the Saddam government, but they failed.

---

6. These leaders included those in charge of the First Ba'thist regime (February–November 1963), the regime of the Arif brothers (November 1963–July 1968), and the Ba'thist regime that followed, first under Ahmad Hasan al-Bakr as president to 1979 and then under Saddam Hussein until 2003. While Arab Shi'a played a role in some of these regimes (especially the First Ba'th regime, led by Shi'a), the political orientation of these regimes was secular and nationalist, eschewing sectarian identity—at least officially.

7. The Kurdish movement under Mulla Mustafa Barzani was given military and financial aid by the Shah in the early 1970s to weaken the new Ba'th government and to make material gains. After compelling Saddam to sign the Algiers Agreement giving Iran half of the Shatt al-Arab in 1975, this aid was withdrawn and the Kurdish movement temporarily collapsed. Most Kurdish leaders, including the Barzanis, took refuge in Iran, where they remained until 1991. The Islamist Da'wa Party, established in Najaf in 1957, was indigenous and had few ties of significance to Iran under the Shah. After numerous challenges to the Ba'th regime in the 1970s, it was repressed and outlawed. However, in 1979, its leader, Muhammad Baqir al-Sadr, sided with the Iranian revolutionaries and, in 1980, was brutally executed. This domestic Shiite challenge was a major factor, but not the only one, in Saddam's decision to go to war with Iran.

The new political order represents a dramatic change in the dominant parties in power and consequently in relations with neighbors. Shi'a, mainly from the Islamist opposition parties who spent years in Iran, and Kurdish nationalist parties with previous ties to Iran, are in control of the government. Arab Sunnis and secularists (whether Sunni or Shiite), especially those with ties to the previous regime, have largely lost out, although since their rout in the January 2005 election some are making a modest comeback. The 2010 elections gave a secular, nationalist ticket, strongly backed by Sunnis, a slight plurality of votes. However, it is important to remember that none of these large ethnic and sectarian blocs is homogeneous; all are split into parties or factions that draw on ethnic and sectarian identity for their support. Moreover, an elaborate set of checks and balances among the various parties competing for power has emerged in the new Iraqi politics (based on an implicit ethnic and sectarian quota system) for important positions, known as *muhassasa* (share). This keeps any one group from dominating but also makes it difficult for the Iraqi government to develop coherent policy.

It is this shift in political parties and the underlying change in the ethnic and sectarian basis of their support that has resulted in a concurrent shift in Iraq's relations with its neighbors and in the threats the neighbors perceive to be emanating from Iraq.

The Shiite Parties with Ties to Iran. As indicated, the new Shiite leaders who have dominated government since 2005 not only spent decades in exile in Iran but also continue to receive support from the Iranian regime. This is primarily the case for ISCI and its associated Badr Corps militia, technically disbanded but with many members absorbed into the security forces. Both were created and organized by the Islamic Republic to fight against Saddam during the Iran-Iraq War.[8] Da'wa's links to Iran are weaker, as the party was fragmented in exile and resistant to Iran's effort to control the Shiite resistance, but some wings of the party, such as Da'wa–Iraq Organization have stronger ties with Iran. Nonetheless, two of Iraq's elected (Da'wa) prime ministers, Ibrahim al-Ja'fari and Nuri al-Maliki, and some of their key advisers have spent significant time in Iran and maintain active ties there. Finally, though Sadrists have been anti-Iranian in rhetoric and spent their time prior to 2003 inside Iraq, Iran has funded and cultivated various Sadrists factions to act as surrogates against the United States and as a balancing force against other Shiite parties. In 2007, Muqtada al-Sadr went to Iran to study for advanced clerical status and has since come under

---

8. ICG, *Shiite Politics in Iraq*, 10–11.

increased Iranian control and influence.[9] In 2010, Sadrists joined the second Maliki government.

In varying degrees, these parties share religious and ideological aims with the Islamic Republic. ISCI has historically supported clerical rule on the Iranian model (*wilayat al-faqih*), although in recent years it has distanced itself from this model because of its unpopularity in Iraq. Sadrists also support a form of *wilayat al-faqih*, although one led by themselves, not by Iran.[10] Da'wa, though it has deemphasized religious rhetoric since 2007, nonetheless remains a proselytizing party committed to Islamizing Iraqi state and society. These Shiite leaders, although competitive, want to remain in power. To do so, they have drawn on a new historical and political narrative that appeals to their Shiite constituency. It emphasizes the fact that Iraq's "Shiite majority" has been discriminated against politically since its founding, never achieving top political or military positions or adequate political representation in the state's governing institution, and that the time has now come to rectify this situation. Emphasis on Shiite identity as part of the electoral process helps ensure a majority for Shi'a in Parliament and, as a result, the top government positions. Hence, this narrative has some appeal, even for secular Shi'a who do not like sectarianism or the religious agenda of the main Shiite parties. In addition to the political logic of this narrative, these parties, with a still fragile hold on power, carry with them a bitterness over their repression by the Ba'th, their long exile, and their victimization by the previous regime.[11] They do not want the Ba'th—or their Arab Sunni supporters—back in power. Stressing Shiite identity helps prevent this.

The dominance of the Shiite religious parties also helps account for the critical political role of Ayatollah Ali al-Sistani, the leading Shiite cleric and *marja' al-taqlid* (source of emulation) in the new system. Indeed, he played a major role in ensuring an early electoral process in Iraq that would achieve a Shiite majority and in assembling and supporting the grand Shiite coalition, the United Iraqi Alliance, which achieved a Shiite victory in Iraq's first and second elections in January and December

---

9. Kenneth Katzman, *Iran's Activities and Influence in Iraq* (Washington, DC: Congressional Research Service, June 4, 2009), 4; Babak Rahimi, "The Rise of Ayatollah Moqtada al-Sadr," *Foreign Policy*, July 27, 2009.

10. ICG, *Iraq's Muqtada al-Sadr: Spoiler or Stabilizer?* (Brussels: ICG, July 11, 2006), 4.

11. Anti-Ba'thism was a theme of both of the predominantly Shiite coalitions—the Iraqi National Alliance and Prime Minister Maliki's State of Law Coalition—in the 2010 elections. For a portrait of the 2003 Iraqi political class and particularly the importance of the exile vs. insider dynamic, see Phebe Marr, *Iraq's New Political Map*, Special Report no. 179 (Washington, DC: United States Institute of Peace Press, January 2007), and Phebe Marr, *Who Are Iraq's New Leaders? What Do They Want?* Special Report no. 160 (Washington, DC: United States Institute of Peace Press, March 2006).

2005.[12] Though Sistani does not believe in the direct rule of clerics—as in the Iranian system—he has nonetheless played a critical indirect role as consultant of last resort by all political figures in times of crisis. While he was more active in intervening openly in the political process in the 2003–5 period, he remains a critical player, as demonstrated by his advocacy for the adoption of an open-list electoral system in the 2010 national elections. He has thus helped keep Shiite Islamist parties in power and also helped shape the government's social agenda in directions compatible with Islamic religious norms.

The Shiite Islamist parties can find support in Iran for these aims and goals. In theory and to a considerable extent in practice, this religious, ideological, and political congruence provides Iran with greater leverage and ability to influence Iraqi politics than other neighbors. It also gives Iran prior contacts and access in Iraq and organizational depth (through parties and militias), together with a network of influential people who often speak a common language (Persian), who are shaped by years of interaction, and who work together toward a common goal. At the very least, these factors greatly decrease the likelihood, if these parties remain dominant, that Iraq will return as Iran's greatest threat.

Nonetheless, there are serious limits on Iran's abilities to influence Shiite politics in Iraq. Iraq's Shiite parties are decidedly Arab and Iraqi in orientation and, like all Iraqis, are suspicious of Iranian attempts at hegemony and efforts to control Iraq; not all of their experiences in exile in Iran were positive. As the Iraqi state grew in confidence and ability after 2007, the Shiite leaders in power began to feel strong enough to strike a more independent course from Iran. There was increased evidence of this in cooperation between the Iraq Security Forces (ISF) and U.S. forces in operations against Iranian-funded "special groups" in 2007 and 2008 and in the conclusion of a Security Agreement and a long-term Strategic Framework Agreement with the United States, both actions strongly opposed by Iran. As reconstruction of the Iraqi oil industry in the south began in earnest in 2010, contentious border issues with Iran resurfaced, reminding Iraq's Shiite leaders of strategic issues that set them apart from Iran.[13] Ultimately, the Shiite parties would like to balance Iranian influence with that of the

---

12. Sistani personally played the leading role in determining the composition of the United Iraqi Alliance (UIA), drafting its platform and mobilizing the Shi'a public to vote in the January 2005 elections. In the December 2005 elections, Sistani and his deputies played a more behind the scenes and subtler—but nonetheless critical—role in ensuring the UIA's victory. For a detailed account, see Ali Allawi's superb history of post-2003 Iraqi politics, *The Occupation of Iraq: Winning the War, Losing the Peace* (New Haven, CT: Yale University Press, 2007), 340–344 and 439–440.

13. "Iraq, Iran Agree to Solve Dispute over Border Oil Field," *Dow Jones Newswires*, January 9, 2010.

United States and other neighbors, while continuing to capitalize on Shiite identity to remain in power.

The Kurdish Nationalist Parties. The main Kurdish parties, the Kurdistan Democratic Party (KDP) and the Patriotic Union of Kurdistan (PUK), have taken advantage of the instability and political fractiousness of the rest of Iraq, their disproportionate influence in the new political system, and their relationship with the United States to maximize their long-term advantage. They were instrumental in drafting and passing an Iraqi constitution that guarantees the KRG substantial autonomy. They occupied territory during the U.S. invasion that they did not control prior to 2003 (the disputed areas) and have worked hard to annex it legally into the KRG. They have passed their own hydrocarbon law and concluded oil contracts not approved by the central government, although the KRG still depends for much of its budget on 17 percent of Iraq's oil revenues (i.e., the Iraqi federal budget) sent north by the central government. And they have played a key role in Baghdad politics, particularly in the legislative arena, to secure their own interests, often at the expense of the central government. Arab leaders resent what they perceive as Kurdish overreach.[14]

Growing Kurdish autonomy and the attendant rise of Kurdish nationalism are of key significance to Iraq's relations with Turkey (and to a lesser extent with Iran and Syria). Turkey fears the spillover of Kurdish nationalist sentiment and the example of a successful KRG government on its own Kurdish population. But Turkey also has two specific concerns in the north: the fact that the PKK (the most militant Kurdish movement) has a haven in the KRG from which it has waged attacks across the border, and the possible incorporation of the oil-rich province of Kirkuk into the KRG, making future KRG independence more likely. Turkey has intervened to contain both of these threats, the former by both overt and covert military means and the latter by supporting political groups and initiatives, like the Iraqi Turkman Front and al-Hadba, to counter Kurdish ambitions in Kirkuk and Ninewa.[15] These concerns and subsequent interventions were most pronounced in 2006 and 2007, when the KRG was strong and the rest of Iraq weak.

---

14. The most detailed and cogent analysis of the disputes over territory and oil can be found in ICG, *Oil for Soil: Toward a Grand Bargain on Iraq and the Kurds* (Brussels: ICG, October 28, 2008); and ICG, *Iraq and the Kurds: Trouble along the Trigger Line* (Brussels: ICG, July 8, 2009).

15. ICG, *Turkey and Iraqi Kurds: Conflict or Cooperation?* (Brussels: ICG, November 13, 2008), 16, and ICG, *Iraq's New Battlefront: The Struggle over Ninewa* (Brussels: ICG, September 28, 2009), 12.

Since that time trends in Iraq and Turkey have moved in the opposite direction. Inside Iraq, the balance of power has gradually shifted in favor of the central government in Baghdad. A strong Arab Sunni provincial government was elected in Ninewa in 2009; the referendum on Kirkuk, constitutionally mandated for 2007, has been continually postponed, and in 2009, the central government successfully challenged the KRG's independent oil contracts.[16] At the same time, the strength of the united Kurdish front has been weakened by a fragmentation within the PUK and the emergence of Gorran (Change), an opposition party, which captured a strong minority position in the KRG Parliament in the 2009 KRG election. On the Turkish side, trade between Turkey and the KRG has grown markedly and Turkish investment in the KRG is increasing.[17] The Turks and Kurds are using development as an insurance policy on the future. U.S. tolerance of Turkish strikes across the border has sent a message on the limits of PKK activity. While these factors worry the Kurds, they have reduced Turkish anxiety about the perceived Kurdish threat and increased Turkish openness for engagement. Indeed, as Henri Barkey notes in his chapter, some Kurds in the KRG are even looking at Turkey as a possible alternative to U.S. protection, if that should be necessary after withdrawal.

Like their Shiite partners in government, the Kurdish leaders in power since 2005 also have long-standing relations with Iran, although they do not share a religious affinity with the Iranians. (The main Kurdish leaders are staunchly secular and distrustful of mixing religion and politics.) They too spent years of exile in Iran and got Iranian support in opposing Saddam. The PUK, whose territory abuts Iran, long had pragmatic relations with Iranian leaders who supported it against its KDP rivals in the Kurdish civil war of the mid-1990s. But these Iranian ties are balanced by longer and stronger U.S. relations, especially after 1991. It was the United States that created and supported the Kurdish safe haven in 1991 and the northern "no-fly zone" (1991–2003) that enabled the two Kurdish parties to establish a semi-independent entity in the north. After 2003, the United States also helped the Kurds establish the KRG, with strong provisions for their autonomy in the transitional administrative law (TAL) and the Iraqi Constitution. This support, however, stops well short of

---

16. In June 2009, foreign oil companies under contract with the KRG began exporting oil from two fields, Tawke and Taq Taq, through the northern pipeline of the central government-run State Oil Marketing Organization (SOMO). The proceeds went to SOMO, which is the sole body legally empowered to sell Iraqi oil. However, Baghdad refused to pay the companies for the oil, declaring the contracts illegal. See William MacNamara, "Kurdish Oil Drama Reaches Breaking Point," *Financial Times,* October 7, 2009.

17. ICG, *Turkey and Iraqi Kurds,* 12–15.

independence. The Kurdish leaders must also balance their reliance on the United States with their need for good relations with Iran.

The Arab Sunnis. The Arab Sunnis were largely the losers in the political shift that resulted from the 2003 occupation and subsequent events.[18] Most educated Sunnis who had remained inside Iraq had worked for the Ba'th government—as bureaucrats, army officers, academics, or professionals— though only a small percentage were Ba'th Party members or relatives and supporters of Saddam. But in the de-Ba'thification process that followed the occupation (and the fallout from the 2005 election that put Shiite and Kurdish parties in control), they were thoroughly displaced in the new political order. Not surprisingly, many rejected it. They were the backbone of the failed insurgency aimed at driving the United States out of Iraq, and they boycotted the first elections of January 2005 for a National Assembly. The violence of the post-2003 period, especially the sectarian civil war of 2006–7, further diminished their influence and even their numbers in the country. But as Shiite Islamist parties came to dominate the process, they reluctantly concluded it was better to leverage U.S. assistance to get some power than face a future in which they would be permanently marginalized. Gradually, most, but not all, moved from a position of militant opposition to participation in the political process with the aim of changing it in a direction more to their liking. But as latecomers to the political process, and with the Ba'th Party (the only one they had known) outlawed, they were at a disadvantage. As a result, they have been fragmented and—with the new highly ethnic and sectarian narratives advanced by Shi'a and Kurds—in search of a new political orientation.

Most Arab Sunnis favor a stronger central government, a more unified state, and greater independence—but not until they can achieve a position of greater strength in the system. However, this may be gradually changing, as some Sunni leaders are coming to the realization that a decentralized state that gives Sunnis (and others) more authority in their provinces may be in their interest. In their emerging narrative Sunnis are the new victims. They dislike accepting sectarian (Sunni) identity and claim discrimination by the new political leaders on "spurious" grounds of Ba'thist

---

18. Some Sunnis and secularists had been in exile, mainly in the West or in other Arab countries, such as Syria, Lebanon, or the United Arab Emirates, and returned to head political parties after 2003, but they did not do well in the elections of 2005 and some have since vanished from the scene. Chief examples include Ayad Allawi, a secular Shi'a, a resident of England, and former Ba'th member who defected in the 1970s and later formed al-Wifaq al-Watani (National Accord Party); Hajim al-Hasani, a resident of the United States and a pragmatic former member of the Iraqi Islamic Party; and Adnan Pachachi, a Sunni who had been a former Iraqi foreign minister in the 1960s and was a liberal and a moderate Arab nationalist. Of these, only Allawi remains a significant player.

connections. Many fought in the long Iran-Iraq War against these same politicians and resent their ascent to power. They accuse the "exiles" of having lived in ease abroad while they suffered under sanctions in the 1990s. Elections and U.S. support for Awakening Councils have provided opportunities for Arab Sunnis to gain a foot in the door, locally and provincially, but the process has been slow at the national level. Distrust between those in power before 2003 (mainly Sunnis) and those who gained power afterward (Shiite and Kurdish parties) remains deep and will subside only slowly. The elections of 2010 produced ample evidence of continuing suspicion and distrust between these groups, along with increased violence, often viewed in the Iraqi and international media in ethnic and sectarian terms.[19] However, the Iraqiyya ticket, supported by most Sunnis, did get the highest number of votes, and Arab Sunnis were given several key positions in the new government, including the presidency of the Council of Representatives and finance minister, showing the gains they are making.

This fundamental change in ruling groups and their constituencies and the new emphasis on ethnic and sectarian identity has resulted in a dramatic shift in relations with the neighbors. Relations with most Arab neighbors since 2003, although not uniform, have been relatively cool. The Arab Sunni political contingent, which has lost power, are more internally fragmented than either the Shiite or Kurdish blocs, but one constant among them (particularly the core of former Ba'thists) is opposition to Iran and its influence in Iraq. They have traditionally emphasized Arabic language and culture and want strong relations with the Arab world to balance Iran and to help in supporting their domestic position. Their emphasis on unity also causes them to look askance at Kurdish moves toward strong local and regional autonomy, which some regard as a prelude to dismemberment. These views find strong resonance in many Arab states, which have been reluctant to give support to the new political regime in Iraq. Arab regimes provide some support and exert some influence over Arab Sunni parties, but their activities pale in comparison to Iranian support for and attempts to influence the Shiite parties. As this volume illustrates, the reasons for this reluctance vary but there are a few constants. Most Sunni-led Arab neighbors, particularly Saudi Arabia,

---

19. The run-up to the national elections was dominated by the decision of the Iraqi Accountability and Justice Committee to bar the participation of over 500 candidates due to ties to the Ba'th Party and by the ensuing controversy. While the candidates were eventually allowed to run, the episode contributed to an atmosphere of intense anti-Ba'thist animosity and rhetoric. Though the barred candidates included many Shi'a, the decision was widely interpreted as being anti-Sunni in nature. See Reidar Visser, "Blacklisted in Baghdad," *Foreign Affairs*, January 27, 2010. For detailed analysis, see the January–February 2010 entries on Reidar Visser's blog, "Gulf Analysis," http://www.gulfanalysis.wordpress.com.

share Arab Sunni fears of Iranian dominance in Iraq and the control of Iraq, a major "Arab" state, by Shiite Islamist parties; they also dread any domestic policy that might lead to state failure or collapse. Their reactions have ranged from coolness to neglect and avoidance, rather than proactive intervention.

Saudi Arabia, threatened by both Iranian hegemony and Shiite dominance, has taken the most negative position to the new order. This negativism was exacerbated when Saudi Arabia (with other Gulf Cooperation Council [GCC] states) sent forces to help Bahrain quell demonstrations in February and March 2011 among its Shiite population, which, as part of the "Arab awakening," was demanding reforms (and, in some cases, a change of regime). A number of demonstrators were killed or wounded; many more were arrested. The Iraqi government protested these GCC actions, whereupon the GCC states privately refused to attend a forthcoming Arab League summit in Baghdad, forcing its postponement. The summit had represented a thaw in relations between Iraq and its Sunni Arab neighbors. The repercussions of these events are unclear, but more turbulence in Bahrain could sharpen the regional Sunni-Shi'a divide and undermine the progress made on accommodations between Iraq and its Sunni-led Arab neighbors, especially Saudi Arabia.

Nonetheless, by 2010, all of Iraq's neighbors except Saudi Arabia had reestablished embassies in Baghdad, and trade and diplomatic relations were growing, especially with Jordan and the United Arab Emirates. By 2010, the United Arab Emirates was the largest investor in Iraq, exceeding even the United States and the United Kingdom.[20]

The Secular Middle Class. In the past, the educated middle class was the backbone and the professional core of all Iraqi regimes. This group often crossed the sectarian and even the ethnic divide, was generally more secular in outlook, and had gradually come to espouse an "Iraqi" identity over and above more parochial loyalties. Since many worked for the state (directly or indirectly), they generally supported a strong state and the independence of Iraq.

Over the past few decades, this class has been decimated. Since the 1960s, Iraq has been undergoing a brain drain, which accelerated following the 1991 Gulf War and the ensuing misery and oppression of sanctions. Even more members of the Iraqi middle class (particularly those responsible for governance under the Saddam regime) fled as a consequence of

---

20. Dunia Frontier Consultants, *Private Foreign Investment in Iraq* (Washington, DC: Dunia Frontier Consultants, November 2009), 8.

the U.S. invasion. Post-2003 violence created yet another flight of middle-class professionals to neighboring countries and the West, as well as huge numbers of internally displaced. Despite an improved security situation after 2007, Iraqi professionals, including those who have worked for the United States, continue to leave in large numbers for neighboring countries, Europe, and the West. Reflecting this loss, secular parties, which cross sectarian lines and could bridge the sectarian gap, have also been losing ground politically. The most significant example is the coalition put together by Ayad Allawi, a secular Shi'a and a long-time opposition leader, for the January 2005 elections. Despite his position as prime minister at the time, his group won less than 10 percent of the vote. This electoral weakness prevents secularists with a more pragmatic bent from influencing the political system and its foreign policy direction. In 2010, however, Allawi's coalition did much better, winning the highest number of seats—91 out of a possible 325—indicating a secular resurgence.

Iraq will likely suffer the consequences of this brain drain for at least a generation—inexperienced leaders, the absence of a professional military and civil service, corruption, and ineffective institutions. The public and the political process have been left more ethnic, sectarian, and tribal in orientation and more radicalized. Moreover, low levels of education and experience among the Iraqi political elite, combined with continued political flux in Baghdad, will make Iraq a difficult and unpredictable partner in international relations for some time. Iraqis, too, will have difficulty developing a coherent vision, as their neighbors desire.

The New U.S. Partnership

Perhaps the most striking change between the old and new Iraq is the country's new partnership and military support relationship with the United States, epitomized by the Security Agreement and the Strategic Framework Agreement signed in 2008. This kind of strategic tie with a Western power stands in contrast not only to Iraq's isolation in the 1990s but also to its entire post-1958 history, during which Iraq depended mainly on the Soviet Union and the Eastern bloc for its military and security requirements. One has to go back to the monarchy to find an Iraq on good terms with the United States and dependent on it (and other Western powers) for military and other needs.[21]

---

21. The exception was a brief period of French military and U.S. intelligence support for Iraq during the Iran-Iraq War, but this was short-lived and abruptly ceased with Iraq's invasion of Kuwait in 1990.

The Security Agreement, which defines this relationship, calls for a withdrawal of all U.S. forces from Iraq by the end of 2011. However, most of Iraq's defense establishment and politicians dealing with Iraq's security have indicated their openness to maintaining U.S. forces in Iraq beyond this deadline.[22] This is a concession to reality: Iraq will face substantial needs in air defense, military equipment and training, intelligence, logistics, protection of ports, and a range of other tasks essential to its security and defense for years to come. A three- to five-year U.S. military presence after 2011 would allow Iraq to address these gaps far more quickly, cheaply, and efficiently than would be the case without such a presence. However, regardless of whether U.S. forces remain in Iraq after 2011, Iraq will likely continue to look to the United States as its primary source of military equipment and training and as its principal security partner, for at least the next five years. Politicians, however, may have difficulty selling this relationship to a public traditionally conditioned to reject foreign ties or control, especially with the United States. Despite the clear need for the military relationship, Iraqi politicians will have to manage the public diplomacy of the relationship well.

If handled properly, this relationship can be mutually beneficial to both Iraqis and Americans. The chief priority of the United States is to help Iraq develop a stable society and state, with normal, peaceful relations with the neighbors, and to support the viability of the political process. The United States can help ward off harmful interference from the neighbors and at the same time counteract the ill effects of the conflict in Iraq in the neighborhood. The United States will also use its influence to encourage better economic ties to and investment in Iraq and support Iraq's reintegration in international and regional organizations. The United States can also use its influence to get neighbors to engage more positively with Iraq, such as through the forgiveness of debt by Kuwait and other Gulf countries.

The strategy of the current Iraqi regime, likely to continue, is to use its relationship with the United States as a means of buttressing its hold on power domestically. It can also use the United States to balance unwanted interference by neighbors and other regional actors, particularly Iran. Most

---

22. Prime Minister Maliki indicated his openness to a post-2011 military presence "for further training and further support" in an address at the United States Institute of Peace in Washington, DC, on July 23, 2009. See Spencer Ackerman, "Iraqi Prime Minister Open to Renegotiating Withdrawal Timeline," *Washington Independent,* July 23, 2009. Deputy Prime Minister Rafi' al-'Issawi (an Arab Sunni from Anbar Province) publicly indicated a similar position in an address at the United States Institute of Peace on June 10, 2009. See Elizabeth Detwiler, "Iraq Beyond 2011: Remarks by Deputy Prime Minister Rafi' al-'Issawi," United States Institute of Peace, June 2009, www.usip.org. For the view of a senior Iraqi Army official, see Eli Lake, "Iraqi Army Wants U.S. Help Past Withdrawal," *Washington Times,* December 8, 2009.

Iraqi political actors, even those historically connected to Iran, want to ensure Iraq's independence, a desire the United States shares. The United States will continue to provide Iraq with sufficient military support on favorable terms to increase the likelihood of that independence. However, there are several cautions about this evolving U.S. relationship. Historically, there has been a deep distrust of foreign, "colonial" ties; this dates from the British imperial era.[23] Although Kurds generally welcome and even court the U.S. presence, there are several domestic Iraqi constituencies that are fiercely opposed to it. Chief among these are the Sadrists. Arab Sunnis still harbor resentment over their fortunes, although they are relying on the United States to support their inclusion in the political process. Even ISCI, which has encouraged U.S. support in post-2003 Iraq, has a past history of suspicions of the West and its embrace may be limited. These tensions can be expected to reassert themselves and future agreements are likely to meet stiff parliamentary debate in any open political system. Continued close relations and a military support relationship must be managed, politically, by both Iraqis and Americans.

The new U.S. role also has some problems from the regional perspective. A continuing military support relationship with Iraq represents a significant shift in the strategic balance of power in the region—in the United States' favor. This factor must now be considered by all neighbors in their own policy calculations. While the shift may be welcome to some allies (Israel, the GCC), all regional states, and even more their publics, look with disfavor—even dismay—at what appears like the reassertion of imperial control over a major Arab state. Indeed, Iraq's relations with some neighbors may even be harmed. This is clearest in the case of Iran, where Iraq could fall victim to the conflict between the United States and Iran over the nuclear file. Should this issue go badly, one could foresee a number of negative developments, including Iranian attempts to retaliate against U.S. forces and interests in Iraq and renewed domestic instability or collapse in Iraq with heightened tensions in the region.

There are negative implications beyond the Iranian issue. A close relationship with the United States could serve as an impediment to more normal relations between Iraq and various neighbors, particularly on the Arab-Israeli fronts. Iraq needs to concentrate on domestic reconstruction and cannot afford to be drawn into the politics of that issue; if the peace

---

23. Several governments in that era were overturned by popular uprisings or upheavals over the British tie. One was the cabinet of Salih Jabr, Iraq's first Shiite prime minister, in 1948 after an uprising (the *wathba*) against a new (and revised) Anglo-Iraq Treaty. In 1958 the pro-British monarchy was overthrown in a military coup caused, in part, by rising attacks, domestically and regionally, by pro-Nasser Arab nationalists against the 1955 Baghdad Pact, which tied Iraq to the West.

process continues to lag and the United States is perceived as too one-sided, Iraq could suffer from the backlash.

Continuities in Post-2003 Iraq

Despite these profound changes, as Iraq stabilizes and the state is gradually reconstituted, traditional concerns and problems are reemerging. These are likely to exhibit numerous continuities with the past in Iraq's interactions with its neighbors and the international community, as state interests gradually reassert themselves. Chief among these will be the facts of Iraq's geography and its strategic position in the region.

Border Issues

Reconstituting domestic order in the state, maintaining its territorial integrity, and regaining its sovereignty will be principal aims of any new government, regardless of who is in control. Above all, this will mean regaining control of the country's borders. Iraq must protect long borders with no less than six states. In the near term, this will mean preventing infiltration across borders and even preventing neighbors, such as Saudi Arabia and Iran, from exercising a destabilizing influence among domestic political opponents. A highly decentralized state and a fractured and divided government may make management of this process more difficult.

Iraq considers that the way in which its borders were drawn by "colonial powers" has left it (alone among its neighbors) almost a landlocked country with no independent access to the outside. Its twenty-six miles of Gulf shoreline is not suitable for a port, and its access to the Gulf is controlled on one side by Iran and the other by Kuwait. Hence, it must depend on neighbors for road transport of goods and for the export of much, though not all, of its oil through pipelines running through neighboring territory. This requires good relations with multiple countries, some of whom may have conflicting policies, not only with Iraq but also with each other. In 1982, hostile relations with Syria resulted in a shutdown of Iraq's Syrian pipeline, with substantial losses to its economy. During the Iran-Iraq War, when Iraq's access to the Gulf was blocked, relations with Jordan were crucial for use of the Red Sea port of Aqaba.

Borders between Iran and Kuwait have been particularly contentious because of Iraq's limited access to the Gulf. As oil exports revive and international companies begin reconstruction of its oil industry in the south, these old controversies are likely to resurface and to affect relations with these neighbors. The controversial border on the Shatt al-Arab, claimed by Saddam as one justification for the Iran-Iraq War, and the offshore territorial waters boundary in the Gulf around Iraq's Khawr al-Amaya terminal may again cause tensions with Iran.[24] In December 2009, Iranian soldiers temporarily occupied al-Fakka, an oil field on the Iran-Iraq border in the south, causing an outcry in Iraq's media and reviving the whole border issue between the two countries. The two sides agreed to settle the issue diplomatically and to demarcate the entire border through meetings of technical committees, but as an indication of the sensitivity of the issue, Sami al-Askari, a member of the Council of Representatives Committee on Foreign Relations, claimed that al-Fakka was in Iraqi territory and Iraq would not give up "one iota (*shibr*) of its land." He also accused Iran of timing the occupation to influence Iraq's upcoming election.[25] The prime minister, in turn, accused the media of exaggeration aimed at damaging "close ties" with Iran.[26]

Border issues are also critical in relations with Kuwait. Many Iraqis feel the British-drawn border with Kuwait cuts off their access to the Gulf through the Khawr Abdallah channel, and several leaders (Qasim, Saddam) have laid claim to Kuwait based on Ottoman borders. This was among the justifications Saddam used for his 1990 occupation of Kuwait. The border adjustment of 1993, made by an international commission after that war, and reluctantly ratified by Saddam's government, is also resented by Iraqis because, in their view, it awarded territory around the Umm Qasr port, which they had developed as an outlet to the Gulf, to Kuwait. The new border also involved disputes over the rich Rumaila oil field in southern Iraq, which tails over into Kuwait territory; in 1990, Iraq accused Kuwait of tapping into this field illegally. In 2009, rights to develop this field were given to an international consortium, involving British Petroleum and the Chinese National Petroleum Company. As oil production rises, this issue may emerge once again.[27]

There are other legacies of Iraq's 1990 occupation of Kuwait that remain unsettled. Most important is the raft of UN Security Council resolutions that impose a range of embargoes on Iraq and prescribe the payment of

---

24. The original boundary between Iran and Iraq, initially delimited in 1914 and solidified by the 1937 Sa'dabad Pact, put Iraq's boundary at the high-water mark on the Iranian side, giving Iraq control over this waterway. Iran has always considered that the Shatt should be shared and insisted that the boundary be drawn down the *thalweg*, the deepwater channel in the middle of the waterway. It finally achieved this goal with the Algiers Agreement in 1975. The Iran-Iraq War temporarily overturned the agreement, but in 1990, when Saddam needed Iranian support for his invasion of Kuwait, he agreed to the boundary, albeit in ambiguous language.

25. "Sami al-Askari: Motakki's Explanations about the Fakka Field Are Unacceptable," *Aswat al-Iraq*, January 7, 2010, http://ar.aswataliraq.info/?p=193834.

26. Hassan Hafidh, "Iraq, Iran Agree to Solve Dispute over Border Oil Field," *Dow Jones Newswire*, January 7, 2010.

27. Both of these issues, including "slant drilling" from the Rumaila field, were among the justifications cited by Saddam for his invasion of Kuwait in 1990. The definitive text on the Iraq-Kuwait border dispute is Richard Schofield, *Kuwait and Iraq: Historical Claims and Territorial Disputes* (London: Royal Institute of International Affairs, 1993).

reparations. Iraq would like to see these removed from the books. Kuwait would like to keep Iraq under UN Chapter VII restraints until certain demands are met: accounting for missing Kuwaitis, returning stolen property, paying reparations, and repaying debt. Iraqis agree to the first two but are committed to removing reparations and debt repayment. As these issues fester, Iraq may once again turn its attention to the border issue and its dissatisfaction with the 1993 settlement. This would certainly raise tensions with Kuwait and the GCC as a whole.

The Iraqi relationship with Kuwait is notable because it is one of the few foreign policy issues that is not divisive in Iraq. Most Iraqis agree on Kuwait. This is primarily because the issues concern core state interests that are largely economic and strategic and affect the state as a whole, not just specific communities. The Kuwaiti file is also one of the clearest cases of continuity with the past.

Regional Trade and Investment

Another continuity—and an important state interest—is development of Iraq's copious resources, including its oil, and their export to the outside world. Even under a situation of improving stability and increased state control of its territory, Iraq will need to concentrate on domestic reconstruction and economic and social development. It will be far too weak to exert any regional hegemony; on the contrary, it will be in need of help and support from all of its neighbors, particularly with respect to cross-border trade and investment.

Cross-border trade can be an important means of improving and sustaining better relations with neighbors, especially since Iraq needs access to neighboring territory for exports. This local trade is often conducted by people of similar background across the borders—Kurds in Turkey, Arab Sunnis and tribal groups in Syria and Jordan, and trading families in Basra and Kuwait.

These trading relations were slow to materialize after the dislocations and violence following the occupation and change of regime in 2003, but they picked up after Iraq stabilized in 2007. Not surprisingly, Iraq's most important trading relationship initially was with Iran, which, by 2009, was one of Iraq's largest trading partners, with bilateral trade estimated at $4 billion a year.[28] Iran exports goods and services to Iraq and invests in tourist enterprises (primarily those associated with religious pilgrim traffic) and in infrastructure projects, such as housing. But Iranian efforts have encountered a negative reaction among many Iraqis who complain that Iranian business is smothering Iraqi industry and agriculture by flooding

---

28. Katzman, *Iran's Activities and Influence in Iraq*, 8.

the market with cheap goods. The Iranian government subsidizes its exports and levies import taxes on inbound goods, making it difficult for Iraqis to compete.[29] Iraqis also blame Iranians for the high price of real estate and monopolizing business in booming tourist areas, such as Najaf, and potential growth areas, such as Basra.

The Turks are another neighbor with strong economic ties to Iraq. They have invested heavily in northern Iraq—in construction, industry, and infrastructure—a development that has been welcomed by the Kurds. The Turks are now expanding elsewhere in Iraq, outside of Kurdish areas. And as Iraq has stabilized, it has reached out to its Arab neighbors, with considerable success. More investment funds have come in, especially from wealthy Gulf neighbors. One dramatic turnaround came from the United Arab Emirates. According to a report issued in November 2009, direct foreign investment by the United Arab Emirates in Iraq more than doubled in 2009, totaling $37 billion, nearly a quarter of all global investments in Iraq, far outstripping that of any other country, including the United States and the United Kingdom. Among other neighbors high on the list of investors were Lebanon ($10 billion), Turkey ($8 billion), and Kuwait ($6.8 billion). Many of these just cited were big investments in oil and gas projects or real-estate ventures, which will take time to spend and may not materialize. In smaller ventures (less than $1 billion)—likely to improve infrastructure, housing, and industry in Iraq and to establish closer cross-border links with Iraq—neighbors played an even greater role, with Lebanon, Iran, the United Arab Emirates, Turkey, Jordan, Kuwait, Oman, and even Saudi Arabia among the top thirteen investors. If neighboring countries follow up on their commitments, over time these cross-border linkages are likely to help diminish tensions and raise the economic costs of cross-border frictions. Time and development will also work in Iraq's favor, with its strong resource base vis-à-vis its neighbors.

Water Resources

Water is another geographic feature that ties Iraq to its neighbors and to continuities in policy. Iraq's major rivers, the Tigris and Euphrates, lie downstream; their headwaters arise in Turkey, with the Euphrates passing through Syria before reaching Iraq. The major tributaries of the Tigris arise in Iran, as does the Karun River, which runs into the Shatt al-Arab in southern Iraq. Thus, Iraq is dependent on these three countries, and especially the first two, for its irrigation and water resources. While developing riparian agreements for water distribution is in the interests of all the neighbors, Iraq—as the downstream power—is particularly vulnera-

---

29. Gina Chon, "Iran's Cheap Goods Stifle Iraq Economy," *Wall Street Journal*, March 18, 2009.

ble. The Tigris and Euphrates have been extensively dammed in Turkey and Syria, as have the tributaries in Iran, with devastating consequences in Iraq. The result has been increasing drought, salination, disappearing marshlands, sandstorms, and a severe decline in agriculture. For example, in the fall of 2009, diversion of the Karun River in Iran created a serious water shortage in Basra and southern Iraq, which Iraq has attempted to mitigate through negotiations. Major frictions have arisen in the past with Turkey and Syria over this issue and the shortage of water in Iraq and the need for agricultural development is likely to be a factor affecting relations with neighbors in the future. It is also an area for potential cooperation.

Oil

Oil production and export and the wealth and power oil may bring to Iraq has been and will continue to be a major factor in Iraq's relations with its neighbors. Current producing fields are located in the north (and a subject of controversy between the Kurds and the central government) and the south. Who controls this oil and how its production and export are managed has been controversial in Iraq and has slowed development, especially in the disputed areas around Kirkuk. The country has 115 billion barrels of proven oil reserves, the fourth largest in the world (behind Saudi Arabia, Iran, and Canada), but in 2010, Iraq ranked twelfth in oil production (about 2.5 million barrels per day [mbd]). This situation began to change with growing stability, especially in the south. During 2008 and 2009, Iraq's Oil Ministry struck a number of deals with international oil companies for twenty-year service contracts on a dozen of Iraq's largest fields. These included contracts with Exxon Mobil to develop the West Qurna reservoir, with British Petroleum and the Chinese National Petroleum Company to develop the Rumaila field, and with a consortium led by the Italian giant ENI to develop the Zubair field. If all goes well, these three deals alone could add 4.5 mbd to Iraqi output.[30]

However, despite outside commitments, raising Iraq's oil field production and export capacity will take time. Oil fields in both the north and the south have been badly damaged from neglect and will require much coordinated work before production can be raised. Getting the oil to market will also involve new infrastructure, such as pipelines and offshore terminals, which involve neighbors as well. The dustup with Iran over the al-Fakka oil fields may be a taste of difficulties to come. Effective operations by international oil companies will also require continued stability, reduced corruption, and a hydrocarbon law to provide a legal framework for long-term production and exports in any quantity.

---

30. Dunia Frontier Consultants, *Private Foreign Investment in Iraq*, 13.

As Iraq's oil begins ⬚⬚⬚ duction levels, pricing, and market shar ⬚⬚⬚ ountries (especially Iran and the GCC ne ⬚⬚⬚ id could be contentious. Given Iraq's rec ⬚⬚⬚ to produce as much oil as it can at whatever price it can get, regardless of OPEC rules, for the foreseeable future. This should not cause much of a problem with neighbors in the near term. However, when Iraq reaches the 4 mbd level, a number of tensions with OPEC neighbors could arise, depending on the global oil market. This policy may affect relations with Saudi Arabia (usually OPEC's swing producer and monitor of last resort on prices) but also with Iran, Kuwait, and other GCC states. Quota and pricing issues have always caused tensions in the past and was the major justification used by Iraq for its invasion of Kuwait in 1990. Indeed, Iraq's development as an oil producer under the aegis of major international oil companies would put neighboring Iran, under international sanctions, at an increasing disadvantage.

Increased oil production will work to Iraq's benefit as well. It will provide wealth—and the power that goes with it—and give Iraq the potential to provide benefits to poorer countries, such as Jordan, Syria, and Turkey. It will also contribute to growing confidence in Baghdad and with it the desire to be more proactive with neighbors—as in the past. And this, in turn, will restore Iraq's more traditional strategic weight in the region and possibly, along with it, the region's more traditional fears of a strong—not a weak—Iraq.

Potential Future Trends and Their Impact on Neighbors

There are myriad ways in which the domestic political contest in Iraq could evolve over the next decade, with differing impacts on relations with neighbors. Three plausible scenarios exist: (1) the emergence of a strong, military-based regime in Baghdad; (2) a collapse of the political system and a return to violence; and (3) a continuation of the current political process with gradual improvement in state consolidation and economic development.

A Strongman in Baghdad

From 2007 to 2010, the Iraqi government under Prime Minister Maliki showed signs of tending in this direction. He increasingly gathered security forces in his own hands; extensively intervened in the composition of the ISF to ensure personal loyalty; eliminated political opponents with spurious and often trumped-up charges of "terrorism"; and used state resources—contracts, jobs, and cash—to cultivate public support. At the same time, he became increasingly assertive in the use of military force within Iraq's borders, taking aggressive measures against Iranian-backed Shiite militants in Basra, Sadr City, and elsewhere, using aggressive rhetoric against the Kurds, and taking actions against *peshmerga* (Kurdish militia) in the disputed territories. In provincial elections he managed to win considerable political support by presenting a tough "law-and-order" image. He did the same in the 2010 national election, and in fact spoke openly about the need for a strong central government. During their years in exile Shiite leaders like Maliki expressed fears of a strong Iraqi state and an aggressive Iraqi Army because they had been oppressed and victimized by both. However, as the state consolidates under their control, their perspective is apparently changing. A strong state that can keep order could consolidate their power and appears to have increasing support from a population weary of violence and instability.

Several developments could accelerate this trend. First, as the United States draws down and loses domestic leverage, Iraqi leaders will face less pressure to include Sunnis, Ba'thists, and other opponents in the political process or to make progress on the Kurdish issue. It is easy to imagine a future government using instability or fears of terrorism as a pretext for more heavy-handed treatment of Iraqi citizens, which, in turn, would engender increased resistance and instability and then further crackdown. Second, as the inefficient, factionalized, and inevitably messy democratic political process continues, it may well fail to meet rising expectations for improved governance and economic development. As the desire for normalcy outstrips tolerance for a slower political process, it is possible that a new Shiite leader, from inside or outside the military, would find ample public support for (or acquiescence in) a military-based takeover either by marginalizing the political process or by dispensing with it altogether. Such an outcome would be consistent with Iraqi history and past regional trends.

Under this scenario, certain continuities with pre-2003 Iraq would emerge: the primacy of the military in Iraq's governing institutions; a "security state" (albeit more benign than Saddam's), and a national identity based on a strong state. While some neighbors might welcome the emergence of order in Iraq, weaker Arab neighbors, such as Syria, Saudi Arabia, and especially Kuwait, would fear that it was only a matter of time before "Iraq was back"—as an aggressive, domineering force in the region. While a new Shiite strongman might be on better terms or even allied with Iran, tensions would undoubtedly emerge here, too. Iran, too, would seek to balance—even weaken—the Iraqi state for fear that a strong sense of nationalism among Shi'a could seek to redress long-standing grievances with Iran (e.g., the Shatt al-Arab) and even compete with its own putative leadership of the Shiite world. Turkey might look more positively on a regime that could keep Kurdish ambitions in check, but it is unlikely to welcome an authoritarian, military regime in Baghdad. Moreover, such a regime is likely to upset an emerging equilibrium in the north between the KRG and Turkey; the Kurds are already raising a warning about any "new Saddam" in Baghdad.

While this scenario has received credence in some circles, it is unlikely to occur—at least in the near to midterm—for several reasons. First is the degree of influence that the United States will probably maintain in Iraq through its mission of training, equipping, and supporting the military, in addition to its nonmilitary forms of support. In short, the United States will work to constrain any movement toward an authoritarian state. Second, given the multiple (and often conflicting) loyalties and lines of authority in Iraq's military command structure, which are only slowly subsiding, any attempt by a leader or leaders to mobilize a military takeover could easily split the military itself. Outside the military, such a government would likely face domestic dissent—even organized violence—from Sunnis, disenfranchised Shi'a, and, most importantly, from an effectively armed Kurdistan. Before it could exert influence abroad, any such government would have to contain opposition at home. Third is the extensive time and resources required to build a military in Iraq that would be truly threatening on a regional scale. Its major arms supplier for the future, the United States, is likely to keep this in mind. Finally, even in the worse-case outcome—a replacement of the United States as Iraq's major arms supplier and ally—the United States will remain the preeminent Persian Gulf power with the responsibility and means to maintain regional security and to protect the borders of neighbors most likely to fall victim to any Iraqi aggression, Saudi Arabia and Kuwait.

A Breakdown of the State

The worst outcome would be a complete collapse of the state and a return of the kind of conflict that gripped Iraq in 2006, or worse. This would be a nightmare scenario for the region. The result of this outcome—essentially a failed state—would be the export of extremism, terrorism, crime, and a host of other social ills to all of the neighbors. Sectarian political identity would spread to neighboring states (especially the eastern province of Saudi Arabia, Bahrain, and Kuwait) and inflame the relationship between Iran and the Arab world. Without the balancing force of the Iraqi Army, the Kurds' relative autonomy and their increased desire for separation would increase the likelihood of Turkish intervention. Such an outcome would also threaten Syria, Lebanon, and Jordan and raise the specter of a regional cold war on sectarian grounds. This scenario has, in fact, nearly occurred. With a weak and collapsing Iraq, Iraq plays little regional role; neighbors intervene politically to protect their interests and their borders. If the situation worsens gravely, the United States, as the chief ally and military supplier of Iraq, would be caught between the unpalatable choice of putting more troops into Iraq to shore up a failing government or getting out and leaving a dangerous political vacuum.

This worst-case scenario—state collapse—now seems improbable. Exhaustion among former antigovernment forces, ongoing government and military consolidation, and the likely continuation of an American presence (at some level) are working against it. So, too, are the prospects for a rise in oil production, increased foreign investment, and an improvement in economic conditions. A breakdown could occur, however, under an exogenous shock, such as an Israeli strike on Iran. In such a situation, Iran could activate its extensive covert networks, escalate its support for Iraqi militants, and undertake other destabilizing measures in order to damage the United States and a U.S.-supported government, either as an act of retaliation or as a means of demonstrating leverage to strengthen its position. This is the most obvious example, but other potential shocks could include terrorist attacks in Iraq or elsewhere in the region on a 9/11 scale, natural disasters, or a major disturbance in the balance of power in the region, either through state collapse or armed aggression. Gradual stagnation in Iraq, failure to address long-term conflicts, and a decrease in U.S. interest and presence in Iraq could produce an explosive climate again in Iraq, but if so, this circumstance is some years away, less likely, and entirely avoidable.

The potential fallout from this scenario has already been faced and partially addressed by the region during the violence of 2006–7. One outcome it clearly seeks to avoid is regional war. One lesson to be learned from the 2006 experience is that while all the neighbors will continue to protect their interests by competing for influence inside Iraq, they share a common interest in trying to keep Iraq's problems confined within Iraq and preventing state collapse, which could affect their own stability. Hence, the most likely regional response to the breakdown scenario is containment, regional balancing, and an avoidance of any partition of Iraq. This response is entirely consonant with U.S. interests.

Stability under a Democratic Process

The most likely scenario is neither collapse nor a new authoritarian regime but one in which the current relatively open and democratic political process, though uneven and uncertain, continues with enough progress in different directions to produce an acceptable level of stability. Problems can be expected to continue and the state consolidation process will be fragile, but there will be sufficient improvement in the economic, political, and military spheres to make these problems manageable. Intense competition among personalities, parties, and demographic groups is likely to continue within some variant of the current constitutional framework, but Iraq will continue to suffer from weak legal institutions, underdeveloped civil society, slow economic progress, and the effects of past isolation. This scenario is effectively a gray area, encompassing a number of outcomes, ranging from tolerable to good, depending on a number of variables. One key variable will be the quality and experience of Iraq's leaders and how successfully they embrace transparency and accountability, put Iraq's broader interests above their own narrowly defined political interests, and find some mutual accommodation on their divisions. They must also deliver services and economic development at a pace that allows this process to continue. Another variable is the cohesion, loyalty, and professionalism of the ISF and, to a lesser extent, the civil service. Yet another may be how well Iraqi leaders manage public perceptions about the U.S. relationship and continue to obtain the kind of security and economic support Iraq needs from the international community to move forward.

Sectarian tensions have lessened since 2007 as Sunnis have gradually become involved in the political process, but distrust remains and key issues—such as amnesty for insurgents, the incorporation of ex-Ba'thists into the political process, and the uneven distribution of resources for reconstruction and economic development—remain unresolved and are sources of tension between the Sunni and Shiite communities, broadly defined. A more stable and developed Iraq will depend on how well Iraq's politicians confront these issues.

The most divisive issue for Iraq's leaders will be the conflict between Arabs and Kurds over territory (particularly Kirkuk) and the KRG rights as a federal region that, if unresolved, will slow state consolidation and Iraq's social and economic progress. Since 2003, these issues have impeded the drafting of a hydrocarbon law conducive to investment by foreign oil companies, the lynchpin of Iraq's economy and its government budget. While the Kurds have moved ahead on oil development in the KRG, they have been stymied by the refusal of the central government to accept their contracts as legal. The Kurds have used their position of power in the central government to derail other legislation and central government initiatives as leverage for their own demands on territory and oil. Until there is a broad resolution of the Arab-Kurd conflict, economic development and government function will continue to be impeded, even beyond the issues at stake.

In the best outcome of this scenario, the KRG and the central government would reach a broad settlement over oil, territory, and constitutional reform. Kurdish leaders know that time is not on their side and that their position will only weaken with the United States' withdrawal and a strengthening of the Baghdad government. Nationalism and resentment at Kurdish overreach is still strong in Arab areas, but most Arabs operating in the political arena understand that their ability to overturn the Kurds' entrenched and institutionalized position in the north is limited and would come at a catastrophic cost. Neither the United States nor the international community is likely to countenance such an outcome or the kinds of actions, such as the Halabja gas attack, that took place under Saddam.

Even the worst outcome of the Kurdish issue does not so much threaten to explode into renewed civil war as to just continue to grind on as a counterproductive zero-sum game. Though at several points friction between the *peshmerga* and central government forces have created sparks that could lead to a broader outbreak of violence, a sustained civil war between the two sides is unlikely given the costs to both sides and the number of U.S. and international actors that will remain engaged. A second security dimension to the problem is that al-Qaida and other rejectionists have been given space to operate in the fissure between the two sides, exploiting rivalries between the two sides that need to be settled. Nonetheless, the main risk is not major fighting but continued political stagnation.

The viability of the emerging Iraqi state will depend on the cohesion, professionalism, and loyalty of the ISF, particularly the army. Though improvement has been considerable since 2004, when the United States began its train and equip mission, early efforts, which involved too rapid an expansion, could not prevent the intrusion of party and sectarian loyalties that compromised the force. Recruitment and training have now improved that situation, but the army has not yet been seriously tested. A key test will be how well the security forces withstand the ongoing political clashes between political parties that may have control over different elements within the ISF, and to what extent the ISF will remain aloof from politics. The Arab-Kurd dispute is a good case in point.

In the worst case of this scenario, Iraq will continue to focus on the internal struggle for power, with insufficient accommodation among leaders to achieve good governance or a rapidly developing economy. In this case, politicians will continue to look for outside help to maximize their advantage, giving neighbors greater opportunity to exert their influence. Iraq's capacity to exert itself on the international scene would be minimal given these internal divisions, but one could see the state acting selectively, particularly in areas like Kuwait, where there is more unity of views. On the negative side, frustration with slow progress and episodic bursts of violence could cause leaders to lash out at perceived adversaries (Syria,

Saudi Arabia), worsening relations and stirring the regional pot. In this case, the United States will have to continue a vigorous behind-the-scenes diplomatic role and a complete military withdrawal could become challenging. But even this modest outcome has advantages—an Iraq unable to challenge its neighbors and still stable enough not to be exporting its problems.

A better outcome in this scenario would see Iraq continuing on a path of state consolidation and political accommodation in which a reasonably transparent political process and credible elections are maintained. Iraq's security apparatus, though still dependent on the United States, would continue to grow in professionalism, Iraqi ministries and other institutions, like the Parliament, would slowly improve in capacity and effectiveness, and the infusions of investment funds and a growth of oil income would create enough economic development to generate more employment and diffuse discontent. This trajectory would give Iraq more time to work out its political problems in a more positive atmosphere. A more effective Iraqi government with a fatter economic budget would be able to chart a more independent course vis-à-vis its neighbors. It would be more proactive, less acted upon. Top Shiite leaders want to avoid involvement in Arab world controversies or become part of Iranian attempts at regional hegemony. More independence would enable them to avoid these pitfalls and even to act as a bridge—as some have said they want—between these two camps. Rather than dealing with the neighborhood in large blocs, Iraq would more likely deal with each neighbor on a bilateral basis. To get to this position, Iraq will need to continue receiving security support from the United States until it is strong enough to be a relatively independent actor. Relations with Turkey will improve proportionally as the Iraqi center strengthens and the underlying Arab-Kurd issues are resolved.

The good outcome in this scenario is entirely possible, but not inevitable. To reach it will require careful handling and considerable attention by both the Iraqis and the United States. Both sides must learn to manage the expectations of their populations and to broaden and deepen their mutual understanding of each others' societies and political cultures. It will certainly require a longer time than the Security Agreement deadline provides, considerable patience, and much more depth in nonmilitary fields—such as education, business, and cultural areas—which would give both sides greater stakes in the achievement of the outcome.

For some considerable time, Iraq will be a relatively weak country with a fragmented leadership over which regional powers—especially its more powerful neighbors—will attempt to exert influence. The United States is now one of these regional players, with an important though diminishing domestic role inside Iraq. Until Iraq gains enough cohesion to become a single-state actor, these forces will have a continuing impact on its policies. But Iraq also has long-standing strategic interests, a historical memory, and a strong desire for a regional role, strong enough to contain and push back on regional attempts at hegemony. But in the near to midterm, it will need help and support. If the United States wants the better outcome outlined in the third scenario, it will have to keep its political thumb on the scale for the foreseeable future.

II
The Neighbors

2

A Transformed Relationship

Turkey and Iraq

Henri J. Barkey

In August 2009, the Turkish government announced that it would undertake a major opening toward Turkey's Kurdish minority. This historic initiative by the ruling Justice and Development Party (AKP) could not have been conceived without the post-2003 transformation of Iraq, the AKP's own makeover of its own policy toward northern Iraq and the Kurdistan Regional Government (KRG), and the decision by both the Bush and Obama administrations to withdraw U.S. troops from Iraq.

The Kurdish initiative, also known as the "democratic opening," is a long-term endeavor that will, as it already has, suffer from numerous and even temporarily crippling setbacks along the way. Nevertheless, at its inception it was a testament to the distance the Turkish government had traveled in its Iraq policy. Throughout modern Turkish history, Ankara had approached Iraq only from the lens of the Kurds in northern Iraq; Kurdish autonomy in Iraq's north represented a particular, some said an existential, challenge to Turkey, which has a sizable Kurdish minority of its own. This worry, in turn, reflected continuous and increasing Turkish Kurdish nationalist political mobilization that, starting in the 1980s, found partial articulation in the Kurdistan Workers' Party (PKK), which initially sought to establish an independent Kurdish state in southeastern Turkey. PKK insurgents took advantage of northern Iraq's uncontrolled areas to ensconce themselves there. Despite its role in the creation of the autonomous Kurdish zone in the immediate aftermath of the 1991 Gulf War, Ankara had vociferously opposed the zone's continued existence and yearned for the return of a strong unitary Iraqi state. In the aftermath of the 2003 U.S. invasion of Iraq, Turkey found itself in the unenviable situation of contending with a transformed Iraq that legitimized the Iraqi Kurds' claims to a federal state in the north. Short of Kurdish independence, this outcome was long thought to be the worst possible conclusion for Turkish policymakers.

More than eight years after the invasion, Turkey, which had spearheaded the opposition to the KRG, has implemented a 180-degree turn in its policy. The two have developed close economic and political ties while collaborating on a gamut of issues, including how to pacify the PKK. Gone is Ankara's highly charged and alarmed discourse on Iraqi Kurds. Today, with a Turkish consulate in Erbil, Turkey has effectively recognized the KRG's legitimacy. In the process, Turkey has emerged as a far more influential actor in Iraq—perhaps not as influential as Iran but certainly one that can give Tehran a run for its money.

It was not surprising that neighbors would adapt their approach to Iraq with the passage of time; Iraq and its problems have posed very difficult challenges for these countries, forcing them to develop policy options under conditions of great uncertainty. In addition to Washington's intentions, they also had to take into account future developments in an Iraqi state that had yet to demonstrate some element of stability. No neighbor has so dramatically transformed its approach to Iraq as has Turkey. A confluence of factors prompted this change, including the articulation by the AKP of a new regional strategic approach, the Turkish military's realization that, after twenty-five years, its military-only strategy would not subdue the PKK or resolve Turkey's Kurdish question, and Ankara's hard realpolitik look at what the American withdrawal would entail for Turkey.

Turkey's Policy toward Iraq and the Kurds, 1958–2009

Turkish officials are fond of reminding everyone that because Iraq was once part of the Ottoman Empire, the two countries enjoy deep historical links. Reality is far more complex. The 1958 Iraqi coup ended both the monarchy and Iraq's participation in the pro-Western Baghdad Pact, which had anchored their mutual relations. During much of the Cold War the two countries were on the opposite side of the global divide. Although Turkey's rendition of history retained the memory of the post–World War I "loss" to the British-created Iraqi state as another perfidy of imperial powers, for the most part Iraq did not figure significantly in Turkey's geopolitical imagination.

Throughout the 1960s and especially in the 1970s, as Mulla Mustafa Barzani's *peshmerga* (Kurdish guerilla forces) went on the offensive following the collapse of the autonomy agreements with Baghdad, Ankara kept a wary eye on Iraq's internal Kurdish problem. Turkey, which had historically refused to acknowledge the existence of its own Kurdish minority, feared a contagion effect. In 1963, for instance, the U.S. embassy in Ankara was informed that Turkish military forces had sealed the Iraqi border to prevent "support for [Iraqi] Kurdish forces from inside Turkey."[1] In the 1980s the collaboration between the Turkish military junta and Saddam Hussein's regime increased as Turkey engaged in cross-border operations with Iraqi permission. In part, the vacuum created in northern Iraq due to the Iran-Iraq War spurred this on; Iranians, having betrayed the Kurds in the 1975 Algiers accords, had restarted their support of the Kurdish insurgency.

Turkish Kurdish nonviolent political activism was a contributing factor to the 1980 military coup. The ruling junta's subsequent wave of repression facilitated the PKK's creation and the reemergence of violent opposition.[2] The PKK took advantage of diminishing Iraqi control over northern Iraq during the Iran-Iraq War to set up bases in Iraq. Throughout the 1980s and 1990s, the PKK insurgency grew rapidly due to accumulated frustrations compounded by government miscalculations and harsh counterinsurgency tactics.[3] The fighting though focused in the Kurdish-inhabited regions of Turkey's east and southeast was quite ferocious. Since its inception, the insurgency has caused the death of some 40,000 people, mostly PKK fighters and Kurdish civilians. In its heyday in 1990–92, the PKK held sway over large parts of the southeast. In 1999, the Turks threatened Syria with military action if it did not force the PKK's mercurial leader, Abdullah Öcalan, out of Damascus. On the run, Öcalan was eventually captured in Kenya with American help. By then the PKK had militarily been on the defensive and, to spare Öcalan's life, it declared a hiatus in its armed struggle. Politically, Turkish officials found it difficult to combat an insurgency against a people whose existence had never been acknowledged. Complicating matters further was the Kurdish question's international and regional dimensions. As the Iran-Iraq War wound down, Iraqi forces

---

1. "Turkish Reaction to Outbreak of Hostilities between Iraqi Government and Barzani Forces," U.S. State Department Cable Embassy Ankara 1963, March 15, 1974, Declassified/Released U.S. Department of State, EO Systematic Review, June 30, 2005.

2. For more on the PKK, please see Aliza Marcus, *Blood and Belief: The PKK and the Kurdish Fight for Independence* (New York: New York University Press, 2007).

3. On the conduct of the counterinsurgency, see Henri J. Barkey, "Turkey and the PKK: A Pyrrhic Victory?" in *Democracy and Counterterrorism Lessons from the Past*, ed. Robert Art and Louise Richardson (Washington, DC: USIP Press, 2007), 343–381.

engaged in their infamous Anfal campaign that primarily targeted Kurdish civilians. In Halabja alone 5,000 civilians perished as the town was devastated by a chemical weapon attack in 1988.[4] There were as many as 200 additional chemical weapons attacks. The Anfal campaign also caused the first significant flow of Kurdish refugees into Turkey. While the numbers were modest in comparison to 1991, their presence on Turkish soil helped further cement the bonds between Kurds on both sides of the border.

The real problem for Turkey emerged following the 1991 Gulf War. Once again, Iraqi reprisals against Kurdish civilians sowed panic among them. This time, however, a million Kurds sought refuge in the mountainous border area with Iran and another half million fled to corresponding terrain along the Turkish border. Confronted with a humanitarian catastrophe and prodded by Turkey, which did not want to let any Kurds enter its territory, the allies inserted a small military contingent into northern Iraq and established a no-fly zone over it.[5] Iraqi troops were pushed out. Kurdish *peshmergas* belonging to the two main Kurdish political parties, the Kurdistan Democratic Party (KDP), led by Masoud Barzani, the son of the legendary Mulla Mustafa, and the Patriotic Union of Kurdistan (PUK), commanded by Jalal Talabani, assumed control over a de facto Kurdish enclave. Allied aircraft stationed in Turkey's Incirlik Air Base patrolled the Iraqi airspace to ensure compliance with the no-fly zone. Turkey was divided between its president, Turgut Özal, a supporter of the war effort who wanted to participate in it, and his military commanders and Parliament, which refused to countenance any aggressive Turkish action against Iraq.

Following President Özal's death in 1993, Turkish policy toward Iraq focused exclusively on containing Iraqi Kurds and the PKK's extensive base network. In addition to these two prongs, Ankara's policy contained an element of "recidivist Ottoman nostalgia and continued resentment at the loss of Mosul and the oil fields of Kirkuk."[6] Turkey strengthened the Turkish-speaking Turkmen population of northern Iraq to gain leverage over the two Kurdish parties. A civil war in the 1990s between the two Kurdish factions over control of territory and customs revenue made the

---

4. Joost R. Hilterman, *A Poisonous Affair: America, Iraq, and the Gassing of Halabja* (New York: Cambridge University Press, 2007).

5. For an account of the development of northern Iraq, see Quill Lawrence, *Invisible Nation: How the Kurds' Quest for Statehood Is Shaping Iraq and the Middle East* (New York: Walker and Company, 2008).

6. Gareth Jenkins, *Turkey in Northern Iraq: An Overview*, Occasional Papers (Washington, DC: Jamestown Foundation, February 2008), 13.

Turks' task much easier. It even provided Turkey with an opportunity to occasionally act as a go-between or even participant in the on-again, off-again intra-Kurdish conflict. During this period Turkey established the Iraqi Turkmen Front (ITC) and also engaged, often with Iraqi Kurdish help, in many anti-PKK cross-border operations.

Almost from the beginning, Turkish attitudes soured on Operation Provide Comfort (later renamed Operation Northern Watch), the Incirlik-based air force effort at maintaining the no-fly zone. This effort became cannon fodder in Turkish domestic political debates with large segments of the Turkish population and political class increasingly convinced that protecting Iraqi Kurds amounted to a nefarious plot by the United States to divide Turkey and carve out an independent Kurdish state. These fears of American machinations, as fantastic as they may have been, were none-theless not only accepted but also propagated by significant members of Turkish officialdom. Bülent Ecevit, a former and future prime minister, eagerly subscribed to this conspiracy theory. Among the most prevalent charges were accusations that U.S. helicopters had been secretly supplying PKK rebels in Turkish mountains. Turkish officials' unwillingness to deny such allegations helped Turkish attitudes against both the Iraqi Kurds and their primary protector, the United States, to harden over time.

Turkey was also in a bind regarding the regime in Baghdad. Although Turkey was an early noncombatant U.S. ally in the war to liberate Kuwait, as the prolongation of the no-fly zone over northern Iraq helped Iraqi Kurds etch out an independent existence, Ankara's sympathies for Saddam increased perceptively. Post-Özal politicians preferred a return to the status quo ante with the Ba'thist regime ridding itself of the crippling UN sanctions and assuming complete control of its territory. Turkey bitterly complained that it had not been fully compensated for its losses incurred during the 1991 war. Yet, for Washington, Turkey's ally, the northern no-fly zone was its single most important weapon to contain Saddam. Therefore, the United States sought means to keep the Turks satisfied; it prevailed on the United Nations to exempt Ankara from trade sanctions.

At the onset of the 2003 Iraq War, the Bush administration painstakingly negotiated a memorandum of understanding with Ankara to open up a second front against Baghdad by dispatching American troops across Turkey to Iraq's northern frontier. As part of the agreement, the Turkish military would insert a sizable force of its own into northern Iraq and planned to arm and train a Turkmen militia whose Turkish military advisers were expected to serve with them on an almost permanent basis.[7]

---

7. Jenkins, *Turkey in Northern Iraq: An Overview*, 16.

Both would serve as a counterweight to Kurdish designs. Happenstance dictated that parliamentary authorization for this agreement would fall victim to the brand new AKP government's inexperience. The AKP, just like the rest of the Turkish public, vehemently disagreed with U.S. objectives in Iraq; it even pushed for a regional dialogue hoping to prevent forthcoming U.S. action. In January 2003, weeks before the onset of the hostilities, Kürşad Tüzmen, the minister in charge of foreign trade, led a large Turkish trade delegation to Baghdad to explore an improvement in ties.[8] Ankara, fearing the adverse impact without the U.S. economic compensation package, felt compelled to go along with U.S. wishes against its own better judgment.

In the ensuing March 1, 2003, parliamentary authorization vote, the AKP, confident of the outcome, freed its parliamentarians to vote their preferences. The outcome was a brutal shock; the authorization was defeated by the narrowest of margins.[9] In retrospect, it was the leadership's miscalculations and inexperience that led to the defeat. Nonetheless, it did create a cloud over U.S.-Turkish relations and led to ill feelings in U.S. Central Command (CENTCOM), the American military command in charge of the Iraq war.[10] Soon thereafter, on July 4, 2003, Turkish Special Forces operating in the Iraqi Kurdish city of Suleymaniyah with American consent were caught red-handed with their Iraqi Turkmen Front clients planning the assassination of a leading figure in the Kirkuk (Tamim) governorate. The captured Turks were subjected to "the al-Qaida treatment," handcuffed and hooded, and sent to Baghdad for interrogation. Absent an official explanation by Ankara, Turks interpreted this event as a deliberate U.S. attempt at humiliating Turkish soldiers as punishment for the March 1 parliamentary vote. The Turkish military's perceived denigration produced a wave of anti-Americanism that continues to affect Turkish opinions of America.[11]

---

8. Not only was the delegation given a red carpet reception in Baghdad, but Tüzmen was also received by Saddam Hussein, though this had not been planned. "Saddam'la Sürpriz Buluşma," *Hürriyet*, January 12, 2003.

9. The government motion had in fact won the day, except for the few abstentions by members of Parliament who were sitting in the chamber. To the AKP's great surprise, these members' abstentions under parliamentary rules had to be counted as negative, causing the motion to lose. Many AKP sources, high and low, charged that in fact it was AKP's Kurdish origin MPs who had voted against the authorization because they feared the trek of American troops from the port city of Iskenderun through Kurdish-inhabited territory would invite the Turkish military to reintroduce emergency law in the southeast Kurdish provinces.

10. Contributing to CENTCOM's unease was Turkish Land Forces commander Aytaç Yalman's opposition to the passage of the authorization in an "anonymous" interview on the eve of the vote. See "The Military Is Uncomfortable," *Milliyet*, February 26, 2003.

11. The irony was that within a year of the incident, the three generals, ranging from a one- to a three-star officer, in charge of the Turkish Special Forces accused of the attempted assassination were all retired or sidelined. See Henri J. Barkey, "Kurdistanoff," *National Interest* no. 90 (July/

Turks wearily watched the Iraq war's progression and Iraqi Kurds' emergence as Washington's sole reliable ally in the conflict. Ankara, to contain the deepening of a demonstration effect on its own Kurdish minority, pursued a rearguard action against the KRG's further legitimization. This was a consensus view that Tarık Oğuzlu calls "the realist-exclusionist approach" supported by the civil and military bureaucracy and the opposition parties, the Republican People's Party and the Nationalist Action Party.[12] Turks bitterly complained that Iraqi Kurds were not expending any efforts to curb PKK activities in northern Iraq; worse, they accused Barzani and the KDP of actively supporting the PKK as a potential source of leverage over Turkey. Turkey also objected to the formation of a federal Iraq with its three Kurdish provinces in the north constituting a single federal entity. Ankara continued to champion Iraqi Turkmen rights and especially their claim to the contested oil-rich city of Kirkuk. Kirkuk had at all cost to be kept out of Kurdish hands because its oil could finance future independence—despite the fact that such a Kurdish state would be landlocked and at the mercy of its hostile neighbors. The Iraqi Constitution's Article 140, which called for a referendum on the future of Kirkuk to be held by the end of 2007, complicated matters further for Ankara.

The concomitant rekindling after a long hiatus of the PKK insurrection strengthened the determination of Turkish authorities to foil Kurdish aspirations in Iraq. The Turkish government's then foreign policy adviser wrote that his government's overriding concern in 2007 was to prevent both northern Iraq from becoming "a breeding ground" for the PKK and for the referendum from going forward because it would engender interethnic clashes. Bizarrely, though, he also argued "it was crucial for Turkey to break down this plot in the making."[13]

Suspicion of American intentions in Iraq permeated all levels of Turkish society; the conspiracy industry's lament usually culminated in the belief that the American occupation had one sole purpose, the creation of a separate Kurdish state. A former commander of the Turkish Land Forces, Aytaç Yalman, opined that the United States began planning its Iraq invasion back in 1998 when Secretary of State Madeleine Albright brought the two warring northern Iraqi Kurdish leaders to Washington to sign a cease-fire.[14] The Turkish military took a decidedly hard-line stance on any

---

August 2007); and Murat Yetkin, "Süleymaniye'de Gerçekte Neler Oldu?" *Radikal*, February 20, 2007.

12. Tarık Oğuzlu, "Turkey's Northern Iraq Policy: Competing Perspectives," *Insight Turkey* 10, no. 3 (2008): 14–15.

13. Ahmet Davutoğlu, "Turkey's Foreign Policy Vision: An Assessment of 2007," *Insight Turkey* 10, no. 1 (2008): 86.

14. Fikret Bila, *Komutanlar Cephesi* (Istanbul: Detay Yayıncılık, 2007), 204–205.

Turkish official civilian contact with the KRG. Iraq became a test of civil-military relations. The military, put on the defensive by the AKP's attempts at civilianizing such institutions as the National Security Council, chose to cast relations with the KRG as one barometer of the government's commitment to national causes.

The officers, suspicious of the AKP, sought to prevent Turkish contacts with Iraqi Kurds out of concern that it would ultimately lead to the KRG's recognition by Ankara. In a well-documented case, the chief of the general staff, Yaşar Büyükanıt, while visiting Washington, publicly reprimanded the government for organizing informal talks between then Turkish foreign minister Abdullah Gül and KRG prime minister Nechrivan Barzani. In an unprecedented bellicose tone he warned that the Turkish military would take a dim view of negotiations with those who had Turkish blood on their hands; the talks were unceremoniously canceled.[15] Ankara's usual discourse on Iraqi Kurds was harsh; most Turkish leaders referred to Talbani (even though he had assumed the presidency of Iraq) and Masoud Barzani, the head of the KRG, not by their titles but as tribal chieftains. This elicited a similarly strong nationalist riposte from the KRG; Barzani every so often would utter statements designed to infuriate Turkish officials and public.

While Ankara considered Baghdad as its only interlocutor, it hedged its bets by establishing links with a variety of Iraqi Arab groups, Sunni and Shiite. Increased involvement in Iraqi domestic politics tracked with AKP's new conception of its role in the region and beyond. A more self-confident Turkey sought to become increasingly active in Iraqi politics. Here too the state bureaucracy's dogged recalcitrance could obstruct sometimes the simplest of diplomatic moves. Turkish president Ahmet Necdet Sezer, an arch secularist and Kemalist, pointedly refused to invite Iraqi president Talabani to Ankara because Talabani was a Kurd and leader of the PUK.

Yet, Turkish officials did nothing to prevent the development of commercial relations between northern Iraq and Turkey. Iraqi Kurds assiduously wooed Turkish firms to invest and participate in large infrastructure tenders. Increase in the volume of cross-border transactions benefited the economically backward southeastern region.[16] Turkish Kurds would even complain that their Iraqi brethren favored Turkish companies at their

---

15. Yasemin Çongar, "Kuşatılmışlık ve 'dinamik güçler,'" *Milliyet*, Februry 19, 2007.

16. In 2007, there were some 1,200 Turkish companies operating in northern Iraq, mostly engaged in construction, but as well as in oil exploration and other services, which generated some $2 billion in business. Some Turkish businessmen even expected that they would get as much as $10 billion of a total of $15 billion worth of contracts the KRG would issue over the next three years. Serpil Yilmaz, "Turks Are Reconstructing Northern Iraq," *Turkish Daily News*, April 12–19, 2007.

expense. Current Turkish trade with Iraq amounts to $10 billion per year, of which half is estimated to be with the KRG.[17]

Ankara's single-minded preoccupation with the demonstration effect Iraqi Kurds could have on Turkey's Kurds and the PKK bases in northern Iraq meant that the U.S.-Turkish dialogue would easily be sidetracked and bogged down over these issues. Turkey insisted, with some justification, that the United States ought to dispose of the PKK's presence in a country that it had just occupied. By contrast, Washington facing an increasingly tough strategic predicament in Iraq with an insufficient deployment of soldiers for the task at hand, demurred. Having only a token force in northern Iraq and unable to deploy any others to challenge the battle-hardened PKK, the United States was unwilling to antagonize Iraqi Kurds or engender a much wider conflict between Iraqi Kurds and Turkey that could undermine its broader efforts in Iraq.

Turkey's New Iraq Policy and Kurdish Initiative: What Changed?

By 2009, the government had effected an almost 180-degree change in its Iraq policy; it began an official dialogue with the KRG, signed agreements, especially regarding the importation of oil, reduced its cooperation with the ITC, opened a consulate in Erbil, and began to approach Iraq comprehensively, often in collaboration with the United States, for purposes of influencing the transition in that country. Turkish prime minister Tayyip Erdoğan and KRG president Masoud Barzani even exchanged visits to each others' capitals. From where Turkey had been an irritant in Washington's conduct of Iraq policy, there emerged much greater harmony between the two.

No single factor accounts for Turkey's policy change. Rather, it was the product of a combination of developments at home, some completely unrelated to Iraq and Iraqi Kurds, changing perceptions of the domestic Kurdish question, the military's reluctant conclusion that the PKK insurrection would continue no matter what efforts it invested, the new geopolitics of the region, including the U.S. decision to withdraw from Iraq, and the AKP's new foreign policy conception that at its core aims to make Turkey a global power of some prominence.

---

17. Amberin Zaman, "Neden, Neden?" *Habertürk*, April 6, 2010. Zaman points out that while Iraq as a whole is Turkey's fourth largest trading partner, the KRG, were it an independent state, would have been among the top ten. Despite all the improvements and attention, including a 300-member trade delegation arriving at the end of April 2010, Zaman further points out that inattention to detail on the Turkish side means that border crossings between the KRG and Turkey are maddeningly slow.

The Geopolitical Context

To argue that the Iraq war profoundly transformed the region would be stating the obvious. However, far more important than the war's unpopularity in the region was the surprise at the insurgents' ability to bloody the U.S. military. With its failures, the Bush administration created a vacuum of influence and leadership in the region. This vacuum, as explored later in this chapter, helped Ankara interject itself into both the region's and Iraq's politics.

The advent of the Obama administration confirmed and accelerated the United States' decision to withdraw from Iraq. This decision, taken without any assurance that the new regime in Baghdad would not perish under the weight of sectarian, ethnic, and regional rivalries, was itself as transformative of the region as the initial decision to invade. The regional powers, which had to originally anticipate the ripple effects of an Iraq refashioned by America, in the aftermath of a sooner than expected U.S. departure have to contend with an Iraq mired in uncertainty.[18] An unstable Iraq could export its instability to the region. Whether such exports take the form of fundamentalist or jihadist organization and violence or nationalist stirrings, their repercussions could create opportunities for either regional cooperation or rivalries that, in turn, could exacerbate conditions on the ground. Even if Iraq were to put its house in order and emerge as a stable state—albeit one with limited influence in the medium term as it rebuilds itself from years of war and ravage—the fact of the matter is that its neighbors and the United States would elect to pursue policies that balanced each other and anticipated and attempted to ward off the worst.

Turkey has been insistent in defending the territorial integrity of Iraq because the prospect of an Iraq getting unglued could set in motion a series of intolerable repercussions. First, this would increase the likelihood of Kurdish independence and the expansion of the Kurdish region to encompass Kirkuk, both the governorate and the city. Despite improvements in Ankara-Erbil relations, such a possibility would be destabilizing to Turkey because it could lead to violence between Kurds and other ethnic groups, primarily Arabs and Turkmen, which, in turn, could spill over into Turkey. Second, a failed Iraqi state could not prevent heavily armed and experienced groups from exporting many of their fighters and knowledge to neighboring countries, including Turkey. Unrest in Saudi Arabia or Jordan or Syria would undermine Turkish economic and diplomatic interests in the region. Third, Ankara worries that greater unrest and insta-

---

18. Kenneth M. Pollack, "The Battle for Baghdad," *National Interest* no. 103 (September/October 2009): 17.

bility on its borders would serve as a disincentive for EU members to accept Turkey as a full member.

Such dire prospects have helped shift Turkey's approach to Iraq. Turkey has also come to accept the fact that the KRG, irrespective of the disputes that continue to swirl around the Iraqi Constitution and its federalism provisions, is here to stay. Save perhaps for some Sunnis, Iraqis have grudgingly become comfortable with the KRG's current status. Iraqi president Talabani too helped by demonstrating to all that as a Kurd he could, through his international contacts and personality, defend Iraqi interests. In turn, this has led Ankara to realize that its ability to influence events on the ground in Iraq is ironically greatest through the KRG. In Baghdad, it faces not just American competition but, far more significantly, an entrenched Iranian presence. However, in the KRG its influence is unrivaled; the Kurds' critical role in Iraq serves to amplify Turkish influence in Baghdad. Ankara's cooperative new approach enables it to rely on a cumulative strategy that privileges cooperation and trade rather than one based solely on threats.

The KRG enjoys immense support among Turkish Kurds. Kurds on both sides of the border are protective of each other. Turkish Kurds do not take kindly to any Turkish government that engages in active hostility toward Erbil. One intended by-product of the engagement with Erbil had been increased Iraqi Kurdish pressure on the PKK. Turks have also come to recognize that northern Iraq, which had been dominated by the two large parties and ruled without much room for dissent against the Barzanis and Talabanis, is now a more differentiated society. In the 2009 KRG provincial elections, an opposition party, Gorran, created a stir by riding an anticorruption wave and making serious inroads into the two families' dominance. Despite the conservative character of Kurdish society, especially in the Kirmanji-speaking areas of northern Iraq and Turkey, Iraqi Kurds resisted attempts by some Shiite groups to infuse the constitution with religious influences. The Kurds' relatively more secular outlook protects Turkey from fundamentalist influences in the rest of Iraq.

Both Turkey and the United States were late in appreciating the benefits of cooperation over Iraq. It took a real crisis in relations with the Turks for the Bush administration to change tactics. Upset at the safe havens the PKK enjoyed in northern Iraq, Turks had continuously upped their pressure on Washington to act. A devastating PKK attack on a Turkish border outpost in October 2007 that resulted in the deaths of thirteen soldiers is what finally triggered a new level of cooperation between Ankara and Washington. As domestic pressure on the Turkish government to intervene militarily in Iraq intensified Washington was left with no choice but to acquiesce. Washington began to coordinate Turkish air strikes against PKK emplacements in northern Iraq and pushed the KRG to be more proactive in its support of Turkish actions.[19] This change in U.S. policy would be a watershed event; Turkish air strikes (and one ground operation) relieved domestic pressure. With the exception of one potential confrontation between Kurdish *peshmerga* forces and Turkish troops based in Iraq, tensions between the KRG and Ankara were managed thanks in part to the more precise bombing raids that minimized collateral damage in northern Iraq.

American acquiescence and cooperation went a long way to reassure both the Turkish government and its military that the United States was unwilling to forsake its relations with Ankara. It helped soothe post–July 4, 2003, feelings. The resulting change in atmosphere and the realization that Washington was seriously looking to extricate itself from Iraq are what got Ankara to work closer with the United States. Turkish diplomacy assumed an active role in helping Washington resolve differences with Baghdad on the relocation of and the withdrawal schedule of U.S. troops. In the process, it also came to better understand the dynamics between the United States and Iraq. The prospect of American withdrawal elicited more positive cooperation from the Turks.

Paradoxically, improved relations with Washington may have also helped the Turks engage the Iraqi Kurds. Without the political cover that the American help provided, the government would have faced even fiercer domestic opposition to extending any olive branch to Iraqi Kurds. Iraqi Kurds for their part toned down their criticisms of Turkey and especially of the air strikes. Turkish Kurds were more vociferous in their criticisms, but, influenced by the KRG, they too ultimately kept their powder dry.

An important change also occurred in Turkish perceptions of the Turkmen issue in northern Iraq. In the 2005 elections, the pro-Ankara ITC did extremely poorly, managing to win less than 1 percent of the vote nationwide. As a result, Turks discovered that the Turkmen, 50 percent of whom are Shi'a aligned with traditional Iraqi Shiite groupings, were not their brethren waiting to be "saved" by Ankara. Moreover, for those Turks who still held on to the dream of a conquering Turkish army capturing Kirkuk, a general in 2007 reminded all that Kirkuk was more than 452 kilometers from the Turkish border.[20]

---

19. In fact, close U.S.-Turkish cooperation on intelligence and counterterrorism efforts were confirmed by both the U.S. ambassador to Ankara, Ross Wilson, and Turkish Foreign Ministry spokesperson Burak Özügergin. See *Today's Zaman*, October 10, 2008.

20. Metehan Demir, "Niye Sınır Ötesi Operasyon Olmaz?" *Sabah* (Istanbul), January 22, 2007.

Turkish Foreign Ministry officials privately share Western concerns on expanding Iranian influence in Iraq. They too would like Iraq to emerge once again as a counterweight to Iran, which has successfully wooed and nurtured many of Iraq's multiple ethnic and sectarian groups. Iran has had a head start because so many of the Iraqi opposition politicians made Tehran their home during Saddam's rule. Even in Iraqi Kurdistan, the Iranians, unlike the Turks until recently, were quite adept at cultivating the two Kurdish parties. While Turkish prime minister Erdoğan and foreign minister Ahmet Davutoğlu have displayed a cordial if not friendly attitude toward Tehran, especially in light of the Iranian nuclear program, Turkey has made serious commercial inroads into northern Iraq. The Free Life Party of Kurdistan (PJAK), the PKK's Iranian affiliate sharing bases and infrastructure with the PKK in the remote northern Iraqi Qandil mountain range, provided Tehran with an opportunity to engage Turkey. Responding to PJAK's bloodying the Iranian military, Iran made a point of shelling PKK/PJAK hideouts in coordination with Turkish military operations. İlker Başbuğ, then the chief of the land forces general, admitted to Turkish-Iranian military and intelligence cooperation.[21]

Since 2003, Iraqi Kurds have had to somewhat balance Turkish and Iranian interests in northern Iraq. Turkey's new relationship with Iraqi Kurds gives Ankara a decisive advantage over Tehran in northern Iraq. Although resistant to KRG entreaties until recently, Turkey recognizes that for Iraqi Kurds Ankara provides a direct gateway to Europe and an indirect one to the United States. Iraqi Kurds seek legitimacy and support primarily in the West. Turkey, both as a NATO member and a EU aspirant, and its prosperous economy offer the Kurds the most desirable strategic option. Iran, with its Islamic regime at odds with the West and a less sophisticated economic base, cannot compete with Turkey in northern Iraq. In effect, a KRG linked to Turkey is likely to be an effective counterbalance to Iran in Iraq.

Finally, the prospect of access to northern Iraq's market in general, but more importantly to its oil and gas potential, has loomed large in the Turkish imagination. Ankara calibrated its position on Iraq's would-be hydrocarbon law; whereas it had sided with Baghdad against the KRG, a frustrated Ankara began in 2009 to directly import northern Iraqi oil. The prospect of a northern Iraqi gas pipeline feeding into the Nabucco pipeline, proposed to carry gas to European destinations, has assumed greater import. Turkey, in its quest to become an oil and gas transit hub, faces direct competition from Russia, and Azerbaijan, Turkey's prime supplier, has insufficient gas

---

21. *CNN–Turk*, June 8, 2008.

quantities to export through Nabucco. The northern Iraqi market may not account for a significant share of Turkish exports, but the prospect of intensive economic relations with the KRG has the added benefit of improving the lot of one of Turkey's most economically depressed regions, the Kurdish-inhabited southeast.

In the final analysis, the Turkish government's change of policy is a calculated geopolitical risk. The most dramatic move that expresses the depth of change is the opening of a consulate in Erbil. As such, the consulate can also be interpreted as an open admission by Ankara that it recognizes the federal structure of Iraq, with the KRG as a constituent element—an admission it had long abhorred to make. Turkish critics charge that in the process Ankara may even be strengthening the KRG's hand and facilitating its irredentist aspirations over Kirkuk and other parts of Iraq to say nothing of Iranian, Syrian, and Turkish parts of the Kurdish-speaking region. Even so, the KRG is landlocked, and its ability to emerge as a viable state with all of its neighbors assuming a hostile stance toward it is quite minute. On the other hand, Turkey's past policies at home and in Iraq manifestly did not work.

The Foreign Policy Contexts

The AKP's new foreign policy vision also underlies the shift in Turkish attitudes toward Iraq. The AKP came to power with the intention of revitalizing Turkey's inward-looking foreign policy. Taking advantage of the vacuum created by the Bush administration's war on Iraq, the AKP began to fashion itself as a regional power acting as mediator in a number of conflicts. In a policy that some have called "new Ottomanism," Turkey has been expanding the contours of its influence in regions that were once part of the Ottoman Empire.[22] The architect of this new foreign policy, Ahmet Davutoğlu, has a far more ambitious agenda: making Turkey a global power. Using its cultural and historical links to its immediate regions and beyond, NATO membership, EU candidacy, a rapidly growing economy, and a willingness to don a leadership mantle, the AKP has furiously been expanding Turkey's role in international organizations, winning for example a seat on the UN Security Council after almost a fifty-year hiatus. In the process, Davutoğlu and Erdoğan have set forth an ambitious policy of "zero problems with neighbors," concomitant with a high level of engagement with the leaders and populations of neighboring states and an emphasis

---

22. Ömer Taşpınar, *Turkey's Middle East Policies: Between Neo-Ottomanism and Kemalism*, Carnegie Middle East Center Paper no. 10 (Washington, DC: Carnegie Endowment for International Peace, September 2008), 11.

on the importance of the internal linkage between security and democracy. Underlying the new Turkish foreign policy is a deep desire to chart a policy distinctly independent of Washington and the European Union. This may appear more discernible when it comes to Iran; Ankara has openly tried to prevent them from imposing further sanctions on that country. In Iraq, despite the current harmony between U.S. and Turkish policy, Erdoğan has been quite explicit in his desire for foreign powers "to leave the region to solve its problems."[23]

Two interlinked problems interfered with this vision: first, Ankara has had serious problems in northern Iraq, specifically with the KRG; second, as an Erdoğan adviser has argued, "the current state of the [domestic] Kurdish issue alone cripples Turkey's ambitions to speak with confidence about democracy, transparency and human rights in the Middle East."[24] Improvement in relations with the KRG would have positive feedback on the domestic Kurdish question and vice versa and improvement on both accounts would remove some of the stigma carried by Ankara and therefore provide it with more clout internationally. Erdoğan's high-level international intercessions have not only won wide acclaim among the Turkish public but have also blurred the boundaries between domestic and foreign policy.[25]

Both openings toward the KRG and the domestic Kurdish minority serve Ankara's foreign and domestic policy purposes. It also strengthens Turkey's hand in Iraqi politics. Its increased sway can also better serve the interests of the Iraqi Turkmen down the road. Finally, both of these lift an important burden in Turkish-American relations from Ankara's shoulders and transforms Turkey into a more valued and ultimately reliable interlocutor on Iraq. However, one danger that lurks in Turkey's new initiatives is the possibility of overconfidence on the part of Ankara. In its zeal to become to go-to address, Ankara risks alienating some of the friends it ultimately needs the most.

On balance, the AKP has played a constructive role in Iraq, establishing relations with groups other than the Turkmen and Kurds. According to senior Turkish officials, Ankara has developed close relations with Iraqi vice president Tariq al-Hashemi, providing him with much-needed support. Similarly, in the run-up to the 2010 Iraqi national elections, Turkish diplomats were influential behind the scenes in the cobbling of the al-

---

23. Speech at the Istanbul Conference, October 19, 2009.
24. Ibrahim Kalın, "Turkey and the Middle East: Ideology or Geo-Politics?" *Private View* (Turkey) (Autumn 2008): 32.
25. Oğuzlu, "Turkey's Northern Iraq Policy," 5.

Iraqiya list of former prime minister Ayad Allawi. Ankara's Sunni outreach occasionally angered the Iraqi Shi'a, especially when some of the hard-core anti-Shiite Sunnis were gathered for a conference in Istanbul. Ankara also facilitated Muqtada al-Sadr's meeting with his followers in Istanbul in June 2008.[26]

The Domestic Institutional Context

The dramatic changes in Iraq policy would not have been possible without significant developments in the domestic institutional context. The AKP's emergence and success as an anti-establishment party set the stage for a showdown between it and the state apparatus. Miscalculations by the civil-military establishment helped undermine its preeminent role in society and politics.

For the civil-military establishment, fearful of society's Islamicization, the AKP's performance on hot-button national security issues could serve as an opportunity to put pressure on the party. However, the AKP, during the early years of its rule, followed Turkey's traditional policy on the Kurdish question broadly defined. The AKP, thanks to the peculiarity of the Turkish electoral system, had with 34 percent of the vote won an overwhelming majority of parliamentary seats in the 2002 elections, including all of the seats in Kurdish majority areas.[27] The AKP parliamentary delegation therefore contained a significant number of Kurdish deputies who were eager to see the AKP improve conditions in the southeast.

AKP's only two exceptions to the traditional policy consisted of the forays of intelligence chief Emre Taner into northern Iraq (discussed in the next section) and a 2005 speech by Erdoğan in Diyarbakir, the heart of the Kurdish southeast, where he acknowledged that Kurds had been poorly treated throughout the republic's history. Expectations raised by the speech soon evaporated because there was no follow-up. Erdoğan would eschew much of the goodwill with his hostile stance against the pro-Kurdish Democracy and Society Party (DTP), which represents the most nationalistic elements of Kurdish society and shares a political base with the PKK.

---

26. Sadr has the added advantage of being an opponent of federalism; he has emerged as an important foe of Iraqi Kurds. He has, however, been known to support both sides, as when he offered Iraqi Kurds support against Turkey when the latter initiated a land incursion. Subsequently, in his June 2008 visit, his subordinates assured Turkish parliamentarians that they fully supported Turkey on Kirkuk. Author's private communication with a Turkish parliamentarian, Ankara, July 13, 2008.

27. Turkey's electoral system has a 10 percent national minimum threshold requirement for parties to win seats in parliament. In 2002, only two parties managed to cross that threshold. Winners, therefore, receive far more seats than their vote share would dictate.

The increasing hostility between the establishment and the AKP came to a boiling point in 2007 and 2008. In what turned out to be a major miscalculation, the military leadership intervened to prevent AKP from electing Abdullah Gül, then foreign minister, as president. Gül's main handicap was the fact that his wife wore a headscarf; for senior officers this constituted a major transgression of secularism for someone who would be occupying the office held by the nation's founder Atatürk. The AKP capitalized from the resulting political crisis and rode a wave a resentment in early elections in which it substantially increased its share of the vote, from 34 to 47 percent. This was the first time an incumbent party had increased its share of the vote in Turkey since 1954. In effect, the military had received its comeuppance from the Turkish voters, triggering a crisis of confidence in its ability to offer unchallenged views of all things political.

The 2007 elections changed the political landscape in a decisive way. Although the establishment made one more attempt at ridding the country of the AKP by instituting a court case aimed at banning the party, it failed. As a result, the AKP emerged far stronger from the bruising battles with the military and its allies. Its parliamentary opposition was also more varied: instead of two parties, three had crossed the 10 percent threshold and some twenty independent Kurdish candidates who once elected organized themselves under the DTP banner.[28]

Reform of civil-military relations had always been at the top of the AKP's priorities. Its early push for EU membership had been motivated by its need to curtail the military's vast prerogatives and indirectly protect the party's own future from "meddlesome generals." Resolving the Kurdish issue was another facet of this agenda; the PKK insurgency had enabled the military to maintain its critical role in society. Political mistakes committed by officers were compounded in 2007 when PKK attacks from across the border in Iraq inflicted significant casualties on border garrisons. Later revelations in this and other cases questioned the military's competence and truthfulness. These missteps helped to redress the lopsided nature of civil-military relations although the Turkish military continues to exercise significant influence in matters relating to national security and foreign policy.

---

28. The Constitutional Court closed the DTP in December 2009; it was quickly replaced by the Peace and Democracy Party (BDP).

Key Agents of Change

There is no question that the most important drivers for the change in Turkish policy toward the Kurds arc Erdoğan, Gül, and Davutoğlu. None of these individuals are new to these issues. Gül had been very active in foreign policy in previous incarnations of the AKP, when he served as a state minister in the government of Necmettin Erbakan (1996–97) and advised the then prime minister on foreign policy. Indeed, beginning in the 1990s, he was the principal foreign policy thinker and spokesperson for the Islamist parties, while in 1991 Erdoğan penned one of the most progressive reports on the Kurdish situation for his then party leader Erbakan.[29] Erdoğan's 2005 Diyarbakir speech represented his first formal foray into the Kurdish issue. As mentioned, the expectations generated from that speech ultimately faded away due to his own inability to follow through and the much tougher climate in Ankara in that period, as well as to a renewal of PKK violence.

The AKP and its much more Islamic predecessor parties have traditionally downplayed nationalist discourse when dealing with their Kurdish populations, preferring instead to emphasize the religious unity of Kurds and Turks. For conservatively inclined Kurds, this has been a winning message historically. The AKP has received an important share of the Kurdish vote and includes numerous—perhaps as many as seventy—parliamentary members of Kurdish origin. Whereas these MPs are a source of pressure on their political leadership, they are also constrained from articulating their grievances in public by rigid party rules and Erdoğan's total dominance of the party. Still, many are within Erdoğan's close circle, with a chance to provide him with a current account of how his policies are received among Kurds. Erdoğan, however, is prone to extemporization and verbal mistakes. For example, his self-confident rhetoric in advance of the municipal elections in 2009, when he promised to "conquer" the DTP fortress of Diyarbakir, caused a backlash, resulting in a resounding victory for the DTP.

The AKP remains a fiercely nationalistic party that subsumes some of its nationalist rhetoric under a more general rubric of tolerance and values. As noted, its foreign policy is ambitious and designed to transform Turkey and the Kurdish question, on both sides of Turkey's border. Although the AKP's foreign policy faces formidable obstacles, Syria and Iraq are two places of consequence where the AKP thinks that Turkey can play a substantial role. Hence, the AKP leadership should be expected to continue to invest time and resources in both of these countries.

---

29. Belma Akçura, *Devletin Kürt Filmi* (Ankara: Ayraç Kitabevi Yayınları, 2008).

Even so, much of the change in Turkey's Iraq policy—more specifically, its northern Iraq policy, which has constituted the core of Turkish concerns—would not have come about without the acquiescence of the military, the initiatives undertaken by Ministry of Foreign Affairs personnel, or the efforts by the Turkish National Intelligence Organization. To be sure, new conditions on the ground and opportunities unquestionably set the stage for changes in policy. That said, however, in Turkey, where ideology matters and the discourse on Kurds and Kurdish rights has been taboo, individuals within these critical institutions have played critical roles. Specifically, without the consent of İlker Başbuğ, the chief of the Turkish General Staff (2008–10), the new Kurdish initiative would not have gotten off the ground. The Turkish military views itself as the guardian of not just the security of the Turkish state but also of its character and the ideological legacy of Atatürk. Much of this legacy was constructed on a denial of the existence of Kurds in Turkey. Turkey was imagined to be a country only inhabited by Turks, and those who were not Turks had little choice but to accept this designation. The military was at the forefront of numerous attempts at the social engineering of Kurdish areas.

The military also took a hard-line against any attempts at or even suggestion of a domestic opening toward the Kurds, insisting that the problem in the Kurdish areas was one of terrorism—that is, the struggle against the PKK—and poor economic conditions, which were driving people to rebel. Despite his hard-line reputation, General Başbuğ, unlike his predecessors (with the possible exception of Hilmi Özkök), sought diverse opinions on the Kurdish issue. In a wide-ranging speech in April 2009, Başbuğ articulated a clear message on Kurdish identity. Emphasizing that "those who formed the Turkish republic are the people of Turkey," he affirmed that it was perfectly fine for an individual to have a sub- or a secondary identity, though he maintained that these identities ought not be constitutionally recognized. Still, in an indirect recognition that nonviolent means should be considered in Turkey's fight against the PKK, Başbuğ suggested that legal changes enabling some PKK fighters to return to society ought to be envisioned.[30] Başbuğ's speech ploughed new ground due to his non-confrontational tone toward Turkish Kurds and his attempt at differentiating the average Kurdish citizens from the PKK. Başbuğ also came to the realization that after twenty-five years of struggle, the Turkish military was not any closer to defeating the insurgency and impeding the flow of

---

30. In his speech, Başbuğ quoted a variety of foreign and Turkish thinkers, including Samuel Huntington, Eliot Cohen, Morris Janowitz, Max Weber, and Chaim Kaufmann.

new recruits for the PKK.[31] Most importantly, in its August 20, 2009, meeting, the National Security Council, Turkey's main civil-military coordinating body, provided the government with a green light to continue its Kurdish policies. Başbuğ told those who were anxious about the Kurdish opening not to worry because "the Turkish military, with the power it derives from the people, is hard at work."[32] Such statements represented the clearest possible endorsement of the policy that civilians could get from the Turkish military.

Başbuğ's tacit support for the domestic Kurdish initiative and change in Iraq policy also came with some fine-tuning. As the discussion of the initiative has gathered steam, he intervened to define the contours of the changes;[33] in so doing he ironically acted as a bulwark from the nationalist elements who opposed the policy but look up to the military as the regime's and the status quo's guarantee. He was careful to draw redlines on the use of Kurdish language in education and on altering the constitution. By quelling such anxieties, these redlines enabled the process to go forward without the opposition resorting to street demonstrations and even violence. The subtle role played by Başbuğ, though very constructive, was also the product of the unnatural evolution of civil-military relations in Turkey. This relationship is on track for further significant changes, of which Başbuğ has been acutely aware. He often reiterated his institution's role in Turkey's democratic system, yet the Turkish military is not a civilianized institution. Ever since the 1960 military coup, when lower-ranking officers overthrew not just the government but also their own hierarchy, officers have been careful to maintain the military chain of command and defend the institution's prerogatives. Just as Başbuğ undid years of military practice on the Kurds, his successor, Işık Koşaner, is in no way compelled to follow through on the opening or reforms, although the military is in a much weaker position today than it has ever been.

The Turkish intelligence organization played critical roles in changing the perspectives of many of the influential actors in the policy discussions over Iraq. The head of Turkish intelligence, Emre Taner, started to secretly engage the Iraqi Kurds in 2006. At a time when Turkish officials shunned the KRG, Taner's missions were critical for keeping tensions from overheating and preparing the groundwork for future talks. Taner, now retired, and his colleagues at the Turkish National Intelligence Organization (TNIO) had long been convinced that the hard-line tactics of

---

31. Author's private communications with a number of Turkish journalists and academics.

32. Fikret Bila, "Org. Başbuğ: Siyaset ve Terör Ağalarından Kurtulmak Lazım," *Milliyet*, September 22, 2009. See also Ahmet Altan, "Belirsiz Duygu," *Taraf*, September 22, 2009.

33. Murat Yetkin, "Başbuğ'un Mesajı, Erdoğan'ın Yöntemi, Gül'ün Konumu," *Radikal*, August 26, 2009.

the Turkish military against Iraqi Kurds were counterproductive. In the Ministry of Foreign Affairs, meanwhile, two diplomats played an important role in convincing the military that a change in policy in Iraq was in Turkey's best interests. Murat Özçelik, the special Iraq coordinator and later ambassador to Baghdad, and Feridun Sinirlioğlu, former deputy under secretary for Middle East affairs and later under secretary, had regional credentials and, perhaps more importantly, were perceived by all to be independent thinkers and actors. As such they could work both sides of the system, the AKP and the military, and work on the military's phobia of Iraqi Kurds.

The Limitations of the New Policy

Turkey's new Iraq policy contains both defensive and expansionist elements. It is defensive in so far as it was constructed on a platform of containment of Kurdish nationalism, a traditional concern of Ankara dating almost to 1926 when it consented to Mosul's integration into Iraq. It is also expansionist in that it seeks to maximize Turkish influence throughout the region and in Iraq in particular with an eye to earning a status commensurate with what Turks think they deserve.

For all of Turkey's newfound enthusiasm for its immediate region and Iraq in particular, the fact of the matter is that Iraq in the end is mostly an Arab country. With the obvious exception of Iraqi Kurdistan, Iraq perceives itself as being part of the Arab core. Turkish inroads into the Arab world have not been as significant as they have been touted to be; for all its successes, there have also been reverses or states angered by Turkish forays in what they perceived to be their zone of influence. In the eternal divide of East versus West, it is unclear if the Arab states consider Turkey as being closer to them or to the West despite AKP's Islamic antecedents.

Iraqi Kurdistan has no choice but to expand its economic ties to Turkey. For the Kurds, the rest of Iraq, as a vestige of a rentier oil state, pales in comparison to Turkey in terms of commercial opportunities. Turkey also offers consumer and durable goods and even a hospitable environment for Iraqi Kurd tourists. Still, as Iraqi Kurdistan moves forward and expands its economic connections to Turkey—as it must—it will remain a part of Iraq in ways that are uniquely binding. They include the institutional structure of the Iraqi state and, more importantly in the medium term, the power of language. For Kurdish students in the north, Arabic will continue to be the most important language for their personal future advancement.

The AKP's new foreign policy that had Ankara offer its good offices at any sign of trouble around its borders raised Turkey's standing. However, as demonstrated by Davutoğlu's August 2009 attempt to reconcile Syria and Iraq following devastating bombings in Baghdad's Green Zone, which Baghdad blamed on Damascus, well-meaning efforts may often not amount to much. Iraqis were not keen to see the Turks interfere despite the honeymoon in Syrian-Turkish relations. Some issues in inter-Arab politics will, for a variety of reasons, remain beyond the reach of outsiders.

One looming time bomb in relations is water, particularly as relates to Iraq, the proverbial Land of the Two Rivers. The danger in Iraq to not just agriculture but to a whole way of life is quite severe. The two rivers—the Euphrates and the Tigris—both originate in Turkey. The Euphrates traverses Syria before entering Iraq, and the Tigris for a short distance delineates the border between Iraq and Syria and then flows into Iraq. Upstream damming and irrigation projects, especially the Turkish multidam Southeast Anatolia Project, have sharply reduced the quality and quantity of water flowing to Iraq and Syria. Already in the 1980s and 1990s, differences over water allocations were construed as the grounds for Syrian leader Hafez al-Assad's support for the PKK and Öcalan. Iran as well has dammed some of the tributaries feeding into the Tigris.

"Decades of war and mismanagement, compounded by two years of drought, [were] wreaking havoc on Iraq's ecosystem, drying up riverbeds and marshes, turning arable land into desert, killing trees and plants, and generally transforming what was once the region's most fertile area into a wasteland."[34] The results were sandstorms and falling agricultural production. The decline in water flows is causing a rise in the sea level and salination, forcing people to abandon their villages in the south.[35] Similarly, in northern Iraq, declining water levels are playing havoc with farming, forcing migration as the traditional underground aqueducts disappear.[36] Between the ravages of climate change and declining water flows, Iraq will continue to become more urbanized and more dependent on food imports.

Once Iraq is stable, Iraq could choose, in conjunction with Syria, irrespective of their differences, to apply pressure on Turkey to release more water. This is unlikely to produce results because water scarcity is a regional

34. "Iraq in Throes of Environmental Catastrophe, Experts Say," *Los Angeles Times*, July 31, 2009.
35. "Water-Short Iraq Faces New Peril: The Sea," *United Press International*, September 23, 2009.
36. UN Educational, Scientific and Cultural Organization (UNESCO), "Crise dans le nord de l'Irak: L'assèchement des karez fait fuir des milliers de paysans," *Diplomatie* no. 42 (Janvier–Février 2010).

problem where upstream countries, especially if they perceive themselves to be powerful, tend to latch on to their right to exploit such resources first. Depending on the severity of the water shortage, relations between Iraq and Turkey could be adversely affected. The Iraqi Parliament in 2009 held up "the ratification of a comprehensive trade and cooperation agreement between the two countries. Members of parliament insist[ed] that a provision guaranteeing Iraq's share of water of the two rivers should be included in the agreement."[37]

The collapse of the Kurdish reform proposals in Turkey could have very serious ramifications for relations between the two countries. There are already visible signs that the AKP has lost much of its enthusiasm for continuing its domestic Kurdish initiative, at the very least, until after the next elections scheduled for summer 2011. This has been driven home with the resurgence in PKK attacks on military outposts in the southeast and even in Istanbul's environs in the summer of 2010. More importantly, perhaps, it has also been driven home by an increase in the Kurds' political mobilization and in their attempts to engender democratic autonomy—that is, to develop governance structures in the southeast that are separate and perhaps even independent of Ankara. An outright collapse of the reform efforts would obviate the PKK's need to demilitarize itself, but, more importantly, a return to more repressive measures by Ankara in Turkey's Kurdish areas would complicate KRG-Ankara relations, leading to a return to Turkey's Baghdad-centric policies. However, conditions having changed dramatically, it is no longer certain that Baghdad would unconditionally back Turkey for fear of repercussions at home. The reverse is also true: if the Kurds were to choose not to keep their faith with Baghdad, any ensuing conflagration between Iraqi Kurds and Baghdad would not automatically enlist Ankara's support for Baghdad. Ankara will have to assess its options in light of its own domestic Kurdish situation. Were the initiative in Turkey to succeed, Turkish Kurds will emerge as an important political constituent block whose preferences can no longer be ignored. The wild card here would be the pro-Turkish elements within the Turkmen population, as their preferences and future prospects are likely to have an impact on Turkish policy, especially regarding Kirkuk. Conflict over Kirkuk, depending on who starts it and how it proceeds, will mark a major watershed in Turkish-Iraqi relations.

Disputes between Baghdad and Erbil over the exploration and, more importantly, export of oil may put Ankara in a very untenable situation.

---

37. Nimrod Raphaeli, *Water Crisis in Iraq: The Growing Danger of Desertification*, Inquiry and Analysis no. 537 (Washington, DC: Middle East Media Research Institute, July 24, 2009).

Paradoxically, if Iraqi Kurds were to insist on exporting their hydrocarbons through Turkey when Baghdad prefers non-Turkish options, then Turkey will be far more positively disposed to Erbil than to Baghdad, an awkward predicament for Ankara, which is a proponent of a stronger Iraqi center. Generally speaking, instability in Iraq is likely to reflect poorly in Turkish-Iraqi relations, as Ankara will seek to shield itself from any violence, especially of the sectarian variety, emanating from south of the border.

Most analysts' assumptions about Iraq are pessimistic; it is seen as a country that will remain on the brink of civil war and mired in violence and instability for the foreseeable future. Although this is undoubtedly a safe supposition to make, it is important to consider what a resurgent Iraq could mean for the region. Oil will remain the commodity of choice for energy; the demand for more oil is predicted to rise as China and India push the limits of prosperity. Iraq's oil potential may be far greater than what the current figures for reserves suggest; for most of the period since 1980, the various wars and stiff international sanctions have stood in the way of oil exploration. Hence, some experts believe that Iraq's undiscovered recoverable oil reserves are quite large. An Iraq that can export 4 million barrels of oil a day or more may once again formulate a foreign policy that is at odds with one or more of its neighbors. It may decide to rearm. Alternatively, an Iraq with limited military capabilities may, at some point in the future, ask the United States to provide it with security, including through the establishment of military bases. All these are hypothetical scenarios that would have an indelible impact on how Turkey and, of course, the region as a whole, will see Iraq.

Finally, there is always the possibility of either Turkey or Iraq overplaying their respective hands. At this stage it is far more likely that Turkey will do so with its rather aggressive foreign policy initiatives. Can it inadvertently alienate Iraq or one of Iraq's Arab allies? As much as the new Turkey, which in Middle Eastern eyes is one that is at peace with its cultural heritage, is welcome in the region, it is after all still a non-Arabic-speaking society that had throughout most of the twentieth century ignored the pull of the Muslim world. There are costs to both becoming a surrogate superpower in the region and making an inordinate effort to belong. Turkey's uncertain reaction to the "Arab Spring," the revolts that swept the Middle East in 2011, especially with regard to both Libya and Syria, demonstrated the difficulties associated with becoming a regional power. Ankara has had to balance its economic and political interests and strong linkages built with the regimes in power against the yearnings of Arab populations for greater freedom.

Turkey, Iraq, and the United States: Long-Term Compatibility of Interests

In the short to medium term there is no question that the new Turkish approach to Iraq and U.S. interests are completely compatible. Gone are the days of U.S. fears that Turks will try to undermine the north and thereby indirectly do the same to U.S. objectives in Iraq. Both countries agree on the need for Iraq to remain united, and the differences over the federal nature of the Kurdish northern Iraq have disappeared. On the contrary, Turkey, with its close cooperation with the KRG, helps stabilize Iraq.

A U.S. withdrawal from Iraq will accelerate competition among the neighbors for influence in Iraq as each seeks to develop its own sphere of influence. For Washington, Turkey, a traditional ally, would be a welcome asset in this competition. This said, the creation of spheres of influence in Iraq and interference in Iraqi politics from neighbors, in the long run, could make for an unstable Iraqi polity, strengthen ethnic and sectarian divisions, and prevent the emergence of a responsible and accountable political system. Turkey and others may find it to be too difficult to resist the temptation or to ignore calls from prospective clients in Iraq to intervene.

During the period of Iraqi government formation in 2010–11, Washington and Ankara sought similar outcomes: the construction of a broad-based Iraqi government with significant Sunni inclusion, even a government led by Allawi that excluded or minimized Sadrist participation. This would not come to be. However, one arena where cooperation with the Turks could bear fruit is in getting the Saudis to engage with Baghdad. Riyadh has had deep misgivings about Iraq's government. More significantly, like many Sunnis in Iraq, Saudis have interpreted the ascendancy of the Shi'a in Iraq as an Iranian strategic victory that will enable Tehran to sow seeds of dissension in Iraq and the region in line with its revisionist aims. While the Saudis have tried to help with Sunni tribes, their efforts have disappointed U.S. officials. Turkey, despite its new foreign policy emphasis of "zero problems" with its neighbors, would like to balance Iran in Iraq.[38] Behind the scenes, Turks often lament the insurgent nature of the Iranian regime and the need to counter it; they think that their approach is better suited but claim to share Saudi and American concerns regarding Iranian behavior.

But the Arab Spring is a complicating factor. It is yet too early to discern long-term patterns. Still, the resurgence of Egypt as a political actor in the region may cap Turkey's ambitions. On the other hand, the challenge to the dominance of the Ba'th regime in Syria has already altered the calculus

---

38. Veysel Ayhan, "Türkiye-İrak İlişkileri: Bölge Ülkelerinin İrak Politikası Bağlamında bir Analiz," *Ortadoğu Analiz* 1, no. 9 (September 2009): 22–31.

of all. What Turkey desires most is a return to stability. Its strong suit is its economic prowess and penetration of local markets. Hence, in Iraq, like Washington, Ankara wants stability and with it the opening up of Iraqi markets and the exploration of oil and gas fields.

U.S.-Iraqi dealings have been anything but predictable. "Since World War II, the United States and Iraq have never enjoyed close relations. There is no deep history of solidarity or deeply held shared values on which to build a new relationship. In fact, the U.S.-Iraq relationship has been fraught with mistrust, and successive generations of Iraqi leaders, while wanting the approval and economic attention of the West, have felt ambivalence if not hostility toward the United States and its global influence."[39] While the impact of the occupation and the American investment in blood and treasure will continue to figure in the bilateral relationship, Iraqi leaders have an incentive to demonstrate their independence from Washington. Even the Shi'a, who have gained power, harbor deep bitterness toward the poor execution of the war's aftermath; some may even see the Americans as the only obstacle to a complete takeover of Iraq. Hence, the likelihood of future antagonisms cannot be discounted.

Were Iraqis to turn against America, Turkey may well find itself between a close neighbor and a close ally. A similar scenario has played itself between Washington and Ankara over Iran's nuclear program. Turkey, as a member of the UN Security Council, has resisted sanctions on Iran and gone out of its way to obstruct the adoption of additional UN sanctions against Iran angering U.S. officials. Prime Minister Erdoğan, contrary to his Western allies, repeatedly vouched for the peaceful intentions of Iran's nuclear program.[40] Turkish behavior over Iran will provide clues to its future conduct in Iraq in the event of U.S.-Iraqi disagreements that affect Turkish interests. The AKP is keen on demonstrating its independence from the United States, especially on issues relating to the Middle East. Turkey's assiduous courting of all factions in Iraq and its concomitant construction of institutional, political, and commercial ties there bode well for its continued influence. Turkey, unlike the United States, is after all a neighbor and there to stay.

Iraq has, of course, another option, and that is to reintegrate itself into the Arab world. The Kurds in Iraq have resisted the definition of Iraq as an Arab state but have agreed that it should continue as a member of the Arab League. It remains unclear how an Iraq closely aligned with and in-

---

39. Ellen Laipson, *America and the Emerging Iraqi Reality: New Goals, No Illusions*, Century Foundation Report (Washington, DC: Century Foundation, 2008), 9.
40. "İran'a Haksızlık Yapılıyor," *Hürriyet*, September 27, 2009.

tegrated into the Arab world would interact with the United States. Washington would benefit politically (and morally) if Iraq were to stabilize its politics and emerge as a politically diverse and tolerant society. However, there are numerous issues on which an Arab cover will enhance Iraq's disputes with not just the United States but also with Turkey, such as those related to water or oil.

The region is in flux, more so than ever. Washington and Ankara are, for different reasons, status quo powers. In Iraq (as in Syria), they are compelled to work together. Both have much to lose from an Iraq that fails to find its sure footing.

3

Iran's Strategies and Objectives in Post-Saddam Iraq

Mohsen M. Milani

The emergence of the Islamic Republic of Iran as a formidable player in Iraq and the closest regional ally of the U.S.-backed government of Nuri al-Maliki, at a time when thousands of American troops are stationed there, is a paradoxical and unintended consequence of the U.S. occupation of Iraq. Prior to the 2003 U.S. invasion of Iraq, Washington considered the Islamic Republic a member of the "axis of evil" and an enemy to be contained. Under the paranoid leadership of Saddam Hussein, who viewed the Persians as mortal enemies, Iraq was an effective bastion against the expansion of Iranian power in the Persian Gulf. By removing the Sunni-supported Saddam Hussein from power, the United States empowered the historically marginalized Shi'a of Iraq—Iran's natural allies—and set in motion a dynamic process that has shuffled the strategic landscape of the oil-rich Persian Gulf. Iran took advantage of the chaos created by the American occupation tsunami to gain strategic depth in Iraq and expand its influence in the Persian Gulf and the Levant. Having fought with Iraq for eight bloody years in the 1980s, Iran, particularly its Revolutionary Guards, gained a treasure trove of valuable lessons that it has used to advance its complex agenda while navigating the fault lines of the post-Saddam era. The agenda combines clear strategic goals with tactical flexibility, and soft power with hard power.

Iran's policy toward Iraq is somewhat different from other aspects of its foreign policy. On one hand, the clerical leadership and a significant percentage of the population have a deeply religious attachment to southern Iraq, home to the holiest shrines of Shiism. On the other hand, there is a popular sense of anger, if not revulsion, toward Iraq, the country that invaded Iran in September 1980 and caused a great deal of death and destruction. These conflicting feelings have influenced Iran's Iraq policy in ways more subtle than are usually recognized.

Iran's policy toward Iraq is also intimately and directly linked to its relations with the United States and its perception of threats emanating from the United States. Ever since the invasion of Iraq in March 2003, Iran has been competing with the United States for influence in Iraq. An Iran whose legitimate security needs are threatened by the United States is likely to act more mischievously in Iraq and undermine U.S. interests than an Iran whose relations with the United States are improving.

Iran's goals in Iraq are complex and evolving. First, Iran wants to help establish, preferably through elections, a friendly, Shi'a-dominated government in Baghdad that does not pose a serious security threat to Iran but is sufficiently strong to prevent the Sunnis from once again dominating the government and to maintain Iraq's territorial integrity and inhibit its Balkanization. Uncertain about the future of Iraq and American plans and intentions, Iran has hedged its bets by supporting as many Shiite groups as possible and antagonizing as few Sunni groups as possible, all in the hope of being on the winning side of the ongoing power struggle in Iraq. Although the most desirable outcome for Iran is an Islamic federal system of government with a weak center and strong and semiautonomous provinces, Tehran would settle for any form of government as long as it is dominated by Shi'a and is not a security threat to Iran. Second, Iran wants to create a "sphere of influence" in southern Iraq, mainly through increasing trade and engaging in economic, financial, and religious activities. Third, Iran wants to develop a deterrent/retaliatory capability to be used against the United States in the event of an attack on Iran's nuclear facilities, while avoiding any direct confrontation with the United States, and to prevent the United States from establishing a permanent military presence. Recognizing the vulnerabilities of the Shi'a-dominated government in Iraq as well as its close security, political, and economic relations with Washington, Tehran had to adapt to the United States playing a significant role in Iraq. Fourth, Iran wants to dismantle the infrastructure of the Mojahedin-e Khalq, an Iranian dissident group based in Iraq that Tehran believes has been engaged in subversive and terrorist activities and is collecting intelligence to overthrow the Islamic Republic.

To what extent has Iran achieved each of these four goals, and how has it achieved them? This chapter addresses these intriguing questions.

Iran's Tortured Relations with Iraq—1921–2003

From 1921, when Britain installed Faysal Ibn Hussein as the king of the newly formed Iraq (formerly known as Mesopotamia, which was part of the Ottoman Empire), until 2003, when Saddam Hussein was overthrown, Iraq was Iran's most hostile neighbor. Their bilateral relations were often shaped by mutual suspicion and bitter territorial disputes and, sporadically, by fleeting cooperation.[1]

After the Ba'th Party seized power in Baghdad in 1968 and after the British troops withdrew from the Persian Gulf, Iran and Iraq became engaged in a fierce rivalry to dominate the Persian Gulf. Washington, too, was intensely interested in the region, but faced two dilemmas: Mohammed Reza Shah (1941–79) opposed the presence of foreign troops in Iran's backyard, and the American people had no appetite for new troop commitments at the height of the Vietnam War. Consequently, Washington developed the "twin pillar" strategy, offering the U.S. indirect control and relegating the task of maintaining regional security to Iran and Saudi Arabia.[2] Ultimately, it was the Shah who became the dominant power or the region's "policeman."

As Iran's regional power increased in the 1970s, so did its tensions and rivalry with Iraq, the only country that belligerently challenged Iran. Iraq formed a united Arab front against Persian expansionism, increased support for separatist elements in Iran's Khuzestan and Baluchistan, which had significant Sunni populations, gave a safe haven to the communist Tudeh Party of Iran and other dissidents, expelled thousands of Iranians living in Iraq and thousands of Shiite Faili Kurds, and signed a friendship treaty with Moscow in 1971. Iran's policies toward Iraq, however, were even more belligerent. To undermine Iraq, the Shah, who called Iraq "that miserable little dwarf," organized an abortive coup against Saddam Hussein in 1971.[3] To contain Iraq in the region, he developed close relations with Arab sheikhdoms and helped Sultan Qabus of Oman defeat a separatist movement that Iraq supported. With clandestine support from Wash-

1. Mohsen M. Milani, "Iran's Relations with Iraq, 1921–1979," *Encyclopedia Iranica*, vol. 13 (New York: Columbia University, 2006), 564–572.

2. James Bill, *The Eagle and the Lion: The Tragedy of American-Iranian Relations* (New Haven, CT: Yale University Press, 1988), 183–216.

3. Assadollah Alm, *The Shah and I: The Confidential Diary of Iran's Royal Court, 1969–1977* (London: I. B. Tauris, 1992), 82, 176.

ington and Tel Aviv, he provided weaponry and lavish financial support to the Iraqi Kurds, particularly to Mulla Mustafa Barzani. The Kurds waged a military campaign against Saddam that, by the mid-1970s, ended in a stalemate—exactly what Iran wanted. Forced into an unsustainable position, Saddam Hussein met the Shah in Algeria in March 1975 to sign the Algeria Protocol. Under the new agreement, Iran and Iraq at last agreed to exercise joint sovereignty over the Shatt al-Arab waterway (Arvand Rud), a power Iran had demanded for decades, and Iran terminated its support for the Kurds. Consequently, bilateral relations became friendly, but only fleetingly.

The Islamic Revolution of 1979 fundamentally changed Iran's foreign policy and created a power vacuum in the Persian Gulf. Ayatollah Khomeini's strategy of exporting revolution sent shivers up the spines of every Arab leader in the region. Iraq was exceptionally vulnerable to Khomeini's call to Islamicize the region, because 60 percent of its population was Shiite. Thus, in September 1980, Iraq invaded Iran. Saddam Hussein's goals were to dismantle or cripple the infant republic and assume the Shah's mantle as the hegemon of the Persian Gulf. Most Arab countries in the region gleefully began to lubricate Iraq's aggressive war machine. They provided an abundance of petrodollars that helped sustain a dazzlingly brutal and insane war that Saddam Hussein started and Khomeini refused to end. When Iran and Iraq accepted a United Nations brokered cease-fire in July 1988, there was no victor, only two losers: tens of thousands of people had died, millions had been injured and displaced, and the financial damage had exceeded the two countries total oil revenues for the twentieth century.[4]

After the cease-fire, the two countries chose different paths. Iran, having no major foreign debt, began to reconstruct its ruined economy and proceeded with a cautious rapprochement toward the West. Iraq, with tens of billions of dollars in foreign debt, refused to relinquish its quest to dominate the region. This time, Kuwait, a tiny and defenseless country that had magnanimously financed Iraq's war against Iran, was the victim. Iraq's fatal miscalculation was that Kuwait, unlike Iran, was not isolated and had a strategic ally in the United States. Washington quickly declared that the Iraqi aggression "shall not stand" and sent some 500,000 troops to the Persian Gulf, its first major deployment of troops to the region.

Iraq's occupation of Kuwait created a strategic quandary for Tehran. It unequivocally denounced Iraq's aggression and demanded its unconditional

---

4. Kaman Mofid, *The Economic Consequences of the Gulf War* (New York: Routledge, 1996). He claims that the cost of the war was a staggering $1.1 trillion.

withdrawal from Kuwait, but it was vehemently opposed to the presence of U.S. troops in the region. The United States and Iraq each offered incentives to entice Tehran either to take their side or remain neutral. Saddam Hussein pledged to improve relations with Tehran and called for "Islamic solidarity" to expel the "army of the infidels" from the region. Washington declared that "goodwill begets goodwill." Ultimately, Tehran pursued "active neutrality" to enhance its interests and avoid entanglement with either the United States or Iraq.[5]

Iran's active neutrality remained intact even after the expulsion of Iraqi troops from Kuwait. When the demoralized Iraqi Army mercilessly quashed two uprisings by Kurds and Shiites (both uprisings had been encouraged by the United States), Iran remained virtually silent. Although there were reports that Iran provided limited support to the rebellious Shi'a, publicly Iran called only for Saddam's resignation.

Iran's neutrality paid good dividends. Iraq, having invaded two countries in one decade, was relegated to a state of suspended animation under UN-imposed sanctions. As the UN inspectors disarmed it, Iraq became a mere nuisance, with Saddam Hussein a virtual prisoner in his own country. At the same time, Iran projected its power more confidently and continued its support to the dissident Iraqi Shi'a and to a lesser extent the Kurds who, thanks to U.S. support, had created an autonomous government in northern Iraq.

Iran's Shi'a Card

In the early 1920s, as Britain was establishing Iraq, Iran faced a conundrum: should it play or not play its Shi'a card in Iraq? At the time, the majority of Iraq's population was Shiite, and a substantial concentration of Persians or those of Persian linage were living in southern Iraq. In addition, there were many highly influential and popular Persian clerics in Iraq, and the clerical establishments of the two countries were intimately linked. Although the temptation was strong to use the Shi'a card, Iran made the strategic decision not to do so—a decision that survived until the 1979 revolution. Thus, Iran remained silent when, in a popular Shiite uprising against the British Mandate in Mesopotamia in June 1920, some 9,000 people were slaughtered by the British.[6] Even when roughly 40 prominent clerics, many of them Persians, left Iraq for Iran protesting the British

---

5. Mohsen M. Milani, "Iran's Active Neutrality During the Kuwaiti Crisis: Reasons and Ramifications," *New Political Science* nos. 21–22 (Spring–Summer 1992): 41–60.

6. J. N. Wiley, *The Islamic Movement of Iraqi Shias* (Boulder, CO: Lynne Rienner 1992), 17.

policy of placing the Sunni minority at the helm of the new Iraqi state, the Iranian government welcomed the clerics with much fanfare but refused to help them.[7]

The fact is that Iran in the 1920s did not and could not play the Shi'a card because it was too weak, was going through an unpredictable transition of power from the Qajars to the Pahlavi dynasty, and was dominated by Britain. Once the Pahlavis were in power (1926–79), they pushed for secularization and had no incentive to use the Shi'a card in Iraq. However, politics in Iran changed dramatically after the 1979 revolution, and by 2003, Iran was an established theocracy ruled by clerics, not dominated by any foreign power, and an emerging regional power.[8] This time around, Iran used its Shi'a card unabashedly and forcefully, counting on the support of Iraqi organizations it had previously supported.[9]

It was in the 1980s, during the Iraq-Iran War, that Tehran began helping dissident Iraqi organizations. They established informal networks of Shi'a and Kurds to influence events in Iraq and develop retaliatory capability on Iraqi soil. In 1981, the Islamic Da'wa Party, or the Islamic Call Party (henceforth, Da'wa), moved its headquarters from Iraq to Iran and began to receive support from the government. The small party, originally formed in 1957 in Iraq, engaged in terrorism against the Iraqi government in the 1960s and 1970s. The party was violently suppressed by the government and was declared illegal. In the early 1980s, its members bombed the French and American embassies and attempted to assassinate the amir of Kuwait. As a concession to Iran when he occupied Kuwait, Saddam Hussein freed the seventeen Lebanese and Iraqi Shi'a who had been convicted of the crimes in Kuwait. They were reportedly turned over to Iran.

There were, however, ideological tensions between the Da'wa and Iran's ruling ayatollahs. The Da'wa's theological foundation was laid by Ayatollah Muhammad Baqir al-Sadr in the 1960s.[10] Although an ally of Ayatollah Khomeini, he emphasized the centrality of "governance by the people" in an Islamic government. (He was tortured and executed by Saddam Hussein in 1980.) That view was not consistent with Ayatollah Khomeini's doctrine of the Vilayat-e Faqih, or direct governance by clerics. Moreover, Khomeini was an institution builder who preferred to create new

---

7. Massoud Kuhestani-nejad, *Calesha wa ta'molat-e Iran wa Eraq dar nima-ye nakost–wsada-ye bistim* [Challenges and interactions of Iran and Iraq in the second half of the twentieth century] (Tehran: Markaz-e Asnad va Khadamat-e Pazoheshi, 2005), 31–33.

8. Mohsen M. Milani, "Iran's Persian Gulf Policy in the Post-Saddam Era," in *Contemporary Iran: Economy, Society and Politics*, ed. Ali Gheissari (New York: Oxford University Press, 2009), 349–355.

9. For an excellent analysis of the Iraqi Shi'a, see Yitzhack Nakash, *The Shias of Iraq* (Princeton, NJ: Princeton University Press, 1994).

10. See, for example, Muhammad Baqir-as-Sadr, *Lessons in Islamic Jurisprudence*, trans. Roy Mottahedeh (Oxford: Oneworld Publications, 2005).

institutions and staff them with those near and dear and loyal to him. To this end he helped establish the Supreme Council for the Islamic Revolution in Iraq (SCIRI), an umbrella group comprised of a few organizations that embraced the doctrine of the Vilayat-e Faqih. The organization celebrated its creation in Tehran in 1982.

Under the leadership of Ayatollah Muhammad Baqir al-Hakim, SCIRI became Iran's most trusted Iraqi dissident group and was lavishly funded.[11] Moreover, the armed wing of the party, the Badr Brigade, was created and trained by Iran's Revolutionary Guards. In fact, the two organizations grew together during the Iraq-Iran War and continued to work closely for years. On the eve of the U.S. invasion, the Badr Brigade was transformed into a disciplined, well-armed militia, with 12,000 to 15,000 fighters.

Iran's Fears and Concerns on the Eve of the U.S. Invasion

Iran's strategic calculations changed in reaction to the U.S. liberation of Afghanistan and invasion of Iraq. These two momentous events, which placed thousands of American troops on Iran's eastern and western borders, created new opportunities and fears for Iran. In October 2001, Iran's Revolutionary Guards rubbed shoulders with U.S. troops as they both worked with the Northern Alliance to free Afghanistan from the clutches of the Taliban—Iran's nemesis. Iran also played a constructive role at the Bonn conference in 2002 that placed Hamid Karzai in power in Kabul. President Mohammed Khatami's moderate administration hoped its tactical cooperation would lead to a strategic cooperation with the United States and a perceptible improvement in U.S.-Iran relations. But that was not to be. Only three months after Afghanistan was liberated, President George W. Bush declared that Iran, Iraq, and North Korea were a grave national security threat and labeled them as members of the "axis of evil."

Washington's harsh rhetoric reinforced Tehran's perception that the United States posed an existential threat to the Islamic Republic, weakened the position of the reform-minded Khatami, and strengthened the hands of the security forces and the Revolutionary Guards who warned of possible U.S. aggression and imposed their bunker mentality on the country. The commander of the Revolutionary Guards proposed that Iran and

---

11. After Ayatollah Hussein Burojerdi, the undisputed grand ayatollah of his time, died in Iran in March 1961, a number of ayatollahs began to compete to replace him, including Khomeini. Mohammed Reza Shah sent a telegram of commiseration to Ayatollah Muhsin al-Hakim, the father of Muhammad Baqir al-Hakim, practically recognizing him as the grand ayatollah and hoping to move the center of Shi'a Islam from Qom to Najaf, Iraq, where Muhsin al-Hakim was residing.

the Islamic countries should develop a comprehensive plan to neutralize the United States, or else "one after another we will fall prey to U.S. aggression." Afghanistan was the first, he said, and Iraq would be the second in the new U.S. policy to dominate the region.[12] Even Hassan Rouhani, the moderate chair of the Supreme National Security Council, denounced the United States for planning to create chaos and destabilize the Islamic Republic.[13] As the drumbeat of the American war against Iraq became ever more deafening in Washington, Tehran quickly concluded that Iraq, not Iran, was the immediate target of the United States. Thus, it found some breathing room to design its Iraq strategy.

Tehran faced a fundamental strategic dilemma before the U.S. invasion: while it supported Washington's goal of overthrowing Saddam Hussein, which Tehran had futilely tried to achieve during the Iraq-Iran War in the 1980s, it feared and opposed the presence of American troops in Iraq. Therefore, Tehran decided to indirectly cooperate with the United States to remove Saddam Hussein, hoping to persuade Washington not to directly interfere in Iraq. In fact, Tehran sought to influence American policy principally through the SCIRI and to a lesser degree through the Da'wa Party, the two main Kurdish parties, and Ahmad Chalabi—they all had their offices in Tehran.

President Mohammed Khatami denounced Saddam Hussein as an aggressor that must be overthrown but without the use of force.[14] Mohammed Reza Khatami, the brother of the president and a reformist leader, said that the day Saddam Hussein is overthrown, by any means possible, would be "one of the happiest days for Iran."[15]

The consensus in Tehran was that Washington should use the same model in Iraq it had successfully employed in dislodging the Taliban: avoid a full invasion and help Iraqis overthrow the incumbent regime. That position was advocated by the SCIRI as well. From Tehran, the leader of SCIRI, Ayatollah Muhammad Baqir al-Hakim, argued that, "We don't believe regime change in Iraq through total war is the right thing to do and it would be a grave threat to the Iraqi people and the region. . . . We believe that the Iraqi government must be overthrown, but at the same time we believe that the people of Iraq should take the responsibility for any regime change, and this should not be done from outside. . . . We have our unique plan to overthrow the Iraqi government, and we have shared this plan with America, even before America sought to overthrow the

---

12. *Hamshahri*, September 22, 2002.
13. Ibid.
14. *Hamshahri*, September 18, 2002.
15. *Hamshahri*, September 29, 2002.

Iraqi government. We are not ready to become a force dependent on the U.S."[16] Eventually, Washington rejected the SCIRI's model and, therefore, both the SCIRI and Iran recalibrated their strategies for an Iraq free of Saddam and occupied by the U.S. military.

Iran's Iraq Policy: The Two Phases

Iran's complex policy toward post-Saddam Iraq has gone through two phases. The first one began when the war started in March 2003 and ended with the victory of the Tehran-supported, Shi'a-dominated United Iraqi Alliance in the elections for the Transitional National Assembly in January 2005. In those unsetting years, when the moderate Mohammed Khatami was president, Iran held a defensive and reactive posture. He favored cooperation with the United States in Iraq, as Iran had done in Afghanistan, arguing that that the new opportunities in Iraq would enhance Iran's national interests. Ayatollah Ali Akbar Hashemi Rafsanjani, chair of the Expediency Council, epitomized that line of thinking when he said, "If the U.S. stops its colonial and hegemonic policies, the Islamic Republic is prepared to cooperate with the U.S. Iran is one of those countries that is prepared to have all kinds of cooperation with the U.S. Afghanistan was a good illustration of such cooperation, and the Americans themselves were grateful for Iran's cooperation."[17] What surely helped the moderates convince the hard-liners to accept this accommodationist policy was the fact that the ruling ayatollahs were in a state of "shock and awe," as they had witnessed the thunderous speed with which the American troops reached Baghdad and overthrew Saddam Hussein. Their fear was, if the United States succeeded in Iraq with little pain and little cost, Iran, as a member of the "axis of evil," would be the next target.[18] In short, Iran proceeded cautiously in that phase; it supported its Shiite allies, called for national elections to choose a legitimate government, avoided any direct confrontation with the United States, and began to build a network inside Iraq to manage its operations and develop a retaliatory capability in Iraq to be used against U.S. troops should it be attacked.

In the second phase, beginning in 2005 Iran has been more interventionist in Iraq. Although the U.S. strategy of the "surge" somewhat stabilized Iraq in 2007–8, Iran's more emboldened strategy evolved in the

---

16. *Jomhouri Islami*, Farvardin 22, 1381.

17. *Kayhan*, August 23, 2004.

18. The National Intelligence Estimate asserts that Iran stopped its nuclear weapons program in 2003. If the assertion is correct, fear of U.S. attack must have had a profound impact on that pivotal decision. See National Intelligence Council, "Iran: Nuclear Intentions and Capabilities," National Intelligence Estimate, November 2007, www.dni.gov/press_releases/20071203_release.pdf.

preceding years as the violent Iraqi insurgencies against the U.S. occupation grew in strength and effectiveness. In 2005, Mahmoud Ahmadinejad won the presidency and altered the balance of power in the Supreme National Security Council, where the country's foreign policy is determined, in favor of the hard-liners. Two discernable approaches to Iraq crystallized. Both agreed that the United States was in a quagmire and needed Iran to stabilize Iraq. Accommodationists, like Khatami and Rafsanjani, believed that Iran should cooperate with Washington to improve its relations with the United States. The hard-liners, like Ahmadinejad and the Revolutionary Guards, insisted that Iran's bargaining position would only strengthen as the United States sank deeper into the quagmire of Iraq, and that escape for Washington would inevitably require an arrangement with Tehran. They believed that "the U.S. has now become a hostage of Iran in Iraq," and therefore, Iran needs to be on the offensive, and demand concessions from Washington. At the end, Ayatollah Seyyed Ali Khomeinei, the supreme leader and the decider, chose a strategy that contained elements of both approaches but leaned toward the hard-liners. In short, Tehran's huge investments in Iraq began to pay dividends during the second phase: a friendly, Shi'a-dominated government was established in Baghdad, U.S.-Iran dialogue about Iraq's security took place, and Iran emerged as Iraq's closest regional ally and a power to be reckoned with in Iraq.

The Irony of Expanding Power through Elections

The overarching strategic goal of Iran since the U.S. invasion has been to help establish a friendly, Shi'a-dominated government in Baghdad powerful enough to prevent the country from descending into chaos—which could metastasize into Iran—but not powerful enough to pose a security threat to Iran.[19] Iraq's invasion of Iran in 1980 was a defining moment that exposed Iran's inability to deter foreign aggression. The enduring lesson of the war was to prevent Iraq from ever again being in a position of invading or posing a fatal security threat to Iran. After all, no other country in the past five centuries had inflicted as much death, destruction, and pain on Iran than Iraq. In fact, one reason why Ayatollah Khomeini refused to end the war when Iran had gained the upper hand in 1982 was to "teach" Iraq never again to think of aggression against Iran.[20]

---

19. For a good discussion of Iran's Iraq policy, see Anoushirvan Ehteshami, "Iran-Iraq Relations after Saddam," *Washington Quarterly* 26, no. 4 (Autumn 2003): 115–129, and Babak Ganji, *A Shia Enclave: Iranian Policy toward Iraq* (Surrey, UK: Conflict Studies Research Centre, March 2006).

20. Mehdi Bazargan, former prime minister of the Provisional Revolutionary Government, in an interview with the author, Tehran, Iran, August 19, 1993.

To achieve its strategic goal, Iran promoted elections and federalism. Iran has consistently called for national elections as the prelude to stability and ending the occupation. After the failure to find any weapons of mass destruction in Iraq, President George W. Bush, perhaps to appease his critics, called for establishing a democratic Iraq in the heart of an undemocratic Middle East. This was an unintended gift to Tehran, for democracy cannot develop without elections and elections were what Tehran saw as the fastest and most enduring path to increase its own power, because Iran's most valuable asset in Iraq was the country's majority Shiite demographic. In addition, the SCIRI and Da'wa, Iran's friends, were the largest Shiite organizations, with massive popular support and huge financial resources to mobilize the electorates. It is ironic that a theocratic Iran became a champion of democratic elections in Iraq—strange bedfellows indeed! No less ironic was that Washington and Tehran were on the same side, calling for parliamentary elections in January 2005. At the same time, some U.S. allies, such as Saudi Arabia and Egypt, questioned the wisdom of elections, fearing they would consolidate Shiite rule, marginalize their Sunni brethrens, and expand Iran's influence. Gradually, as violence increased, the voices of these allies held sway and Washington began intimating that perhaps the elections should be postponed, ostensibly to restore order.

The chances for conducting the elections were significantly diminished when, in August 2004, a bloody confrontation took place in Najaf between U.S. forces and the Jaish al-Mahdi militia loyal to Muqtada al-Sadr, a young Shiite cleric. Unlike the major Shiite parties and Iran, whose strategic priority was to hold elections, Sadr's main agenda was to end the occupation. Iran pressured Sadr to end the uprising, as did Ayatollah Kadhim al-Husaini Ha'iri, who resided in Iran and was his mentor and "source of emulation." Eventually, however, it was Ayatollah Ali al-Sistani, an Iranian living in Najaf and Iraq's most popular cleric, who brokered a ceasefire and insisted that elections must be held as scheduled.[21] And they were.

The results of the January 2005 election for the 275-seat Transitional National Assembly could not have been more gratifying to Iran. The results laid the foundation for Iran's growing influence. Despite an election boycott by many Sunnis, the Shi'a-dominated United Iraqi Alliance won 140 seats and formed an enduring alliance with the Kurds, who had the second largest bloc of seats. The assembly selected Jalal Talabani as the first Kurdish president of Iraq and Ibrahim al-Ja'fari, a Shi'a from Da'wa,

---

21. It was after the Najaf crisis in 2004 that the so-called special group criminals split from the Jaish al-Mahdi, accusing Sadr of capitulation to the Americans.

as prime minister. In the elections for National Assembly in December 2005, the United Iraqi Alliance emerged victorious again, and the Shiite-Kurdish alliance remained intact. Talabani retained his position, and Maliki from Da'wa became prime minister. Tehran achieved its central strategic objective through popular elections: a Shi'a-dominated, Tehran-friendly government in Baghdad, the first of its kind since Iraq's birth in 1921. Moreover, this Shiite victory strengthened Iran's regional standing and energized the repressed Shi'a of Lebanon, Bahrain, Saudi Arabia, Afghanistan, Pakistan, and elsewhere.

The formation of Prime Minister Maliki's second government in 2010, which preserved much of the power of the Shi'a-affiliated parties, was also viewed favorably in Tehran. The outcome of the 2010 election and the drawn-out process of government formation may not have been ideal from Iran's perspective, but on balance the outcome was seen by Iran as preserving its interests and influence in post-Saddam Iraq. Iran's second goal was to push for a federal system of government in the new Iraqi Constitution. Iranian leaders, as did Iraqi Shiite leaders, recognized that the United States and Iraqi Sunni Kurds would never tolerate a Shiite theocracy in Iraq and, therefore, opted for the second best alternative, a federal system of government.[22] The committee that drafted the constitution was selected by the Transitional National Assembly, which was dominated by the United Iraqi Alliance. While the SCIRI and the Kurds favored a federal system, Arab Sunnis and some Shi'a, including Sadr, opposed it. They feared that it would lead to Iraq's disintegration and loss of character as an authentic Arab state and would augment Iran's power in the Shi'a-concentrated regions. In the end, a tenuous compromise was reached. The new constitution, approved by voters in October 2005, did not endorse regional autonomy but empowered the provinces to hold referenda to declare autonomy. Although the inclusion of this key provision was a victory for Iran, it has yet to be fully implemented, except in the Kurdish areas. Still, many Iraqi provinces are under the control of the SCIRI and Da'wa and enjoy relative autonomy.

A federal Iraq would make it easier for Iran to expand its sphere of influence in the Shiite regions. A federal system would allow the Shi'a to impose their own laws, traditions, and even a legal system without antagonizing the Sunnis and Kurds. In the long term, however, such a system in Iraq is fraught with potential dangers for Iran. While Iran has supported the territorial integrity of Iraq, any meaningful empowerment

---

22. In 2007, the Supreme Council for the Islamic Revolution in Iraq changed its name to the Islamic Supreme Council of Iraq. The dropping of the words "Islamic Revolution" was presumably designed to emphasize the organization's commitment not to create an Islamic government modeled after Iran's.

of the provinces at the expense of the central government could be a recipe for the eventual Balkanization of Iraq along ethnic and sectarian divisions. This would certainly not be a desirable scenario for Iran as it is most likely to incite Iran's own rich, and occasionally restless, ethnic populations to demand autonomy, if not secession. This is why, despite having friendly relations with the Iraqi Kurds, Iran has adamantly opposed an independent Kurdistan in Iraq. Such an entity might entice Iran's Kurds to seek autonomy and then join their brethren in Iraq, Turkey, and Syria to create a Greater Kurdistan.

Iran Hedges Its Bets

It is virtually impossible for Iran to predict the future of Iraq. Moreover, Iran is uncertain about the reliability and durability of its relationships with the Iraqi Shiite organizations that are deeply divided and represent different socioeconomic constituencies.[23] This lingering uncertainty about Iraq's future and the dependability of its Shiite brethren explains why Iran has proceeded cautiously and hedged its bets by backing both the Shi'a-dominated government and those that challenge it and oppose the U.S. occupation. This strategy is designed to decrease Iran's chances of being unpleasantly surprised in Iraq and increase its prospects of being on the side of the winner in the unpredictable struggle for power. (In Afghanistan, Iran was shocked by the Taliban's meteoric rise to power.[24]) In addition, it provides Iran with leverage to foment trouble in Iraq should it so desire, or mediate among warring groups when it needs to. In both cases, Iran's power and credibility are increased.[25] The danger of such a strategy is that, in pleasing and appeasing different groups, Iran will have to spend a considerable amount of its human and financial capital, and it could easily alienate some of these groups and ultimately find itself with few true friends.

Iran's evolving relations with Muqtada al-Sadr illustrate the complexity, nuances, benefits, and dangers of this double-edged strategy. When the young Muqtada (born in 1973) gained international notoriety for his

---

23. For Iran's take on the security situation in Iraq, see Mohammad Vaezi, *The Importance of Securitization in Iraq* [in Persian] (Tehran: Center for Strategic Studies, Khordad 1387), www.csr.ir/PrintDetail.aspx?cid=1145&did=44&type=ar.

24. For a discussion of how Iran misread the situation in Afghanistan and did not take the challenge of the Taliban as seriously as it should have, see Mohsen M. Milani, "Iran's Policy towards Afghanistan," *Middle East Journal* 60, no. 2 (Spring 2006): 215–256.

25. For details about this aspect of Iran's policy, see the excellent essay by Joseph Felter and Brian Fishman, *Iranian Strategy in Iraq: Politics and "Other Means,"* Occasional Paper Series (West Point, NY: Combating Terrorism Center, October 13, 2008). This section has benefited enormously from this study.

violent opposition to the U.S. occupation in 2003, he was no mystery to Tehran, as he was to Washington. After all, Iran's top leaders had had personal relationships with the Sadr family for decades. Tehran saw the young Sadr as a "useful idiot," a "loose cannon," and a "rising star" who should neither be ignored nor too closely embraced.[26] He was and is vigilantly, but indirectly, handled. He is cautiously supported so that he remains a viable player in Iraqi politics and is being carefully groomed for the future. Having invested heavily in the SCIRI and Da'wa, Iran could not abandon them in favor of Sadr. And yet, for Tehran, Sadr's assets outweighed his liabilities. He opposed the U.S. occupation, as did Iran. He was immensely popular among the youth and impoverished Shi'a. He controlled the Sadr family's huge fortune and its networks of mosques and charitable organizations. Early on, during Iraq's civil strife, he had close connections to the Sunni insurgency, a connection Iran probably used to develop indirect relations with the insurgency. His secret militia probably helped Iran settle old scores with the Iraqi Ba'thists who fought Iran in the 1980s and violently confronted the Wahhabi-inspired al-Qaida in Iraq that was hell-bent on killing as many Shi'a as Americans. Finally, Sadr's radicalism was a counterweight to the more conservative views of Ayatollah Sistani, whose opposition to the Khomeinist version of the Vilayat-e Faqih worried Tehran.

Sadr's liabilities were more symbolic than substantive and did not pose an immediate threat to Iran. He was an unabashed Iraqi nationalist, who openly expressed his utter contempt for those, like the leaders of the SCIRI and Da'wa, who went into exile in Iran while his family audaciously challenged Saddam Hussein and paid with its blood. Nor did he hide his blatantly anti-Persian sentiments, questioning Iran's design for Iraq. He even ridiculed Ayatollah Sistani for his Ajami or Persian accent. Despite these tensions, Sadr recognized that Shiite Iran was his best and most natural ally and, therefore, he entered into a "marriage of convenience" with Tehran; a marriage that both sides initially preferred to keep hidden but, despite its inherent tensions, became stronger with each passing day. In the early days of the insurgency when Iran feared being attacked by the United States, Iran praised Sadr and the Sunni insurgency for their violent operations against the Coalition Forces. In fact, Iranian television programs, aired in Iraq in Arabic, glorified the insurgency as a national liberation movement. Ayatollah Hashimi Shahrudi, an Iraqi-born chief of the Iranian judiciary, declared that "no one can question the legitimacy of the just struggle of the Iraqi people against [the] foreign occupiers," even calling it "the

---

26. On August 29, 2003, Ayatollah Hakim was mysteriously killed in Iraq. This temporarily weakened the SCIRI and allowed Sadr to expand power.

beginning of a new Intifada [uprising] against foreign occupiers and aggressors."[27] When the history of the American invasion is written, the tremendous difficulties the U.S. military faced in suppressing the Iraqi insurgencies is likely to be viewed as a major hurdle that prevented the United States from going after Iran.

While Iran supported Sadr and the Shiite insurgency, it intervened when the conflict between the Shi'a and the U.S. military reached a dangerous level that threatened Iran's major strategic goals in Iraq, and when it seriously angered Iran's friends (SCIRI and Da'wa), which were collaborating with the United States. It was in that spirit, in mid-2004, that Iran sent a delegation to mediate between the Coalition Forces and Muqtada al-Sadr, which resulted in the assassination of an Iranian official. In the same vein, Iran pressured Sadr to end his August 2004 uprising in Najaf against the Coalition Forces because it was endangering the prospects of the scheduled election in January 2005. In April 2008, Prime Minister Maliki and the Mahdi militia were engaged in a ferocious fight over the control of the port city of Basra. Initially, the Sadrists made impressive advances, but then U.S. and British forces intervened and the Iraqi security forces reversed the situation. Sadr, who was living in Iran at the time, agreed to an Iran-brokered cease-fire in March 2008.

Iran had no interest in turning the political conflict in Iraq into a Shiite-Sunni conflict and encouraged both sides to cooperate. With its ambitions, Iran has sought to transcend the Sunni-Shiite divide, recognizing that the Shi'a constitute not more than 20 percent of the population of the Islamic world. (Iran's support for the Sunni Hamas and Islamic Jihad is often used by Tehran to prove that it has transcended the Shiite-Sunni divide.) Iran was less alarmed about the Iraqi Sunnis than the Wahhabi-style fundamentalists, many who came from Saudi Arabia. Iran, having seen the operation of the Wahhabi-inspired Taliban in Afghanistan, quickly recognized the game plan of Abu Musab al-Zarqawi, the notorious leader of al-Qaida in Iraq. He performed spectacular terrorist attacks against Shi'a to turn the conflict into a war between all Arab Sunnis and the Shi'a. He called Shi'a "the insurmountable obstacle, the lurking snake, the crafty and malicious scorpion, the spying enemy, and the penetrating venom" whose ultimate hope is to "establish a Shi'i state stretching from Iran through Iraq, Syria, and Lebanon and ending in the Cardboard Kingdom of the Gulf."[28] When in February 2006 his organization destroyed the golden dome of the Askariyya Mosque in Samarra, one of the holiest Shiite shrines,

---

27. *Hamshahri*, August 24, 2004.

28. Coalition Provisional Authority's English translation of a letter by Musab al-Zarqawi, which was obtained by the U.S. government in Iraq, February 2004.

Iraq descended into a full-blown sectarian war. Condemning the attack, Iran, however, reminded its Shiite brethren to avoid falling into the trap and to avoid a sectarian war.

Sadr's periodic conflict with the Maliki government, the repeated defeat of his militia at the hands of U.S. troops, and his debilitating fear of being arrested or killed by the Coalition Forces eventually forced him to do what he had criticized the SCIRI and Da'wa leaders for having done: seek sanctuary in Iran. After "renouncing" violence, he reportedly left Iraq sometime between March and August of 2007. Since then, he has been completing his religious studies in the city of Qom, presumably under Ayatollah al-Ha'iri.

Sadr's sanctuary in Iran can potentially help Iran address one of its major concerns, namely, the impact of Najaf seminaries on Iran's domestic politics. The seminaries in Iraq historically have had a profound impact on Iranian politics. It was, for example, from Najaf where Ayatollah Khomeini delivered his important lectures about the role of the Vilayat-e Faqih in an Islamic government. Today, what alarms Iran's ruling ayatollahs is the growing popularity of Ayatollah Ali al-Sistani in Iraq and Iran. Sistani does not embrace the notion of the Vilayat-e Faqih and instead champions the "quietist" tradition of Shiism. Although Sistani has been cautious not to publicly say anything critical about the Islamic Republic and was remarkably silent during the presidential dispute in Iran in June 2009, when millions of people took to the streets of the major cities, the Islamic Republic is, nevertheless, determined to undermine the "quietist" tradition and to lavishly support the Iraqi clerics who support its own version of Shiism. Toward that end, Sadr is potentially a useful tool as well. It is not, therefore, unreasonable to expect that Sadr, still in charge of his family's massive network, will return to Iraq as an ayatollah and as a critic of the "quietist" tradition of Shiism. The achievements of the Sadrists in the 2010 election, most notably their kingmaker role in securing a second term for Maliki, their deep antipathy toward an American military presence, and their growing influence on the ground, are all viewed favorably in Iran. For Tehran, the best days of Sadr, with his nationalistic credentials and his anti-occupation stance, are yet to come. Stay tuned.

Iran's Sphere of Influence in Southern Iraq

A pivotal component of Iran's strategy to neutralize the United States' containment policy and expand its own power is to support pro-Iranian organizations and networks beyond Iran's borders, creating spheres of influence. Iran relies a great deal on its soft power to create such spheres of influences, including engaging in a variety of economic, cultural, and social programs. In Afghanistan, Iran has built one such sphere of influence around the city of Herat. It is doing the same in Shi'a-dominated southern Iraq, home to some of the holiest shrines of Shiism. That region offers fertile ground for expanding Iranian power. Not only does it have a large population of Persians or those of Persian lineage, but it also has deep historical ties with Iran. Iran has pledged to spend more than $1 billion for Iraq's reconstruction, most of it in the southern region of Iraq. Ultimately, it hopes to transform the region into a kind of southern Lebanon, creating a ministate within a state—that is, within the Iraqi state.

Since 2003, Iran and Iraq have signed a number of agreements designed to improve their economic, cultural, political, and security relationships. Today, Iraq has become the second largest nonoil export market for Iran. Nonoil exports from Iran to Iraq have increased from a mere $184 million in 2003 to $4 billion in 2008, a whopping 2,173 percent increase in five years, and exports are expected to continue to grow rapidly.[29] Iran has a significant surplus in its trade relations with Iraq. In 2007, Iraqi imports from Iran stood at $2.7 billion, while its exports to Iran were $37 million.[30] As Iraq's reconstruction proceeds, this imbalance will certainly decline.

Iran is also heavily engaged in Iraqi infrastructure investment projects. Iranian technicians and entrepreneurs are involved in various projects, building refinery and petrochemical facilities, hospitals, roads, hotels, and telecommunications towers.[31] Iran has signed contracts to build power plants in Iraq and to link Iraqi cities to the Iranian electricity grid. In 2007, Tehran signed a $150 million contract to build a 300-megawatt power plant in Baghdad.[32] In March 2008, during Iranian president Ahmadinejad's first visit to Iraq, the two countries agreed that Iran will provide "a 400-megawatt electricity line running from the Iranian port city of Abadan to the Iraqi town of Alharasa . . . [and] on a transmission line that will run from the Iranian Kurdish city of Marivan to Panjwin in Iraqi Kurdis-

29. "Iran-Iraq Trade Facts," FARS News Agency, March 2, 2008, http://english.farsnews.com/newstext.php?nn=8612120433; Gina Chon, "Iran's Cheap Goods Stifle Iraq Economy," *Wall Street Journal*, March 18, 2009, http://online.wsj.com/article/SB123732669334561799.html; "Iraq-Iran Trade Meeting Pledges $5 Billion," *United Press International*, February 12, 2009, www.upi.com/Energy_Resources/2009/02/12/Iraq-Iran-trade-meeting-pledges-5-billion/UPI-99931234478117; "Official: Iran-Iraq Trade Volume to Reach 4bn US Dollars This Year," *Mathaba .net*, June 21, 2008, www.mathaba.net/news/?x=595969.

30. Chon, "Iran's Cheap Goods."

31. "Iran Says Ready to Help in Iraq's Reconstruction, Security," Xinhua News Agency, August 8, 2007, http://news.xinhuanet.com/english/2007-08/08/content_6497963.htm.

32. Marisa Cochrne, "Iran's Soft Power in Iraq," *Irantracker*, August 4, 2009, www.irantracker .org/analysis/iran%E2%80%99s-soft-power-iraq.

tan." Iran also helped to build a new airport near Najaf, which opened in August 2008, and which helps host about 20,000 Iranian pilgrims per month.[33] Iranian pilgrims contribute to the local economy of Iraq. At its peak, there were days when up to 7,000 pilgrims visited Iraq. By September 2009, the numbers declined because of inadequate quality of service.[34] (A significantly fewer number of Iraqi pilgrims visit Iran's holy cities in Mashad and Qom.)

Iran is also heavily involved in the port city of Basra, which has a strategic significance for Iraq and its oil industry. It currently supplies power to Basra, and has agreed to "build pipelines between Basra and Iran's city of Abadan to transport crude and oil products for their swap arrangements." In 2009, "An Iranian firm won a $1.0 to $1.5 billion contract to build a new town, Haydar Ali, in Basra. The town will include 5,000 housing units, and amenities like schools and health facilities."[35] Iran seeks to develop a "free trade zone" in Basra and is building a highway to connect Basra to Iranian cities.

Partly because of the Iranian involvement in southern Iraq, the region has enjoyed more economic growth and prosperity than other regions of Iraq, with the exception of the Kurdish areas.

Iran's U.S. Strategy on the Battlegrounds of Iraq

While it is being extremely careful to avoid a direct military confrontation with the United States, Iran has devised a strategy to deter a perceived threat from the United States.[36] One element of this strategy is to build a deterrent network within Iraq that could be activated, at will, to retaliate against U.S. troops if Iran is attacked.

When Saddam's regime was overthrown and chaos and looting prevailed, Iran quickly sent its agents, as well as thousands of pilgrims, to southern Iraq to build a network to direct its operations in Iraq. Moreover, the 15,000- to 20,000-strong Badr Brigade, created and trained by the Islamic Republic, moved back to Iraq, giving Iran a powerful stronghold there. Having fought with Iraq for eight years, and previously supported Iraqi dissident groups, and with thousands of Iranians and those of

---

33. "Kenneth Katzman, "Iran's Activities and Influence in Iraq," *Congressional Research Service*, June 4, 2009, 8, www.fas.org/sgp/crs/mideast/RS22323.pdf. There are reports that Iraq never received the funds from Iran for the airport. See Cochrne, "Iran's Soft Power in Iraq."

34. *Azzaman.com*, September 7, 2009, www.azzaman.com/english/index.asp?fname=news\2009 -09-07\kur.htm.

35. "Iran Wins $1.5B Basra Construction Contract," *FARS News Agency*, February 18, 2009, www .payvand.com/news/09/feb/1206.html.

36. See Mohsen M. Milani, "Tehran's Take: Understanding Iran's Policy toward the U.S." *Foreign Affairs* 88, no. 4 (July/August 2009): 46–62.

Iranian descent living in southern Iraq, Iran operated in a known territory and quickly expanded its influence and network.

The key moment for the expansion of that network came when Paul Bremer, the head of the Coalition Provisional Authority that ruled Iraq from May 2003 until June 2004, dissolved the Iraqi Armed Forces. The goal of creating an army free of the Ba'thists was surely an imperative, but the timing and the way it was carried out were imprudent. Iran took advantage of the vacuum created by dissolving the Iraqi Armed Forces and expanded its network. Compare Bremer's actions with the way Ayatollah Khomeini dealt with the American-trained and -equipped armed forces upon his triumphant return to Iran in 1979. He did not dissolve the armed forces, even though he feared they could stage a coup against him. Instead, while he ordered the execution and imprisonment of members of the top echelons of the armed forces, and purged its "unfriendly elements," he also built the Revolutionary Guards. He then used the Guards to consolidate his power and neutralize any coup attempt by the army.

On one hand, dissolving the Iraqi Army opened the doors to integrating Shi'a, including those of the Badr Brigade, into the new armed forces. That only increased Iranian influence. On the other hand, the power vacuum provided some breathing room for the anti-occupation militias to proliferate and grow, as many of the unemployed personnel of the army joined the insurgency. By developing close relations with some of the Shiite militias, Iran strengthened its network. Then it watched the bleeding U.S. forces from the sidelines and identified their vulnerabilities.[37]

It appears that the Islamic Republic has ordered its military personnel to avoid, at all costs, direct involvement in any operations against the U.S. military. In fact, Iran claims that there is no direct evidence implicating Iranian military personnel, including its Revolutionary Guards, in any direct military operations against the United States. However, some Iraqi officials and the U.S. military have consistently accused Iran of providing weapons to Sadr's Mahdi Army and some of its offshoots and to other Shiite militias. Moreover, the United States has accused Iran, and the Iranian-supported Lebanese Hizballah, of training Iraqi militias inside Iranian territory, and of establishing a secret network to provide a variety of weapons to the Iraqi militias, including rockets and mortars. The deadliest of these weapons are the explosively forced projectiles (EFPs), which have been responsible for 200 U.S. deaths since 2003. The United States

---

37. Prior to becoming the new commander of the Revolutionary Guards, Mohammad Ali (Aziz) Jaffari served as the commander of the Army Section of the Revolutionary Guards. In that capacity, he claims to have observed and identified the vulnerability of the U.S. forces in Afghanistan and Iraq. See Iran News Agency, October 7, 2009, www.irna.ir/View/Fullstory/Tools/PrintVersion/ ?NewsId=719269.

also believes that the Revolutionary Guards, particularly its Qods Force, is responsible for implementing Iran's policies in Iraq. According to U.S. sources, Iran spends about $3 million per month supporting the Iraqi militias, including "death squads" or special group criminals (SGCs). The United States has arrested as many as twenty Iranians inside Iraq, claiming that they belonged to the Revolutionary Guards.[38]

The Islamic Republic has denied these allegations. It would be naive to deny that Iran has provided support to the Mahdi Army and the major Shiite militias, although the quality and impact of that support is open for discussion. It is harder, however, to establish the support given to the Shiite militias through the informal Shiite networks that exist between the clerical establishments of the two countries. Clearly, supporting the major Shiite militias is consistent with Iran's strategy of hedging its bets and developing retaliatory capabilities against the United States inside Iraq.

After Iraq descended into a civil war, it became rather clear that Iran could play an important role in stabilizing the country. Many Iraqi leaders urged Washington to negotiate with Iran about Iraq, but these calls landed on deaf ears. Even after the 2006 James A. Baker and Lee H. Hamilton–led Iraq Study Group prudently recommended that the United States should engage Iran to stabilize Iraq, its advice was ignored. Eventually, the Bush administration changed course and met with Iranian officials, in Baghdad, to discuss Iraq's security. The first meeting took place in May 2007 between U.S. ambassador Ryan Crocker and Iranian ambassador Kazemi Qommi. The two countries subsequently met a few more times in Baghdad. After these meetings, and after the U.S. government launched its surge strategy in Iraq, the level of violence in Iraq subsided. Iran played a role in stabilizing the situation by pressuring its allies, including the Mahdi Army, to refrain from violence against Sunnis or U.S. troops. The State Department argued that diplomacy with Iran had contributed to the decline of violence; the Pentagon believed that the tough measures by the United States against Iranian agents were the cause for the relative stability.

A Thorn in Iran's Side

A source of persistent anxiety for Tehran is the effort of the armed, disciplined, and Iraq-based Mojahedin-e Khalq to destabilize the Islamic Republic and collect intelligence. Therefore, dismantling the Mojahedin organization from Iraq has remained one of Iran's main objectives.

---

38. The information in this section is from Felter and Fishman, *Iranian Strategy in Iraq.*

The organization, which engaged in terrorist operations against Americans living in Iran in the 1970s, was part of the coalition that overthrew the Pahlavi regime in 1979. After bloody clashes with the Islamic Republic in 1980, its top leadership escaped from Iran and eventually found sanctuary in Iraq during the Iraq-Iran War. They subsequently moved their headquarters to Camp Ashraf, in the Iraqi city of Khalis, some 120 kilometers from the Iranian border. Saddam used the group for subversive activities against the Islamic Republic. The organization, labeled as terrorist by the U.S. Department of State, has essentially created a "government in exile."[39] It has its own "elected" president in Maryam Rajavi (the wife the organization's "leader"), its own "Liberation Army," its own radio and television stations, and its own intelligence arm.

After the U.S. invasion, Camp Ashraf was brought under direct American control. (The Mojahedin claimed that under the Fourth Geneva Convention the United States is legally obligated to protect them.) Tehran quickly condemned the U.S. failure to disarm the Mojahedin as "hypocrisy" in the conduct of the war on terror. For a long time, Tehran has been convinced that the United States uses the Mojahedin to destabilize Iran, just as it directed the Contras to destabilize the Sandinistas in Nicaragua. There were rumors that Iran, which held several al-Qaida members, wanted to play the "al-Qaida card" to strike a deal with Washington—al-Qaida operatives in exchange for Mojahedin agents.

Iran believes that even before the United States took over Camp Ashraf, the Mojahedin were outsourced to provide intelligence to the United States. In August 2002, for example, the Mojahedin claimed that it had discovered the Natanz uranium enrichment facility, which became the catalyst for imposing UN Security Council sanctions on Iran. When in September 2009, the United States announced the discovery of another uranium enriching facility in the vicinity of the city of Qom, Iranian foreign minister Manochehr Motaki quickly pointed to the Mojahedin and British intelligence, and not the Central Intelligence Agency, for providing "misinformation" to the United States.[40]

Since 2003, Iran has repeatedly pressured its Iraqi friends in the government to remove the Mojahedin from its camp, disarm it, and even extradite its members to Iran, but to no avail. In 2008, the situation changed drastically after the United States and Iraq signed the status-of-forces agreement that gave sovereign authority to the Iraqi Armed Forces to maintain internal order. After the signing of the agreement, the U.S. military

39. On January 26, 2009, the Mojahedin-e Khalq was removed from the European Union terrorism list.
40. *BBC Persian*, September 29, 2009, www.bbc.co.uk/persian/iran/2009/09/090929_he_nuc_mottaki_lavrov.shtml.

withdrew from the camp and later there were violent clashes at Ashraf Camp between the residents and Iraqi Armed Forces. Both Shi'a and Kurds had their own reasons to confront the Mojahedin, which had reportedly been used by Saddam Hussein to suppress them, particularly during their respective uprisings in 1991 when Iraq was expelled from Kuwait. When in July 2009 the Iraqi security forces tried to enter into the camp, which had 3,416 people living in it, the Mojahedin resisted.

After two days of fighting, "eleven members of the [Mojahedin] were killed and around 200 injured. 200 Iraqi security forces were injured as well."[41] Dr. Muwaffiq al-Ruba'i, Iraq's national security adviser, describes the Mojahedin as "an indoctrinated and tightly disciplined organization of extremist zealots who have employed terrorism and at times even self-immolation to secure their aims. In normal everyday language we can say that they are brainwashed."[42]

The 2009 attack on Camp Ashraf, and the subsequent tensions that have persisted since, are a partial but important victory for the Islamic Republic. As yet, the Iraqi government has been unable to inspect the compound, to extradite the Mojahedin, or remove it from Iraqi soil. According to a report, the government of Iraq "has good reason to be angry with the US Embassy and military which are in many ways actively supporting the MKO."[43] The accuracy of this report notwithstanding, it is clear that for the United States the Mojahedin offers leverage in its negotiations with Iran. Moreover, any drastic measures taken against the Mojahedin would be viewed as a major setback for Washington.

Conclusion

Orchestrating Iran's policy toward Iraq is one of the most sensitive priorities of the country's overall foreign policy. This is true both because southern Iraq is deeply and uniquely important to Iran's clerical leadership and, more importantly, because it is also linked to Iran's main security concerns, such as its relations with the United States and its nuclear program. This

---

41. For the status of the Mojahedin prior to the attack on Camp Ashraf, see "Special Report from Baghdad: Camp Ashraf and the Mojahedin-e Khalq," *Iran Interlink*, February 2008, www.iran-interlink.org/?mod=view&id=4224. For the history of the organization, see Ervand Abrahamian, *The Iranian Mojahedin* (New Haven, CT: Yale University Press, 1992). For a more recent account, see Jeremiah Goulka, Lydia Hansell, Elizabeth Wilke, and Judith Larson, *The Mujahedin-e Khalq in Iraq: A Policy Conundrum* (Santa Monica, CA: RAND Publishing, 2009), www.rand.org/pubs/monographs/MG871/

42. Massoud Khodabandeh, "Second Report on Camp Ashraf and Mojahedin-e Khalq Cult Led by Massoud Rajavi and Maryam Rajavi in Iraq," *Iran Interlink*, August 2009.

43. Ibid.

linkage means that Iran views Iraq as a valuable card it could effectively exploit in its possible negotiations with the United States. If Iran believes it is making satisfactory progress in these negotiations, it is more likely to cooperate with the United States in Iraq. If Tehran concludes that its interests are being ignored, it is likely to act mischievously to undermine U.S. interests. Right or wrong, Iran is convinced that it can manage undermining U.S. interests in Iraq without damaging its good relations with the Iraqi government and without inciting the United States to take retaliatory military actions against Tehran.

Iran has made significant progress in achieving some of its major goals in Iraq. There is now a Tehran-friendly, Shi'a-dominated government in Baghdad, something that had not happened in Baghdad since Shiism was established as a state religion in Iran in 1501. Iran has created a sphere of influence in southern Iraq by engaging in a variety of economic, religious, technical, and developmental projects that are financed both by the Iranian government and the private sector. Iran, through the Iraqi government, has made some progress in undermining the Mojahedin in Iraq. It is unlikely, however, that the United States would allow the Iraqi government or Iran to dismantle the Mojahedin. After all, the Mojahedin is also a card Washington can play against Iran.

Although it is hard to accurately assess the effectiveness of Iran's secret policy of developing a retaliatory capability inside Iraq against U.S. forces, it is clear Iran failed to prevent the United States from establishing military bases or from reaching an agreement with the Iraqi government on the status of U.S. military forces. This is one area where there are clear limits to Iran's influence. When the United States and Iran signed their own status of forces agreement in 1963, Ayatollah Khomeini condemned Mohammad Reza Shah for signing the document, which, he insisted, had turned Iran into a "U.S. colony." More than half a century later, in 2008, the Islamic Republic futilely pressured the Maliki government to refrain from signing the agreement. In so doing, Tehran recognized the limits of its own influence in Iraq, even among its allies. At last, Iran acquiesced to the new agreement, albeit reluctantly. The agreement, however, contained two key provisions that pleased Tehran. First, the agreement stipulated that U.S. forces would withdraw from Iraq no later than December 2011, something Iran had publicly called for. Second, the agreement stated that "Iraqi land, sea, and air shall not be used as a lunching or transit point for attacks against other countries," which allayed Iran's fears that the United States could use Iraqi territory to attack Iran.

Surely, the meteoric rise of Iran's power in Iraq would have been unfathomable without the U.S. invasion. It stretches credulity, however, to argue that the United States has "handed over" Iraq to Iran,[44] and it is dangerous hyperbole to suggest that Iran will shortly transform Iraq into a "colony."[45] It is worth mentioning that some Iraqi leaders, as well as the regional powers who are concerned about the rise of Iran in the Middle East, have played the United States and Iran against one another and have often exaggerated Iran's involvement in actions against the United States to enhance their own interests. Clearly, Iran exercises more influence today in Iraq than other neighbors of Iraq, and more so today than at any other time since Iraq's birth in 1921. Iran's power, however, should not be exaggerated; it is limited and reversible and it faces serious hurdles in Iraq. The United States will continue to be the most powerful impediment to Iran's ambitions in Iraq. As Iran learned during the Iran-Iraq war, Iraqi Shi'a are Iraqis first and Shi'a second. To stay in power, many of the Shiite parties Tehran has supported will inevitably move closer to the United States and will become more independent of Tehran. The Shiite block is divided and Tehran has had trouble keeping it cohesive, as evidenced with the 2010 elections. There is also the age-old suspicion and mistrust of Persians by Iraqi Sunnis as well as by many Iraqi Shi'a. There is the growing allure of Iraqi nationalism that will continue to profoundly limit Iran's power and could swiftly turn Iran's assets into liabilities. In fact, Iran worries about a resurgence of Arab nationalism and the now-banned Ba'th Party. It worries about the decision by the United States to retain members of the "Iran section" of Saddam's intelligence services who could reignite old hostilities with Iran. Iran has been complaining that the Iraqi government has given safe haven to members of the Party for a Free Life in Kurdistan (PJAK), a separatist group that has engaged in violent clashes with Iran's security forces.

Territorial disputes, most importantly over the sensitive issue of the sovereignty of the Shatt al-Arab waterway, which provides Iraq with its only access to the Persian Gulf, and Iran's claim of war reparations form Iraq, could easily be reignited and poison Iran-Iraq relations. In 1975, Iran and Iraq signed the Treaty Concerning the State Frontiers and Neighborly Relations between Iran and Iraq, which reflected the broad agreement the two countries had reached regarding territorial disputes, including their

---

44. Saud bin Faisal bin Abdal-Aziz Al Sa'ud, Saudi Arabia's foreign minister, said in 2006 that "we are handing the whole country [Iraq] to Iran without reason." See Megan K. Stack and Borzou Daragahi, "Iran Was on Edge; Now It's on Top," *Los Angeles Times*, February 18, 2006.

45. The quotation is by General Muhammad al-Shahwani, the head of Iraq's intelligence service, who quit in August 2009, ostensibly because of the growing influence of Iranian agents in Iraq. See David Ignatius, "Behind the Carnage in Baghdad," *Washington Post*, August 25, 2009. Shahwani, a Sunni who was trained in the U.S. Army Ranger School in the 1960s, was in charge of a Republican Guards helicopter unit in Iraq and fought Iran during the Iraq-Iran war. He defected to London in 1990.

explicit adherence to the thalweg principle (the middle of a waterway) and joint sovereignty over the Shatt al-Arab. As Iraq continues to increase its oil exports and its dependence on the Shatt al-Arab, the sovereignty of that strategic waterway could create friction between the two countries. These issues, however, are unlikely to create a major rift between Iraq and Iran as long as some form of a Shi'a-led coalition remains in power in Baghdad.

The June 2009 electoral dispute in Iran has unquestionably created complications for Iran's foreign policy. The most serious crisis the Islamic Republic has faced in years, it has created major and lingering fissures among the ruling elites and has brought to the surface the anger and frustration of a good portion of the population. The slogan of "Iran First" chanted by thousands of demonstrators in major cities reflected the opposition to Iran's heavy investments in places like Iraq and Lebanon.

The presidential dispute, however, has thus far had no discernable impact on Iran's policies toward Iraq. The same forces that have formulated Iran's strategy toward Iraq since the inauguration of President Ahmadinejad in 2005 are still in charge, namely, Khomeinei, the Revolutionary Guards, and Ahmadinejad, in that order of importance. The medium-term and long-term impact of the ongoing domestic crisis in Iran on its policy toward Iraq, however, is difficult, if not impossible, to predict.

It seems that the lingering fissures among the governing elites will make it more difficult and costly for Iran to sustain its limited and reversible gains in Iraq. Much more important, however, are Iran's relations with the United States. Tehran must recognize that without some kind of understanding with Washington about the future of Iraq, it can lose much of what it has gained in Iraq.

Finally, the Arab Spring—which has touched off political turmoil across the Arab world—and the looming U.S. troop withdrawal from Iraq are the two wildcards that will undoubtedly shape the strategic environment in the years ahead.

The author wishes to dedicate this chapter to Ramak Milani for her love, friendship, and support.

4

Saudi-Iraq Relations

Devolving Chaos or Acrimonious Stability?

Toby C. Jones

R elations between Saudi Arabia and Iraq are marred by deep distrust and simmering hostility. With the consolidation of Shiite
power in Iraq, foremost among Riyadh's fears is that Shi'a-dominated Iraq will serve the interests of Iran, Saudi Arabia's most important
regional rival. It is through this lens—the prospect of an Iranian client on
Saudi Arabia's northern border—that much of the kingdom's anxiety and
its developing cold war with Iraq can and should be understood. Despite
public declarations of support for a strong Iraqi state by Saudi leaders in
the aftermath of the U.S. invasion, the reality is that Saudi and Iraqi officials barely speak to one another. Well after the fall of Saddam Hussein's
regime and the rise of a Shi'a-led government in Baghdad, the two neighbors face the prospect of prolonged frosty relations.

Saudi fears of expanded Iranian influence in the Persian Gulf intensified in spring 2011. Bahrain, the kingdom's closest neighbor, experienced
a wave of pro-democracy protests in February and March. Bahrain's political opposition, made up mostly of the island's majority Shiite population,
took to the streets demanding reform and the creation of a constitutional
monarchy. Alarmed by the specter of Shiite political empowerment in
Bahrain, Saudi Arabia encouraged the Bahraini government and then
lent military support to it as it carried out a brutal crackdown on the protest movement. While events in Bahrain are unlikely to directly shape

Saudi Arabia's relations with Iraq, they have and will continue to further inflame regional sectarian tensions in the Gulf.

The implications of Saudi Arabia's anxieties for U.S. policy in the region are significant. Although the United States created the crisis of instability in Iraq and opened the Pandora's box of Iranian power, the Saudis have made clear that only the Americans will be able to guarantee a stable Iraq in the future. The kingdom would like to see some kind of continued U.S. military presence in the Persian Gulf, just not in Saudi Arabia. Tense relations between Saudi Arabia and Iraq provide one pretext for such an arrangement. The United States almost certainly will not want to choose between backing either Iraq or Saudi Arabia, a dilemma that Riyadh understands well and will seek to exploit.

Mounting tensions between Saudi Arabia and Iraq have played out publicly and relations have soured dramatically in recent years. Although the two countries restored diplomatic ties in 2004, with Iraq even opening an embassy in Riyadh in 2007, the Saudis have made particularly clear their opprobrium for the new bosses in Baghdad. In mid-2007 Saudi leaders confronted U.S. officials with forged evidence that purported to show that Iraqi prime minister Nuri al-Maliki was untrustworthy, motivated more by sectarian calculation than reason. Saudis protested to the United States that Maliki was cultivating close ties with the anti-American Shiite cleric Muqtada al-Sadr.[1]

Saudi animus for Iraq has grown so palpable that King Abdullah has openly snubbed Iraq's prime minister several times in recent years, rebuffing efforts by Maliki to arrange a meeting between the two heads of state. In March 2009 the Saudi monarch reportedly refused to even greet the Iraqi leader at the Arab summit in Doha. The rebuke led Maliki to declare that "Iraq has no intention of making new goodwill gestures towards Saudi Arabia because my initiative has been interpreted in Riyadh as a sign of weakness," and that "there will be no other initiatives on our part as long as there is no sign from Saudi Arabia that it wants to have good ties [with Baghdad]."[2]

Saudi enmity toward Iraq is not a new phenomenon. For much of the twentieth century Riyadh watched its neighbor to the north with paranoia.[3] Even during the Iran-Iraq War in the 1980s, when Saudi Arabia provided significant financial support to Iraq, Saudi leaders remained suspicious of the Ba'thist regime—for good reason. Relations reached a low point in

---

1. Helene Cooper, "Saudis' Role in Iraq Frustrates U.S. Officials," *New York Times*, July 27, 2007.

2. "No More Gestures to Saudis: Iraq's Maliki," *Agence France-Presse*, May 29, 2009.

3. See Joseph McMillan, *Saudi Arabia and Iraq: Oil, Religion, and an Enduring Rivalry*, Special Report no. 157 (Washington, DC: United States Institute of Peace Press, January 2006), 4–6.

1990 when Saddam Hussein's armies stormed and seized Kuwait, bringing Iraq's armies within striking distance of Saudi Arabia's rich oil reserves. Saddam inflamed tensions by launching Scud missiles at Riyadh and the oil-rich Eastern Province during the war. But postwar Saudi acrimony is the immediate result of the U.S.-led invasion of Iraq in 2003 and the political transformations the war set in motion both inside Iraq and across the region.

The war generated several key concerns in Riyadh. The kingdom's leaders have officially claimed that continued instability in Iraq and the ongoing threat of violence and terrorism there have prevented them from pursuing closer and more amicable ties. Fears that combat-hardened veterans of the Iraqi insurgency may find their way into the kingdom to carry out future attacks are genuine. The country paid a price for its support of the anti-Soviet jihad in Afghanistan in the 1980s, after radicalized veterans of that war joined forces with al-Qaida and took up arms in a domestic campaign of terror in 2003–4. Many in Riyadh have feared the specter of a similar turn of events after Iraq. But while it is true that Iraq continues to be haunted by gruesome bloodshed, the reality is that the character of the post-Saddam Iraqi state and its potential role in the Middle East's new balance of power troubles Saudi Arabia more.

Saudi enmity can also be measured outside the halls of power. And, in important ways Riyadh is not in total control of the kinds of relationships its citizens have, are, and will pursue in Iraq. Many of the kingdom's most powerful religious scholars, particularly the unofficial clergy who keep some distance between themselves and the kingdom's rulers and thus enjoy considerable popularity, continue to shape domestic opinion about Iraq, anti-Shiite sectarianism, and the U.S. presence. Far more radical than the Saudi regime itself, these religious scholars represent a powerful force, one that the Saudis cannot completely control. While they do not represent the official policy, Saudi leaders are somewhat beholden to their views and their popularity. Their impact on Iraqi leaders, along with the impact of recruiters and Saudi citizens who actively support or who have participated in sectarian and anti-American violence, explains some of the distance and the distrust that divides Riyadh and Baghdad.

While acrimony between Iraq and Saudi Arabia seemed to have put the United States in a potentially difficult position, the reality is that Saudi-Iraqi rancor will change very little in the region. Although Saudi Arabia does not desire to see the return of significant numbers of U.S. military personnel to its soil, the United States has historically and almost certainly will play a role in the kingdom's pursuit of security. The quagmire in Iraq and even the tensions that divide the kingdom and its northern neighbor have, perhaps paradoxically, ensured that the United States will maintain a large military presence in the region for the foreseeable future. Saudi Arabia will be one of the most important benefactors of such an arrangement.

Beyond geopolitical and regional balance of power concerns, it is unlikely that Saudi Arabia and Iraq will become oil rivals. With Saudi Arabia home to more than a quarter of the world's proven oil reserves, even a powerful oil producing country like Iraq, and Iraq has some way to go before it is capable of exporting oil at full capacity, will not be able to challenge Saudi oil supremacy. It is more likely, as Joseph McMillan has noted, that "the Saudis will probably welcome higher production quotas for Iraq as this would allow them to return some of their own capacity to reserves and maintain their traditional role of swing producer."[4] For the foreseeable future, oil will not be a significant source of tension. The most pressing political challenges are elsewhere.

Iran, Iraq, and the Regional Balance of Power

In the fallout from the September 11, 2001, attacks, Riyadh faced a series of foreign and domestic challenges that worked against it becoming a regional power. By 2003 pressure from the United States converged with a homegrown terrorist threat and an emboldened political reform lobby that compelled the Saudis to focus on internal politics.[5] The domestic focus proved only temporary. In recent years Saudi Arabia has become an influential power in the Middle East, playing prominent roles in the Arab-Israeli conflict and in Lebanese internal politics. For myriad reasons, including preserving regional stability, fostering stable economic markets for its own investors, and providing political assistance for its allies, the kingdom has worked hard to establish itself as the principal Arab powerbroker in the early twenty-first century. Perhaps no issue has motivated Saudi Arabia to assert its influence abroad more than the reemergence of Iran as a regional power and adversary after the U.S.-led invasion of Iraq in 2003. The threat posed by an invigorated and strong Iran has shaped every Saudi move in the region since 2003. Riyadh has struggled to check Iranian influence and to tip the power of balance in the region in the kingdom's favor.[6] So far, the Saudis have worked to avoid an open confrontation with Iran. Still, fears of Iranian influence have affected Saudi decision

---

4. McMillan, *Saudi Arabia and Iraq*, 7.

5. International Crisis Group (ICG), *Can Saudi Arabia Reform Itself?* Middle East Report no. 28 (Brussels: ICG, July 14, 2004).

6. See F. Gregory Gause, "Saudis Aim to Roll Back Iranian Influence in Region, Interview with Bernard Gwertzman," Council on Foreign Relations, March 16, 2007, www.cfr.org/publication/12895/gause.html.

making on Palestine, Lebanon, Yemen, and Iraq. But where the specter of Iranian power and concerns about the regional balance of power have sparked active Saudi involvement in the Levant, they have produced the opposite effect in Iraq, where official Saudi involvement, and particularly any kind of constructive engagement, has been conspicuously absent.

Iran benefited enormously from the fall of Saddam Hussein's regime in 2003. Iran's rise, including its growing influence inside Iraq as well as across the region, has and will continue to shape how and whether Saudi Arabia engages with Iraq. As Vali Nasr wrote in *Foreign Policy* magazine in 2007, "Iranians rejoiced in the fall of Saddam, who fought an eight-year war against their country that killed hundreds of thousands of people, many by chemical weapons. For Iran, the war in Iraq turned out to be a strategic windfall, uprooting Ba'thism and pacifying a nemesis that had been a thorn in its side for much of the 20th century."[7] Tehran's delight goes beyond the fall of the much-loathed Saddam and the satisfaction of seeing a regional rival pacified. Just as important, Iran's regional strategic gains have been significant. In addition to Saddam's downfall, the instability and the civil war that plagued Iraq after the invasion worked to bog down American occupation forces, and opened the door for Iran to become more regionally assertive, free from the fear of a powerful U.S. military reprisal. Nowhere is Iranian truculence more evident than in its ability to successfully frustrate efforts to halt its purported pursuit of nuclear weapons, a development that would significantly expand not only Iranian military power, but also the country's ability to even more effectively impose its political will across the region.[8]

Iran's ascendancy has sparked considerable trepidation in Riyadh. The Saudis have ample reason for worry, even though they remain undecided in how to deal with the challenge. Iran has enthusiastically embraced the opportunity to become a regional powerbroker. Already influential in Lebanon and Syria, Tehran has also emerged as a key player in the Arab-Israeli conflict. Iranian support for Hizballah enabled the network to stand its ground against Israel during its 2006 push into southern Lebanon. Its efforts have been felt in Palestine as well. By providing material and military support to Hamas, Iran has not only influenced intra-Palestinian politics but has also positioned itself as the primary backer for continued resistance against the Israeli occupation, a role historically played by Arab states. The significance of Iran's efforts to support Palestinian resistance is hard to measure, but what is clearer is that Iranian popularity across the region has

---

7. Vali Nasr, "Who Wins in Iraq," *Foreign Policy* (March/April 2007).

8. Toby Jones, "Driven by a Sense of Urgency," *Bitterlemons-international.org* 5, no. 16 (April 26, 2007).

reached unprecedented levels and has also frustrated Saudi Arabia's desire to remain the most important backer of the Palestinian cause.

Saudi and other Arab leaders have come to see Iranian influence everywhere. It is widely believed that Iran maintains considerable power to shape politics and attitudes in Shiite communities across the Persian Gulf, particularly in Saudi Arabia, which is home to as many as 2 million Shi'a. Most Saudi Shi'a live in the oil-rich Eastern Province.[9] Saudi Arabia and the Gulf sheikhdoms have long claimed that these communities are fifth columns for Iran and are preternaturally inclined to heed whatever marching orders are handed down from Tehran.[10] The result is the perennial expression of concern that Iran represents a direct threat to the domestic security of each of these regimes, possessing the potential to meddle at will in the internal affairs of neighboring states and mobilize political activism on demand. Most of these fears are overwrought, the by-product of long-standing anxieties that first emerged in the context of the Iranian revolution. Under the leadership of the charismatic Ayatollah Khomeini, Iran openly sought to export the revolution and topple rival regimes in the region, singling out the Saudi royal family as particularly corrupt, beholden to American imperial interests, and ripe for overthrowing. In late 1979 efforts to whip up revolutionary fervor around the Gulf seemed to yield results, when Bahraini and Saudi Shi'a took part in revolts against their Sunni masters. While the rebellion in Saudi Arabia was partly motivated by events in Iran, it was mostly an expression of frustration over local issues.[11] Whatever the underlying issues that sparked outrage in 1979, Saudis continue to claim that it has historically been and continues to be the case that there is a hidden Iranian hand at work in the kingdom's Shiite communities.

Similar fears emerged in Yemen in 2009, Saudi Arabia's unstable southern neighbor. Since 2004 the Yemeni government has been engaged in a violent conflict with a group of rebels in the country's mountainous northern border known as the al-Houthis. After a brief lull in the fighting, the war between the government and the rebels, who hail from the Zaydi sect

---

9. In Bahrain the Shi'a make up the majority of the indigenous population. However, they enjoy little political power. The island is ruled by the Sunni al-Khalifa, which has rendered the Shiite community a functional minority. See Juan Cole, *Sacred Space and Holy War: The Politics, Culture, and History of Shi'ite Islam* (New York: I. B. Tauris, 2002); and ICG, *Bahrain's Sectarian Challenge*, Middle East Report no. 40 (Brussels: ICG, May 6, 2005).

10. These claims are mostly misplaced. They do serve important political purposes including justifying continued discriminatory policies against them as well as checking domestic Shiite social and political power.

11. Toby Craig Jones, "Rebellion on the Saudi Periphery: Modernity, Marginalization, and the Shia Uprising of 1979," *International Journal of Middle East Studies* 38, no. 2 (May 2006): 213–233.

of Shiism, intensified in mid-2009. In early November violence spilled across the Saudi-Yemeni border, when al-Houthi rebels raided a Saudi military outpost and killed several Saudi personnel. The Saudis responded dramatically, reportedly launching air raids against rebel redoubts in northern Yemen.[12] Saudi Arabia has supported the Yemeni campaign against the al-Houthis from the beginning. The kingdom's leaders worry that a weak Yemen, one unable to control its northern border, will be fertile ground for al-Qaida–inspired militants to regroup and launch terrorist attacks against Saudi Arabia in the future.[13] Whatever Riyadh's security concerns, there have been additional political considerations at work. Since 2004 Yemeni leaders have insisted that Iran has actively supported the al-Houthis and their rebellion. Even though there is no clear evidence of Iranian complicity, it is almost a certainty that the Saudi decision to order its air force to bomb rebel outposts in Yemen has taken this into account.

It is Iraq, Saudi Arabia's largest and historically most powerful neighbor, that presents the biggest challenge and source of anxiety. And nowhere has Iranian influence been more significant. The fall of Saddam Hussein's regime raised the possibility for unprecedented Iranian influence in Iraq. Although about 60 percent of Iraq's population is Shi'a, Iran enjoyed only thin ties to the community historically. Even during the Iran-Iraq War, most Iraqi Shi'a fought on the Iraqi side, preferring nationalist loyalty over shared religious identity. Key Shiite opposition figures did flee Iraq for Iran in the 1980s, including Muhammad Baqir al-Hakim and his brother Abd al-Aziz al-Hakim, leaders of the Supreme Council for the Islamic Revolution in Iraq (SCIRI), an organization that has since rebranded itself the Islamic Supreme Council of Iraq (ISCI). During the Iran-Iraq War SCIRI members received training from the Iranian Revolutionary Guards and took part in the fighting against Iraq. Iran provided considerable financial, political, and material support to the ISCI and its militia, the Badr Brigades, in the post-Saddam period. In 2005–6, with a leading figure of ISCI at the helm of the Ministry of the Interior, Badr Brigade members took control over much of Iraq's security force and domestic police. Iran came to provide similar training and support for the followers of Muqtada al-Sadr and his militia the Jaish al-Mahdi. Early on ties between Sadr and Iran were virtually nonexistent, but they have expanded over time. Iran has also been supportive of Sadr's religious studies

---

12. Robert Worth, "Yemeni Rebels and Saudis Clash at Border," *New York Times*, November 6, 2009.

13. In August 2009 an al-Qaida operative from Yemen snuck into Saudi Arabia and attempted to assassinate Muhammad bin Nayef, the vice minister of the interior, the first attempt by al-Qaida members to strike at the Saudi royal family.

in Qom, where it is suspected he has spent the last year burnishing his scholarly credentials. At the height of Sunni-Shiite violence in Iraq, many in the U.S. military and political establishment as well as in neighboring states, particularly Saudi Arabia, believed that Iran was training and equipping Shiite Iraqi militants, encouraging their violence against Iraq's Sunnis and U.S. military personnel.[14]

The ebb in sectarian killings in Iraq since 2007 has partly been the result of Iran "reduc[ing] the number of militants it supports" there.[15] Although it pulled back some of its military support, Iran continued to provide backing for a range of militant activity, reflecting what some see as a "fundamental commitment to preventing the emergence of a threat to Iran from Iraqi territory, either from the [Iraqi government] or from the United States. This fundamental objective," the U.S. Department of Defense has claimed, "is reflected in the Iranian Government's preference for a weak, Shi'a Islamist-dominated government that is aligned with Iranian interests and that does not pose a threat to Iran's position in the region."[16]

Saudi Arabia has seen Iranian connections to Iraq as much more than efforts to simply protect Iranian interests. Rather, the Saudis came to view Iranian activity in Iraq as part of an imperial project to turn Iraq into a client state. Even though Iran's role in Iraq developed and became more complicated over time, Saudi leaders expressed fears about its influence almost immediately after the U.S invasion. After the 2003 toppling of Saddam Hussein, Saudi officials expressed open nervousness about Iranian influence. In 2004 Saudi officials expressed fears about Iranian designs to establish permanent influence by purchasing property in predominantly Shiite southern Iraq.[17] Concerns about Iraq becoming an enduring Iranian satellite have most troubled Saudi Arabia. Saudi Arabia's foreign minister, Saud al-Faisal, provided clear evidence of the kingdom's apprehension of Iranian influence inside Iraq just a year later. In remarks he delivered at the Council on Foreign Relations in New York in September 2005, he argued that

> the Iranians now go in this pacified area that the Americans have pacified, and they go into every government of Iraq, pay money, install their own people . . . even establish police forces for them. . . . And they are being protected in doing this by the British and the American forces in the area. . . . To us it seems out of this world that you do this. We fought a war together to keep Iran from occupying Iraq

---

14. Kenneth Katzman, "Iran's Activities and Influence in Iraq," *Congressional Research Service*, June 4, 2009.

15. U.S. Department of Defense, "Measuring Stability and Security in Iraq," March 2009, 6.

16. U.S. Department of Defense, "Measuring Stability and Security in Iraq," June 2009, v.

17. See McMillan, *Saudi Arabia and Iraq*, 4.

after Iraq was driven out of Kuwait. Now we are handing the whole country over to Iran without reason.[18]

Faisal's candor provided unusually clear insight into behind-the-scenes Saudi reasoning. The depth of Iranian influence in Iraq has gone a long way in preventing Saudi Arabia from working with the Maliki government. Refusing to pursue strong ties with Baghdad—indeed, refusing even to meet with Iraq's prime minister—suggests that the Saudis view anything more than the minimal level of official engagement (allowing Iraq to open an embassy in Riyadh, for example) as fueling Iran's power grab. The Saudis have deliberately made life difficult for Iraq beyond its refusal to engage with Maliki. After making several promises to write off Iraq's massive debt to Saudi Arabia, the kingdom has backed away from the pledge. Riyadh loaned Iraq over $20 billion during Iraq's protracted war against Iran.[19] Even though Saudi Arabia fully supported the war, with Iran now on top in Iraq, the Saudis almost certainly view any kind of debt relief as serving Iranian interests more than theirs.

Saudi fears about further empowering Iran in Iraq have proven even more powerful than whatever purported ties the kingdom has historically maintained with Sunni and tribal leaders there. These ties have not been strong enough to pull the kingdom fully into domestic Iraqi political affairs. Whatever support Riyadh has provided for its Sunni allies in Iraq has remained furtive. And aside from public declarations about their unhappiness with the marginalization of Sunnis from the political process in Iraq, Saudi leaders have avoided becoming more directly engaged. This is partly explained by Saudi Arabia's anxieties about the short- and long-term consequences of overextending itself in a place that might devolve into violence again. The risk of another civil war or the re-escalation of sectarian violence in Iraq could rebound on the kingdom if it were too heavily invested in the outcome, including through a direct and costly confrontation with Iran. In addition to its fears of blowback from any potential involvement in Iraq, there may be a more basic consideration at work. With the exception of its involvement in Yemen several times in the twentieth century, Saudi Arabia has historically been dependent on outsiders, particularly the United States, to maintain regional security. Long beset with its own domestic challenges, Riyadh has avoided foreign entanglements.

---

18. Prince Saud al-Faisal, "The Fight Against Extremism and the Search for Peace" (address to the Council on Foreign Relations, New York, September 20, 2005), www.cfr.org/publication/8908/fight_against_extremism_and_the_search_for_peace_rush_transcript_federal_news_service_inc .html.

19. Steven Mufson and Robin Wright, "In a Major Step, Saudi Arabia Agrees to Write Off 80% of Iraqi Debt," *Washington Post*, April 18, 2007. See also McMillan, *Saudi Arabia and Iraq*, 6.

The hesitation to become overly involved in Iraq has been consistent with this conservative instinct.

For the most part, Saudi Arabia's emphasis on limiting Iranian gains in Iraq and the region has not been driven primarily by sectarian difference. But there have also been signs that sectarianism is becoming a critical factor elsewhere, most importantly in the aftermath of Saudi Arabia's occupation of Bahrain in March 2011. Fearing Shiite power in the Gulf, Saudi Arabia and Bahrain have justified the crackdown on Bahrain's pro-democracy movement as a response to Iranian meddling. This will almost certainly have an impact on the kingdom's relations with Iraq. Saudi frustrations about Iraq's domestic political disorder, and its anxieties about the shifting balance of power in the region, underscore the potential for sectarian discord to rise to the surface, which work only to further drive Iraq and Saudi Arabia apart.

Saudi Arabia's Sectarian Pasts and Futures

In addition to worries that Iraq will turn out to be an Iranian client, Saudi Arabia has also openly expressed dismay over the dismal state of sectarian relations in Iraq and particularly the continued marginalization of its Sunni minority. Sectarianism has a long history in Saudi Arabia. The official orthodoxy of the Saudi state, known generally as Wahhabism, was founded in part on the belief that many Muslims had strayed from the true faith and corrupted Islam through various forms of innovation. Muhammad ibn abd al-Wahhab, the eighteenth-century scholar from whom Wahhabism takes its name, viewed Shiism as a particularly grave form of heresy, and considered Shiite apostates. Saudi-Wahhabi warriors have historically been infamous for violence against Shiite communities. In 1802 a Wahhabi military mission backed by the Saudi leadership raided the holy Shiite city of Karbala in Iraq. The invaders murdered thousands, razed the city, and destroyed some of its most important shrines. In 1913 the Saudi-Wahhabi militia known as the *ikhwan* (the brotherhood) conquered the predominantly Shiite province al-Hasa on the eastern Arabian Peninsula, home today to virtually all of Saudi Arabia's vast oil reserves. The religious warriors openly advocated expelling or murdering the region's Shi'a. Saudi leaders refused demands that the peninsula's largest Shiite community be wiped out for mostly practical considerations. While the Saudis have forbidden widespread violence against Shi'a at home and abroad, anti-Shi'a sectarianism was a structural feature of Saudi Arabia's social and political life in the twentieth century.

Anti-Shi'a hostility became even more pronounced and more public in the aftermath of the Iranian Revolution. Events abroad and at home sparked a revival of sectarian ferment. The domestic uprising of the kingdom's Shi'a in November 1979 raised domestic security concerns, prompting a violent military response. The politicization of Shiism in Iran and efforts by Khomeini to export the revolution intensified Saudi fears. In response, the kingdom mobilized against Iran by encouraging its mosques and the Saudi clergy to rant against and demonize Shiism. The proliferation of anti-Shi'a fulmination was staggering. The kingdom supported the production of works that portrayed Shi'a as an existential threat to Islam and to Saudi Arabia. In addition to permitting teachers to decry Shiism as a form of blasphemy in schools, the country also backed the distribution of published books that provided validation for the intensification of sectarian rancor.[20]

Iranian-Saudi relations improved in the 1990s, resulting in a decrease in the scope of sectarian antagonism emanating from the kingdom, although it did not stop altogether.[21] Still, the intensity of anti-Shiite fervor paled in comparison to the height of Iranian-Saudi hostility in the 1980s.

The war in Iraq and the empowerment of Iraqi Shi'a has reignited old antagonisms. This is evident both at home and in Iraq. The kingdom's Shi'a enjoyed a brief political opening in early 2003 when then crown prince Abdullah agreed to meet community leaders and called publicly for greater tolerance throughout the country. In the years since, however, the situation has deteriorated. Shi'a inside the kingdom have been subjected to venomous attacks from leading Sunni scholars. In February 2009 hundreds of Shiite pilgrims in Medina were assaulted by members of the Saudi Commission for the Prevention of Vice and the Promotion of Virtue, the religious police. In the aftermath of the Medina violence, religious and political leaders threatened to use violence to protect their interests, prompting state security forces to crack down on predominantly Shiite communities in the Eastern Province.[22]

The reemergence of Saudi sectarianism has also been evident in its relations with Baghdad. For the most part, Saudi leaders have either publicly avoided making sectarian difference an official explanation for their Iraq policy or charged Iraq with being the chief sectarian antagonist. After

---

20. Some of these include Ibrahim Sulayman al-Jabhan's book *Removing the Darkness and Awakening to the Danger of Shi'ism to Muslims and Islam* (1980), which was licensed by the office of the highest religious authority in Saudi Arabia. The 1980s saw the addition of equally spiteful books, including *The Shi'a and the Sunna*, *The Shi'a and the Qur'an*, and *The Shi'a and the Prophet's Family*, all by the Pakistani author Ihsan Ilahi Zahir.

21. See Toby Jones, "The Iraq Effect in Saudi Arabia," *Middle East Report* no. 237 (Winter 2005).

22. Toby Matthieson, "The Shi'a of Saudi Arabia at a Crossroads," *Middle East Report Online*, May 6, 2009; Toby Jones, *Embattled in Arabia: Shi'is and the Politics of Confrontation in Saudi Arabia*, Occasional Paper Series (West Point, NY: Combating Terrorism Center, June 3, 2009).

refusing to meet with Maliki at a 2007 summit in the Egyptian resort town Sharm al-Sheikh, King Abdullah justified the snub by accusing the Iraqi prime minister of "embodying sectarian divisions."[23] But while Saudi Arabia has been slow to find common ground with the Iraqi government, it is widely believed that there are strong private and government ties to the Sunni community in Iraq. Little is certain about the nature of these ties. It is likely that Saudi Arabia has provided financial and material support for its patrons in Iraq. In mid-2007 Bush administration officials claimed that Saudi Arabia had been providing "financial support to opponents" of Maliki and had attempted to press neighboring governments in the Gulf to provide direct financial aid to Iraqi Sunni groups.[24] It is less certain that the kingdom has officially provided weapons or military encouragement, particularly since the principal thrust of the anti-American insurgency has come from within the Sunni community.

In 2006 Saudi frustrations regarding violence against Iraqi Sunnis seemed to boil over. It even appeared possible that the kingdom was poised to take up arms to defend its allies in Iraq if the United States proved unable to protect them. The clearest articulation of this came in an article by Nawaf Obaid, a Saudi security consultant to then Saudi ambassador to the United States Turki al-Faisal, published in the *Washington Post*. Writing in response to calls for the United States to withdraw from Iraq, Obaid suggested "one of the first consequences [would] be massive Saudi intervention to stop Iranian-backed Shiite militias from butchering Iraqi Sunnis." He continued, "to turn a blind eye to the massacre of Iraqi Sunnis would be to abandon the principles upon which the kingdom was founded. It would undermine Saudi Arabia's credibility in the Sunni world and would be a capitulation to Iran's militarist actions in the region."[25]

Obaid's commentary was quickly repudiated by Riyadh and he was subsequently sacked from his position as consultant to Faisal. It is likely that Obaid was punished for a combination of reasons. He exaggerated Saudi Arabia's military intent and overstepped his authority in offering controversial and threatening commentary in a major American newspaper. It is unlikely, however, that Obaid acted on his own or was not representing some powerful faction in Saudi Arabia. It is even less likely that the sentiment behind Obaid's article, that Saudi Arabia was outraged over Iran's influence in Iraq, the plight of its Sunnis, and the new sectarian balance of power inside Iraq, was not widely shared by Saudi Arabia's leaders.

---

23. Sami Moubayed, "Doubts over Maliki's Anti-graft Crusade," *Asia Times Online*, June 2, 2009.
24. Cooper, "Saudis' Role in Iraq Frustrates U.S. Officials."
25. Nawaf Obaid, "Stepping into Iraq," *Washington Post*, November 29, 2006.

The kingdom's ability to work with any Shiite government, in Iraq or elsewhere, is severely restricted by its rancorous history with Iran and the legacy of Iran's revolution inside Saudi Arabia. While the kingdom was able to build workable relations with Iran in the 1990s, during a brief dé-tente, many Saudis continued to harbor deep hatred for Shi'a and for Shi-ism more generally. Much of this intense loathing, particularly its modern forms, is the legacy of the antagonisms of the 1980s. And to a consider-able extent, it is beyond the ability of Riyadh to manage. Popular clerics in Saudi Arabia, including Nasr al-Umar and Safar al-Hawali, who com-mand massive followings and arguably more respect than the Al Saud, routinely decry Shiism as a grave form of apostasy. Both have loudly sup-ported violence against Shi'a in Iraq and encourage it elsewhere.[26]

The Security Paradox

In addition to concerns about Iranian influence in Iraq and the marginal-ization of the country's Sunni minority, Saudi leaders have also feared the potentially devastating consequences of continued Iraqi instability on the kingdom's own domestic security. Riyadh has consistently cited instabil-ity and continued violence as a reason why it has avoided opening an em-bassy in Baghdad, suggesting there is no urgency in putting its diplomats in harm's way. Of greater concern has been the specter of Iraq's internal troubles spilling over the border. At the height of Iraq's sectarian civil war and jihad against the U.S. occupation Saudi leaders were particularly con-cerned by the prospect of battle-hardened veterans of Iraq's insurgency crossing the border to carry out attacks inside the kingdom. Even with the recent reduction in the frequency of terrorist attacks and improvement in security, Iraq continues to be plagued by periodically spectacular violence. The situation is far from settled and the country remains a central front for terrorism.

Shoring up Iraqi security is one area in which Saudi and Iraqi leaders should have already established cooperative relations. But rather than com-ing together over this issue, the two countries remain deeply divided about violence in Iraq and who is responsible. For its part, Saudi Arabia's position on Iraq's internal security challenges has been paradoxical. Fears about the threat of Iraq's violence spreading to the kingdom have been genuine, but Saudi Arabia has, in fact, been slow to address the many ways that it is actually complicit in the problem.

---

26. ICG, *The Shiite Question in Saudi Arabia*, Middle East Report no. 45 (Brussels: ICG, Septem-ber 19, 2005).

Saudi officials have publicly and loudly condemned Sunni-led terrorism, whether carried out by al-Qaida, Iraqi Islamists, or ex-Ba'thists. The kingdom faced its own domestic terrorist threat from 2003 to 2005, when al-Qaida in the Arabian Peninsula (QAP) carried out a murderous terror campaign that mostly targeted Westerners living and working in the kingdom.[27] Initially reluctant to admit that terrorism was either a homegrown phenomenon or a threat to its internal security, the kingdom eventually took significant security measures to rein in Saudi militants. Several of the founders and most important leaders of al-Qaida in the Arabian Peninsula were veterans of the jihad against the Soviets in Afghanistan, where they fought and trained alongside other Arab mojahedin. While the vast majority of those Saudis who spent time in the 1980s and 1990s in Central Asia came home and quietly assimilated back into society, others remained militant.

The makeup of QAP raised alarm bells in Riyadh, sparking concerns that a similar pattern could easily repeat itself in Iraq. And there was considerable cause for alarm. Since the fall of Saddam's regime and the beginning of the U.S. occupation, thousands of Saudi citizens traveled to Iraq to fight in the insurgency and in the sectarian civil war. The number of Saudis who went to Iraq peaked in 2004 or 2005, but many continued to gain access even after the initial deluge.[28] A disproportionate number of insurgents who take part in suicide attacks on American military personnel have reportedly been from Saudi Arabia. Unlike the jihad in Afghanistan, Saudi Arabia did not support the participation of its citizens in violence in Iraq. But the kingdom also proved hesitant to stop the flow. As Thomas Hegghammer has pointed out, "Saudi authorities have acted to stem recruitment, but they are restricted politically by public perceptions of the Iraqi resistance as legitimate."[29] Saudis undertook elaborate measures to get to Iraq, often crossing into Bahrain and then flying to Syria where they would then cross the border into Iraq. Recruiting networks were extensive. Despite the Saudi government's anxieties about Iraq's terrorism problem, recruiters inside the kingdom proved able to attract thousands of militants, provided them with financial support, arranged for their transportation out of the kingdom, and handled logistical support for them once they arrived in Syria.

---

27. For more information on al-Qaida in the Arabian Peninsula, see Stephane Lacroix's and Thomas Hegghammer's report for ICG, *Saudi Arabia Backgrounder: Who Are the Islamists?* Middle East Report no. 31 (Brussels: ICG, September 21, 2004).

28. Thomas Hegghammer, "Saudis in Iraq: Patterns of Radicalization and Recruitment," *Cultures and Conflicts*, June 12, 2008, http://conflits.org/index10042.html.

29. Ibid.

In addition to the flow of people into Iraq, Saudi Arabia has also been a significant source of financial support for the Iraqi resistance. Given the nature of such support, and because it is likely that much of the money that passes into Iraq has been used to purchase weapons or to support the insurgency, the details of the scope of private Saudi support are murky.[30] It is likely that most funds have originated through charitable foundations. Since 2003 the kingdom has made determined efforts to rein and regulate Islamic charities. But the results have been mixed, at least with regard to charitable giving to Iraqi Sunnis. It has also been widely believed in Iraq and even in the U.S. government that Saudi Arabia has also quietly been passing state funds to Sunni groups, some of whom have ties to the insurgency. In July 2007 American impatience with Saudi Arabia's involvement in funding Iraqi Sunni groups led the U.S. ambassador to the United Nations Zalmay Khalilzad to remark on the American television news channel CNN that "Saudi Arabia and a number of other countries are not doing all they can to help us in Iraq. At times, some of them are not only not helping, but they are doing things that is undermining the effort to make progress."[31] These claims, and the implication that Saudi Arabia was officially complicit in the insurgency, proved difficult to substantiate. Such uncertainty did play a potentially important political role, as it allowed U.S. policymakers to apply pressure on Riyadh. In this respect, it mattered less whether the claims were true or not; that U.S. officials were willing to invoke such claims publicly suggested an attempt to use them as leverage. It is far from certain what was gained from doing so.

Iraqi leaders have been even more critical of Saudi Arabia's reported financial complicity in the violence in their country. It is an axiom of Iraqi political belief that despite its claims to innocence Saudi Arabia bears tremendous responsibility for supporting both the Sunni insurgency and the sectarian civil war. After twin suicide bombings killed more than 150 people in an attack on the Ministry of Justice building in Baghdad in October 2009, a devastating attack that took place amid a sharp drop in overall levels of violence, Iraqi leaders renewed their charges that Saudi Arabia was directly responsible for financing and supporting terrorism.[32]

In addition to the flow of people and dollars, Saudi religious scholars have been some of the most vitriolic supporters of anti-American and anti-Shiite violence in Iraq. Like the flow of Saudi citizens into Iraq, Saudi clergy

30. "Saudis Reportedly Funding Iraqi Sunni Insurgents," Associated Press, December 8, 2006.

31. "U.S. Envoy Says Saudi Arabia Is Undermining Iraq," Associated Press, July 30, 2007.

32. Timothy Williams, "Bombings in Iraq, Deadliest since 2007, Raise Security Issue," *New York Times*, October 25, 2009.

were particularly active and virulent in 2004 and 2005. On November 5, 2004, while U.S. forces prepared to lay siege to the Iraqi insurgent stronghold of Fallujah, twenty-six Saudi clerics signed on to an open letter supporting the jihad against the United States. The letter argued that the "*jihad* against the occupation was mandatory for those who were able." The clerics did not explicitly encourage Saudis to travel to Iraq to take part in the insurgency. But it was easy to interpret the letter as doing so, as the clerics exhorted "our Muslim brothers to stand by their brothers in Iraq by . . . supporting them as much as possible."[33]

Saudi clerics have even met with their counterparts in Iraq to push a sectarian and violent agenda. In December 2006 thirty-eight Saudi religious leaders gathered in Istanbul with prominent Sunni Iraqis, including Adnan al-Dulaymi of the Iraqi Accord Front, Harith al-Dhari of the Muslim Scholars Association, and, via video, the Islamic Army of Iraq, to encourage the continuation of the anti-U.S. and anti-Shiite insurgency. A few weeks later several senior Saudi scholars intensified the sectarian campaign. Abd al-Rahman al-Barrak issued a fatwa condemning Shi'a guilty of *takfir* (of being non-Muslim) and Abdullah bin Jibrin, a one-time member of the kingdom's Council of Senior Ulama, issued a declaration of war against Iraqi Shi'a and argued for the necessity of a Sunni victory in Iraq.[34]

As has been the case with sectarian hostility more generally, it remains unclear to what extent Saudi leaders are able to control the messages and vitriol emanating from within the kingdom. Historically, the ruling family has bequeathed significant authority to the religious scholars. Because of the Iranian threat of the 1980s, the Saudis felt compelled to unleash some of the most brutish and radical voices, encouraging an ideological war with Iran and revolutionary Shiism. Much of the sentiment of the 1980s remains as do some of the most committed purveyors of sectarian hate. There has been a noticeable decrease in sectarian ferment since the height of Iraq's civil war, mostly as a result of the decline in violence. Much of the enmity remains, however.

Sources of Saudi Arabia's Leverage over the United States

Neither the Bush nor the Obama administrations proved able to pressure the Saudis into setting aside their frustrations and anxieties about Iranian influence and Shiite power in Iraq. King Abdullah and the core Saudi

---

33. Toby Craig Jones, "The Clerics, the Sahwa, and the Saudi State," *Strategic Insights* 4, no. 3 (March 2005).

34. Toby Jones, "Saudi Arabia's Not-So-New Anti-Shi'ism," *Middle East Report* no. 242 (Spring 2006): 29–32.

leadership have been obdurate, unwilling to compromise on providing aid, canceling debt, or working to strengthen the current Iraqi government. And Saudi Arabia has remained a significant obstacle to Iraqi stability. The reality is that Saudi-Iraqi tensions have and very likely will continue to serve Saudi Arabia's interests. From the vantage point of Riyadh, there is considerable utility in maintaining distant and frosty relations with Baghdad. These tensions have been especially useful in shaping the kingdom's relationship with the United States. Its posture on Iraq provides the kingdom some leverage on key matters of policy, including the Palestine-Israel conflict, oil, and its own domestic political situation. In addition, low-level tensions in the Gulf also serve to continue Saudi Arabia's reliance on the United States as the guarantor of its regional security.

Since the outbreak of the war, Saudi Arabia has been consistently clear that its preference has been to see the United States remain in Iraq. Riyadh also realizes that American efforts to secure Iraq also serve Saudi Arabia's security needs. Long dependent on the United States for its security, Saudi Arabia's leaders have sought to continue the basic framework of the relationship. Riyadh's desire for the United States to continue to protect it from external threats has hardly abated. Historically, American security has come either through weapons sales or through the presence of U.S. military personnel in the region. The kingdom will almost certainly remain a fertile market for arms. And Riyadh also understands that the United States is unlikely to risk its hegemony or "vital interests" in the Gulf by withdrawing its military forces as long as relations between Saudi Arabia, Iraq, and Iran all remain fraught. These tensions require the United States to serve as a balancing force. They do not need to be resolved for Saudi Arabia's interests to be served. In fact, Riyadh may be better served if they are not. Rather, from the perspective of the Saudis, they require management, a role that the United States has historically been eager to play. Saudi Arabia is almost certainly counting on this to continue.

Saudi Arabia's unwillingness to work more closely with Baghdad also provided Saudi Arabia with some leverage on other Arab affairs in its relations with Washington. The kingdom has considered itself the primary Arab backer of the Palestinian cause. Although Iran gained influence through its ties to Hamas, Saudi Arabia has continued to call on the United States to pressure Israel into making important concessions and compromises. While this has produced negligible results, Saudi leaders will likely see any future improvement in the kingdom's relations with Iraq as being tied to the United States' willingness to push Israel.

Tense relations with Iraq also strengthened Saudi Arabia's power as the world's largest oil producer. While Saudi Arabia has hardly been militant in its pursuit of high oil prices—in fact, it has consistently worked to keep prices stable and relatively low—the kingdom does not wish to see the price of oil retreat too far. While the United States may have been able to push the kingdom to expand output or work to lower oil prices in the past, current tensions in the Gulf have made it more difficult for Washington to apply similar kinds of pressure. And as long as political relations between Iraq and Saudi Arabia remain charged, and as long as tensions remain high in the Gulf, it is unlikely that the United States will have the leverage necessary to push Riyadh on its oil production policies.

Instability in Iraq and tensions between Saudi Arabia and its northern neighbor have also helped deflect any potential demonstration effect that the opening up of Iraq's political system might have had. One of the great fictions of the U.S. invasion of Iraq was that a democratic Iraq would generate pressure on other autocratic governments in the Middle East to undertake political reform. In fact, the opposite has been true. Rather than facilitating the democratization of the Middle East, the Iraq War and its fallout has undermined reform elsewhere. This has especially been true in Saudi Arabia. On the eve of the war in early 2003, Saudi Arabia was under pressure from a small but persistent domestic reform movement, one that had grown emboldened in the aftermath of the September 11, 2001, attacks. Saudi reformers called for sweeping political change, opening up the system to greater participation, an end to corruption, and broader political and civil rights for Saudi citizens.

The Saudi ruling family was initially disarmed. Throughout 2003 then crown prince Abdullah made gestures that suggested the kingdom would pursue a bold new reform agenda. It soon became clear that the country's rulers were biding their time, waiting to outflank the reformers, adopt the mantle of reform for themselves, and co-opt the reform movement's leaders.[35] The Iraq War, and particularly Iraq's descent into civil war, played a part in the kingdom's efforts to turn back domestic reformers. Most importantly, it was the sense that American pressure for reform had disintegrated along with the declining fortunes of the U.S. occupation in Iraq that freed the Saudis to take a firmer stand against reformers. As violence in Iraq escalated and particularly as the United States desperately sought support for its mission there, Saudi leaders correctly perceived that the United States had deemphasized—indeed, had mostly abandoned—its call for greater democratization throughout the region. Absent U.S. leverage or at least the perception that the United States would have used its leverage on the matter of reform, the Saudis moved much more deliberately

---

35. Toby Jones, "Seeking a 'Social Contract' in Saudi Arabia," *Middle East Report* no. 228 (Fall 2003); and Toby Jones, "Violence and the Illusion of Reform in Saudi Arabia," *Middle East Report Online*, November 13, 2003.

to crush and co-opt the reform movement. In reality, while pressure from the United States certainly played a role in creating space for Saudi reformers, the importance of any American role in helping move reform efforts forward was minimal. Saudi reform efforts were mostly the result of indigenous efforts by Saudi intellectuals, academics, and activists with no connections to the outside and especially not with the United States.

Even after the peak of violence in Iraq and the decision by the United States to establish a timeline for the withdrawal of its military forces, Iraq's political transformation has had little impact on Saudi Arabia domestically. Tense relations between Riyadh and Baghdad have had some impact. American policymakers have made clear that their preference between stronger Saudi-Iraqi ties or Saudi democratization has been the former.

Neither the continuation of a U.S. military presence in the region nor the strengthening of Saudi authoritarianism should be seen as uncomfortable outcomes for American policymakers. In fact, the militarization of the Persian Gulf, the use of U.S. military might to secure its "vital interests" in the region, and U.S. support for autocrats is entirely consistent with its historic posture in the region. The brief moment that "democracy talk" played in the lead-up to Iraq was historically aberrant. And while Bush administration officials and supporters of the Iraq War have long denied that invasion had anything to do with oil or securing U.S. hegemony in the region, the war was entirely consistent with past foreign policy patterns. The war fit a long-standing pattern, dating back to the 1970s, of seeking to guarantee U.S. military supremacy and military outposts in the Gulf, and securing access to oil either through war or the threat of war.[36] It has been equally true that the United States has also long preferred the insurance and security that seemingly strong authoritarian regimes in the regime have promised. Saudi animus with Iraq, to the extent that it has helped shape the continuation of the United States' historical approach to the Gulf, should not be seen as a departure from the status quo, but part of a broader strategic calculus on the part of the Saudis to keep it in place.

Conclusion

Saudi-Iraqi relations reached their nadir in late 2009, freezing in mutual exchanges of rancor. It remains uncertain where future relations will go, particularly after the United States draws down most of its military pres-

---

36. Sheila Carapico and Chris Toensing, "The Strategic Logic of the Iraq Blunder," *Middle East Report* no. 239 (Summer 2006).

ence in Iraq in 2011. One of the most important unknowns will be what effect any potential breakdown in Iraqi security will have in the future. A return to the civil strife like that in 2006–7 would not only plunge Iraq into chaos but also raise considerable security challenges for the region. But given Saudi Arabia's reluctance to involve itself in the earlier civil war, it is unlikely that the kingdom would radically change course. Even though some Saudi leaders might advocate for more open support for Sunnis in Iraq, such as that advocated by Nawaf Obaid, the potential costs to Saudi stability and its regional primacy are simply too high. The kingdom's leaders do not desire to get bogged down politically or militarily in Iraq. Nor do they desire to see the erosion of their influence in the Arab world more broadly. While Saudis would fear even greater levels of Iranian influence in Iraq wrought by more violence there, the fears of turning Iraq into a proxy war, and the potentially devastating outcomes that such a war might mean for Saudi Arabia, are far greater.

5

Iraq and Its Gulf Arab Neighbors

Avoiding Risk, Seeking Opportunity

Judith S. Yaphe

The tribes and communities that line the Arabian side of the Persian Gulf—today represented by the states of Kuwait, Bahrain, Qatar, the United Arab Emirates, and Oman—have lived in the shadow of larger, more powerful neighbors almost since the dawn of recorded history. Overlooked for the most part by Persian, Greek, Roman, and various Islamic empires, they could afford to ignore and be ignored by the warring tribes and states of premodern times.[1] In the nineteenth century, the growing global dependence on the Gulf's energy resources and its key strategic location brought the five sheikhdoms and their ruling elites international attention and competing claims for their affection. It also brought them unwanted attention from neighbors—the rulers of Iraq, Iran, and Saudi Arabia—and from so-called great powers that promised protection in exchange for access to their oil wealth.

The preferred security policy of these small and vulnerable states was, and still is, to avoid provoking their larger neighbors while seeking ways to engage more distant and powerful allies. They use their assets—oil and money for investment—to buy them protection from feared neighbors and as a hedge against domestic threats. For the greater part of 200 years, the

---

The opinions and analysis presented in this chapter are the author's alone and do not reflect the views of the National Defense University, the U.S. Department of Defense, or any other government agency.

1. Premodern as used here refers to the period up to the nineteenth century.

strategy worked. The exception was Saddam Hussein's invasion and occupation of Kuwait, a lesson seemingly forgotten in the decades since
1990.

The Gulf Arab states face two major external threats: Iraq, whether it
succeeds or fails; and Iran, with or without nuclear weapons. But it is Iraq
that will provide them their ultimate challenge. The people of Iraq and the
Gulf—Sunni and Shi'a, Arab and Persian—have lived together and shared
the poverty of occupation and the sudden wealth that oil can bring. Kuwait in particular has shared oil fields and borders with Iraq as well as
access to the Shatt al-Arab waterway and Gulf waters. Some in Iraq still
covet Kuwait as its nineteenth province—a claim that preceded Kuwait's
declaration of independence in 1961 and survives Saddam Hussein.

Without an Iraq led by a strong Sunni Arab leader, the Gulf Arab
states see a looming threat from an Iranian extremist ideological regime
willing to use its growing military power to extend its power and influence
over the Gulf. This worry is underscored by the perceived threat from a
new Shiite coalition led by Tehran, seemingly backed by the Shi'a-dominated government in post-Saddam Iraq, which is wooing the Shiite and
Persian-origin populations in the Gulf Arab countries. The worry is perhaps greatest for Saudi Arabia, which may be engaged in a proxy war with
Iran for the fate of Lebanon, Syria, and Bahrain, where demonstrations in
early 2011 calling for political reform turned violent. The kings of Saudi
Arabia and Bahrain claimed Iran was encouraging Shiite communities in
both countries to challenge their Sunni rulers. The presence of the U.S.
military has enabled the states to deal with both Iraq and Iran. The way in
which the United States ultimately leaves Iraq will signal to the small Arab
Gulf states whether their long-standing reliance on the United States as
their ultimate protector is still valid.

It is impossible to assess the Gulf states' relations with Iraq without giv-
ing consideration to Iran. Iran's perceived ambitions under both shah and
ayatollah, its offers to protect the Gulf states from danger, and its warnings of its assumed influence over the Gulf's Shiite populations drove
Kuwait, Bahrain, Qatar, and the United Arab Emirates to seek Saddam
Hussein's protection and to support his war on Iran in the 1980s. If the
Gulf Arab states are not careful in how they re-establish relations with
Baghdad, they could be recreating a second angry neighbor to the north
mindful of the lack of respect of these states rather than one accepted and
integrated into regional political and security affairs.

Background

Since the early 1960s, the five Arab states that, along with Saudi Arabia, compose the Gulf Cooperation Council (GCC)—Kuwait, Bahrain, Qatar, the United Arab Emirates, and Oman—have preferred or, more aptly, allowed outsiders to define their security policies and needs. New to acting like states rather than tribes but not yet wealthy from oil, the smaller Arab states of the Persian Gulf were accustomed to letting tradition determine the governance and institutions of civil society, while they looked to Great Britain to protect them from the Arab and Persian storms that periodically swept through the neighborhood. The exception was Saudi Arabia, which enjoyed better relations with the United States than with the United Kingdom.

When the British decided they could no longer afford to protect the Gulf Arabs and withdrew in 1971, the Gulf states turned to the United States to assume the British mantle.[2] Concerned about possible Soviet encroachments in the Gulf, President Richard Nixon created the "twin pillars" policy, which designated Iran and Saudi Arabia as proxies for U.S. military presence in the region.[3] This was followed by the introduction of U.S. forces under the Carter Doctrine and the expansion of American force presence and operations under President Ronald Reagan during the Iran-Iraq War.

Through the 1970s and 1980s the Arab states of the Gulf faced the hegemonic ambitions of Iran, first under the secular and intensely nationalist regime of the Shah, and then under the Islamic Republic of Iran, also nationalist and determined to export its revolution across the Gulf. In between Iranian challenges came Iraqi feints at territorial acquisition as well as attempts to gain influence in decision making on Gulf Arab and regional political, economic, and strategic affairs. In 1981, as the Iraq-Iran War continued and Iran broadened its efforts to export its Islamic revolution across the Gulf, the six states formed the GCC.[4] It was not intended to be a political or security organization similar to the European Union (then the European Community) or NATO; rather, its members focused on common economic interests, such as forming a common customs union and trade zone and cooperating in local police and security matters.

---

2. For a short history of the U.S. military engagement of the United States in the Persian Gulf, see *The United States and the Persian Gulf: Reshaping Security Strategy for the Post-Containment Era*, ed. Richard Sokolsky (Washington, DC: NDU Press, 2003).

3. The United States first entered the Gulf with a small naval presence—the U.S. 5th Fleet—in 1947 in Bahrain and a U.S. Air Force presence in Dhahran, Saudi Arabia, from the 1940s through the early 60s.

4. In 2001, the GCC extended a special status to Yemen but remains reluctant to extend it full membership or to include Iraq or Iran. In May 2011, the GCC announced that Jordan and Morocco were seeking membership in the GCC.

Continuities in the Arab Gulf

The GCC states have been relatively stable over the past half-century. Their patterns of political and social behavior are similar—rule by a single family with a patriarchal and tribal style of decision making, nominal parliaments or councils whose members are handpicked by the ruler, stability purchased by oil wealth and doled out to elites and citizens who form only a very small percentage of the population, and modernization imported from countries whose culture is both desired and derided. Successions for the most part have been unchallenged and populations kept quiescent by generous government subsidies and intimidation.

Until 1990, when Saddam Hussein invaded and occupied Kuwait, citizens of the oil-rich Gulf Arab states enjoyed the kind of security available to wealthy welfare states. They were protected by a strategic balance of power in the Gulf policed first by the Shah and then by Iraq, and guaranteed by the absent United States. Lavish but incompatible arms purchases, eagerness to invest in relatively safe markets, and a bland business climate brought American business interests as well as other foreign patrons. Gulf governments gave little thought to strategic planning, crisis management, meaningful political liberalization, or economic reform. After 1991 and the liberation of Kuwait, the small Gulf Arab states sought to return to the old ways of thinking about security—avoid provoking more powerful neighbors; use investments abroad, oil, and arms sales to acquire international approval and protection; and depend on oil-consuming, arms-selling nations—especially the United States and Western European countries—for protection.

Growing Discontinuities in the Arab Gulf

Less observed or understood are the undercurrents of change that began rippling through the Arab side of the Gulf after the Kuwait war. The first Arab Development Plan of 2002 noted that despite their great wealth and small population base, the Gulf states lagged behind poorer and more populous regions such as Africa in productivity, political reform, and economic diversification.[5] Gulf Arabs, in particular, had limited exposure to the world outside, with too many of its citizens lacking the education and skills necessary for life in the twenty-first century and most work done by expatriate labor. Moreover, more than half the population—women—were politically, economically, and socially disenfranchised. They lacked the educational and career opportunities available to men in their societies and, more to the point, were isolated from politics and denied jobs in the work force.

---

5. UN Development Program (UNDP), *The Arab Human Development Report, 2002: Creating Opportunities for Future Generations* (New York: UNDP, 2002), http://hdr.undp.org/en/reports/regionalreports/arabstates/name,3140,en.html.

Other troubling signs suggested change was coming to the Arab Gulf long before public protests in early 2011 challenged and changed governments and political behavior in Tunisia and Egypt, the so-called Arab Spring. Claims of abuse of privilege by ruling family members had become more common. The impact of the economic downturn in 2009 was cushioned by governments buying up debt, including Abu Dhabi's bailout of Dubai, and the elimination of expatriates at the upper and lower ends of the wage scale. But questions about the need for political and economic reform remained muted, except for the small civil society and human rights organizations that were becoming more outspoken in demanding inclusion in political decision making, protection of basic human and civil rights, and an end to ethnic and/or religious discrimination. The specter of labor unrest among expatriate and local laborers, antigovernment demonstrations, and public criticism of the ruling families, once rare occurrences, also became more common.

In addition to this unease, the Gulf governments face the rise of ultra-conservative tribal and sectarian movements demanding political reform or, in extreme cases, regime change. These factions seek a greater role in decision making, constitutional limitations on ruling family power, adherence to a strict version of Islamic law, and an end to corruption in government. Kuwait is the clearest example of these trends. Before the 1990 invasion, two-thirds of Kuwait's overall population of 1.7 million were expatriates; they still are. Approximately 20 percent of Kuwait's population is Shi'a, and many Kuwaiti families have ties to Shiite Arab families and tribes in Basra and southern Iraq.

Citizenship was open only to those able to trace their grandfathers' presence in Kuwait to the pre-1920 period. Those identified as *bidoon*—those "without" status—had no hope of citizenship, even though many came from tribes that may have originated in Ottoman Iraq. Kuwait today is the only Gulf country with a vibrant elected parliament. Elections for the National Assembly in 2008 saw Islamists and tribal conservatives win nearly half of the seats. These conservative elements are challenging the ruling Al Sabah family for the right to appoint and question cabinet ministers and, ultimately, would like to place limitations on the power of the amir. In Qatar and the Emirates, expatriates comprise approximately 85 percent of the overall population. The states lacking oil wealth—Bahrain and Oman—have smaller percentages of foreign workers and less homogenous populations.

The Terrorist Menace in the Arab Gulf

In the 1980s and 1990s extremist factions seeking to disrupt the Gulf states by violence and terror were seen as more pernicious than the political and economic challenges noted above. Even before the al-Qaida attacks on New York and Washington, D.C., on September 11, 2001, the Gulf states experienced attacks on national and foreign military and security targets. Terrorist attacks by groups affiliated with al-Qaida or seeking to imitate its attacks on the United States occurred in London, Madrid, Riyadh, and Casablanca. The groups were able to recruit and receive financial contributions from wealthy Gulf donors sympathetic to their Islamist and anti-Western goals. Al-Qaida and other extremist elements accuse the Al-Sabah of Kuwait, the Al Khalifa of Bahrain, and the Al-Thani of Qatar, as well as other elite families, of being un-Islamic and puppets of the United States. In the 1980s, terrorists linked to Hizballah of Lebanon and the Iran-based Iraqi Da'wa movement targeted Kuwaiti, American, and French interests in Kuwait. The goal was to aid Iran and obtain the release of prisoners caught in terrorist operations in Kuwait, including an attempted assassination on the amir and the bombing of U.S. and French interests.

In the late 1990s, the terrorists were surrogates of Saudi extremist Osama bin Laden and other Sunni Salafi extremists who sought to replace the Sunni-dominated governments in the Gulf with a more strictly observant Islamic emirate. They criticized the Gulf rulers but conducted terrorist operations on Muslims as well as non-Muslims in Saudi Arabia. Youth from the Gulf Arab states were recruited for operations in U.S. occupied Iraq, and press reports indicate Gulf nationals were caught in counterterrorist operations in Iraq and on their return to the Peninsula states. Wealthy Arabs in the Gulf states, especially in the United Arab Emirates, Bahrain, and Qatar, have donated money to al-Qaida and other Sunni Arab extremists in Iraq. Iraqi exiles, including Saddam loyalists and former Ba'th Party leaders, have also received safe haven and been allowed to raise recruits and money for operations in Iraq.

The Gulf governments are responding with efforts to co-opt their critics, restrict political participation, and, in states like Bahrain, change the demographic imbalance. Bahrain has long been ruled by a Sunni elite representing approximately 25–30 percent of the population that controls the lives and well-being of its 70–75 percent Shiite majority. To maintain power, the government transformed itself into a kingdom, created a parliament, banned political activity in mosques and Shiite prayer houses (*husseiniyah*s), and began talking about measures to expand political participation for women and protect foreign labor. These efforts at political reform were rejected by Bahraini Shiite political factions and some Sunni reformists. According to human rights supporters, however, Bahrain is also trying to alter population demographics by wooing foreign Sunni

Arabs, especially Iraqis, to become citizens. They are offered jobs in internal security, including police intelligence, and education, and receive preference in naturalization over non-Sunni immigrants who have long lived in country.[6]

The Gulf Arabs' Security Vision

Gulf Arab security policies have traditionally been based on risk avoidance, collective reaction, and reliance on nonregional powers to ensure their security and survival. The strategy was to avoid provoking any dominant and more powerful government in the region, especially in Baghdad and Riyadh, to pay for protection, to use arms sales as an extension of foreign policy, and above all, to maintain a balance of power in the Gulf. Iraq's invasion and occupation of Kuwait in 1990 should have exposed the weakness in this form of strategic thinking, but the Gulf governments still prefer to maintain the kind of balance of power they once felt comfortable under—a balance maintained by cordial relations with local powers and backed up by a more distant U.S. commitment and presence.

The Gulf Arab states face threats from Iraq and Iran. The first is from a rearming Iraq led by cranky Sunni and Shiite politicians unhappy with the lack of support given by Saudi Arabia and the Gulf states and eager to participate in Arab and Gulf affairs. Over the next decade, Iran will probably present a greater security challenge than Iraq, but Baghdad is seeking release from its pariah status under Chapter VII of the UN Charter and shopping for military hardware—aircraft and tanks, for example—that are not necessarily needed for internal use, as in Saddam's time. One goal of sanctions after 1990 and the removal of Saddam in 2003 was to ensure that Iraq would not again threaten its neighbors, but the line between a defensive and offensive military capability is probably seen as very thin from Kuwait.

Kuwait-Iraq: Proximity Breeds Contempt

Relations between Iraq and Kuwait probably pose the most serious threat to regional security over the long term. For much of their modern history, the two states have contested borders, territory, and resources. Iraqi leaders have tried to absorb Kuwait as the nineteenth province, claimed possession of uninhabitable islands (Warbah and Bubiyan at the entrance to

---

6. Author interviews conducted in Europe and the Middle East, 2008 and 2009. Admission of Jordan and Morocco to the GCC could open jobs in the armed forces and internal security to Sunni Arab nationals from these countries.

the Shatt al-Arab) and oil fields, and demanded Al Sabah support for its regional wars. Despite Kuwait's devastating occupation by Iraq in 1990 and Iraq's defeat in the brief 1991 Gulf War, neither side appears to have learned any lessons. Many Iraqis today, regardless of ethnic or sectarian loyalties, still blame Kuwait for all the ills that they have suffered since 1991. Iraqi officials understand Kuwait's acceptance and forgiveness is critical to ending their pariah status. Kuwait, too, understands it is the key to Iraq's release from UN restrictions but continues to insist that Iraq fully comply with UN Security Council resolutions first. The issues remain virtually the same, defined by proximity and contempt.

Rancor between the two countries runs deep. Iraq has long resented what it regards as its loss of the Ottoman province of Kuwait, which under the Turks had nominally been part of Basra Province. When Kuwait declared its independence in 1961, Abd al-Karim Qasim, the general who orchestrated the 1958 coup against the Iraqi monarchy, declared Kuwait part of Iraq. First the British deployed troops to Kuwait and then the Arab League sent a force to replace the British. Qasim was forced to withdraw his claim. In the 1980s Kuwait joined Saudi Arabia, the United Arab Emirates, and Qatar in loaning Iraq more than $80 billion to defeat Iran in their eight-year war. Kuwait shared Baghdad's fear of the Islamic Republic's efforts to export its revolution across the Gulf.

Iraq emerged from the war with Iran with its territory and its military intact and with a sense of nationalist pride at its defense of the country. The costs of the war, however, were high.[7] Iraq's offshore oil export facilities were destroyed and the Shatt al-Arab waterway was closed to traffic, filled with sunken ships, chemical weapons, and other ordnance, making Iraq almost a landlocked country. As a result, Iraq had to turn to its Umm Qasr port, bordering Kuwait, as its main shipping terminal.

Most observers assumed Iraq would settle down after the war, rebuild its economy, and repay its debt. It did not. Eager to continue work on expensive military programs, including biological, chemical, and nuclear weapons, and to sustain expensive subsidy programs to his support base, Saddam looked for a new source of money. He found it in Kuwait. In spring 1990 he accused Kuwait of stealing oil from fields that spanned their mutual and contested borders. He also charged that Kuwait and the United Arab Emirates were pumping more oil than allowed by OPEC quotas, thereby depressing oil prices and leaving Iraq unable to meet its debt payments. Baghdad demanded large sums of money from Kuwait and the

---

7. Estimates by scholars and U.S. government reporting place Iraq's war casualties at nearly 500,000, including 150,000 deaths. See, for example, Joost Hiltermann, *A Poisonous Affair: America, Iraq, and the Gassing of Halabja* (New York: Cambridge University Press, 2007).

other GCC states as the price of rescuing them from Iranian efforts to export its revolution across the Gulf. When Kuwait refused to accede to Saddam's blackmail, Iraq invaded Kuwait on August 2, 1990. The invasion was over in less than a day. One week later, Saddam announced that Kuwait had become Iraq's nineteenth province.

Kuwait was devastated by the Iraqi occupation. Led by Saddam's cousin, Ali Hassan al-Majid, known as "Chemical Ali" for his attacks on the Kurds, and Saddam's older son, Uday, Iraqis descended on the so-called nineteenth province and systematically began looting the country. They sought Kuwait's financial assets, natural resources, and Islamic treasures, stripping government offices, hospitals, and private homes of cars, technology, and other moveable objects. An estimated 800 Kuwaitis also disappeared during the occupation and retreat. On January 16, 1991, U.S.-led coalition forces began an air and ground war that resulted in Iraq's retreat from Kuwait. As a final gesture, the Iraqis set Kuwait's oil fields afire as they left, creating an economic, environmental, and ecological disaster that took many months to extinguish.

For the next twelve years, Iraq languished under UN-imposed sanctions and an oil embargo, and occasional coalition military operations to encourage Saddam to comply with UN Security Council resolutions and not threaten his neighbors in the south or the Kurds in the north of Iraq. To further protect Saudi Arabia and Kuwait, the coalition instituted a no-fly zone south of the thirty-second parallel, but Saddam's troops kept control on the ground.

The collapse of Saddam Hussein's regime in 2003 and the election in 2005 of a non-Sunni government in Baghdad heightened Gulf Arabs' security fears. They see risk if Iraq fails and if it succeeds. A failed Iraq will mean more cross-border terrorists entering or returning to the Gulf intent on overthrowing the traditional ruling elites and the expansion of Iranian control of southern Iraq. It also raises the risk of sectarian or ethnic unrest in countries where significant minority populations have long been discriminated against by Sunni and Wahhabi prejudices and Arab nationalist sentiment. If Iraq succeeds in stabilizing under a democratic-leaning, elective form of governance, especially one with a weak central government and strong semi-independent provincial authorities, then the Gulf states will increasingly worry about the export of "advanced" political ideas that they say their countries do not need or are not prepared to adopt.

Either strategically or tactically, Iraq is no longer the eastern flank of the Arab world and protector of the Sunni Arab Gulf against the Persian Shiite crescent. Rather, Gulf leaders perceive Iraq as providing strategic depth for a hegemonic-minded Iran. Some Gulf leaders believe this has already happened. None of the GCC states appear willing to make the kind of gestures toward Iraq that might keep it more Gulf friendly.

Relations between Kuwait and Iraq remain deeply troubled. On the surface, ties appear somewhat cordial—Kuwait sent as its ambassador to Baghdad a retired Shi'a Arab general in late 2008, one of the first Gulf states to do so. Deputy Prime Minister and Foreign Minister Sheikh Mohammad Sabah al-Salim al-Sabah made the first visit by a senior Kuwaiti official to Baghdad in February 2009, when Kuwait and Iraq established a joint ministerial commission. One year later, Iraq nominated Mohammed Hussein Bahr al-Ulum as its ambassador to Kuwait. According to press and Kuwaiti sources, Iraq has paid $13.3 billion in compensation for its invasion and occupation, but it still owes Kuwait $25.5 billion in war damages plus approximately $16 billion for loans during the Iran-Iraq War.[8] Especially galling for the Iraqis is the 1995 UN-brokered border agreement that awarded territory around Iraq's Umm Qasr port to Kuwait, thereby blocking Iraqi access to the Gulf through the Khawr Abdullah waterway. The new border also gave disputed portions of the rich Rumaila oil fields in the south of Iraq to Kuwait.[9]

In 2009, Prime Minister Nuri al-Maliki and Parliament Speaker Iyad al-Samarra'i made separate visits to Kuwait, the first official visits by senior Iraqi officials since Saddam reviewed his troops in Kuwait in fall 1990.[10] The Iraqis urged Kuwaiti leaders in the government and National Assembly to increase cooperation with Iraq and support Baghdad's request that the United Nations lift all remaining sanctions and end its pariah status under Chapter VII of the UN Charter.[11] Prime Minister Maliki assured Kuwait's deputy prime minister Sheikh Mohammed al-Sabah in early 2009 that "there is no way to return to the policy of war and adventures. . . . Iraq has changed. The bad image is over, no more terrorism, no more Al-Qaeda. Our country is an important partner in the region."[12]

Kuwait, for its part, has expressed its willingness to support Iraq's request. Speaking to a UN committee in March 2007, Kuwait's ambassador to the United Nations urged the international community to support the

---

8. Iraq is required to put 5 percent of its oil revenues into a fund created by the UN Security Council to pay reparations for its seven-month occupation of Kuwait. The UN fund has received claims worth $368 billion and has approved payment of approximately $52 billion, based on figures from the fund and Kuwait. The fund has paid out almost $27 billion to claimants, according to figures up to the end of January 2009 posted on the fund's Web site. Khaled al-Mudhaf, Kuwait's public authority for compensation, in an interview with Kuwait News Agency in April 2009; "Iraq Owes Kuwait 25.5 Billion Dollars in War Damages," *Khaleej Times*, April 29, 2009; "Kuwait Presses UN on Iraq Sanctions," *Agence France-Presse*, May 28, 2009.

9. See Phebe Marr and Sam Parker's chapter in this volume.

10. Iraqi president Jalal Talabani visited Kuwait to attend an Arab economic summit in January 2009, but this was not a head-of-state visit.

11. "Parliament Urges Kuwait to Respond to Iraq's 'Positive Initiatives,'" Al-Iraqiyah Television, June 1, 2009.

12. *Arab News*, February 27, 2009.

Iraqi government and prevent interference in its internal affairs, saying that "a free, democratic, united, safe and stable Iraq will serve security and stability of the region and the whole world."[13] The offer, however, is conditional—before Kuwait agrees to forgive Iraq's debt or renegotiate borders, Iraq must first pay all the reparations it owes, agree to the demarcation of land and maritime borders, account for Kuwaitis missing in Iraq since 1990, and return all looted property.[14] In 2010, Kuwait demanded the British seize an Iraqi airliner that had made its first flight to London. This demand was not the action of a government seeking to upgrade relations with a potentially resurgent and occasionally hostile neighbor. Kuwait's position seems unlikely to change.

Is Reconciliation Possible?

The Gulf states probably fear Iraq today under Shiite governance more than they feared Iraq under Saddam. After all, Saddam was a Sunni Arab, a strong-willed determined autocrat who ruled a united Iraq using terror and repression. Like the Sunni Arabs who rule the Gulf states, he abhorred religious and political extremists that he could not control and was especially wary of Iran and its Shiite cohorts in Iraq and the Gulf states. Now the northern Gulf states, in their view, have on their borders a new Islamist state run by a pro-Iranian government to protect Iranian interests and aspirations. Gulf Arabs blame the United States' insistence on democratic practices in Iraq for the Shiite takeover of Iraq, accusing Washington of backing elections to hand Iraq over to Iran and its allies.[15] Like their counterparts in Saudi Arabia, Kuwaiti security officials warn that the sectarian strife in Iraq could spread to other Gulf Arab states. A senior Kuwaiti official in an interview with *Al-Sharq al-Awsat* in 2007 warned that Kuwaitis had three fears centered on Iraq: that it would be divided, that it would descend into a civil war, and that its sectarian fighting would spread to Kuwait. The flames, the official warned, "will reach everybody."[16]

The issue of reconciliation is difficult for both Kuwaitis and Iraqis. In a survey on whether Kuwait should reopen diplomatic relations with Iraq conducted in 2008 by the Kuwaiti newspaper *Al-Watan*, 46 percent of Kuwaiti citizens said that they opposed normalization of relations and would never forget or forgive Iraqi forces' crimes and aggression during the 1990

---

13. Kuwait News Agency, March 16, 2007.

14. "Kuwait Opposes Iraq's Removal from UN Chapter 7 until Obligations Fulfilled," *al-Jaridah Online*, May 26, 2009.

15. Author interviews of Gulf Arabs conducted in Kuwait, Qatar, and Saudi Arabia in 2008 and 2009.

16. "Kuwait Warns of Iraqi Sectarian Strife Spreading," Reuters, February 14, 2007.

invasion, 31 percent said that Kuwait should wait until the intentions of the new Iraqi government are known, and 23 percent agreed that diplomatic relations should be reopened, saying that the old disputes, along with Iraq's aggression against Kuwait, had been over for a long time. Asked whether or not they supported the opening of a Kuwaiti embassy in Iraq, 41 percent opposed the idea, while 38 percent supported it. The remaining 21 percent said that it was still too soon to reopen an embassy in Baghdad but they would support reopening one there in the future.[17]

Iraqi officials say Iraq seeks to resolve all outstanding issues with Kuwait, including missing persons and assets. It wants removal of Chapter VII sanctions that still keep an arms embargo and some financial restrictions in place because, as an Iraqi spokesman for Prime Minister Maliki noted, "the new regime is not a threat to security or peace in the region."[18] Some Iraqis, however, think differently. They blame Kuwait for everything that is wrong in their lives. Kuwait is responsible for all the looting in Iraq, Kuwait is trying to destroy Iraq by keeping it under Chapter VII, everyone in Kuwait is rich and lives off of wealth that belongs to Iraq, Iraq must retake Kuwait because it is Iraq's right and it is the nineteenth province.

Some Iraqi parliamentarians demand that Kuwait compensate Baghdad for its role in the U.S.-led 2003 invasion. An editorial in a pro-Sadrist Iraqi newspaper in June 2009 may reflect the views of a wide range of public opinion. It blamed "the Sheikhs of Kuwait" for the devastating sanctions placed on Iraq in 1990 when they complained to the international community that Saddam "was going to swallow their small country." It warned Kuwait and other Arab states that "the masks are falling off to reveal the ugly faces of some Arabs' hatred towards the sons of Mesopotamia. A hatred that is so deeply rooted in history that it cannot be removed without smashing in their rotten heads to end their poisoned thoughts." Referring to Iraq's request for relief of Chapter VII sanctions, the editorial writer said,

> The Iraqis thought that the first country that would stand by their side would be Kuwait because of what Saddam did to them. However, the Sheikhs who reside in Al Saif Palace have shown their true hatred towards the people of Iraq. Saddam is gone and Iraq always emphasizes that it respects Kuwait's sovereignty . . . but those rotten heads are still trying to take more Iraqi territory and oil fields. We urge our government to stand firm against the Kuwaiti greed. We demand that they stop begging from their Sheikhs. Sending delegations only makes us look weak. The Iraqi government should form a committee to demand compensation

---

17. *Kuwait Times*, August 3, 2008.
18. Ibid.; *Agence France-Presse*, May 28, 2009.

for the sanctions and the occupation. The Sheikhs of Kuwait opened their airspace, land, and seas to facilitate the Americans' unjust invasion of Iraq. We demand that Iraqi journalists and the media to be more strict with this country and expose them for who they are![19]

Another Arab journalist writing in *Al-Sharq al-Awsat* quoted an Iraqi leader asking, "Do we need to invade Kuwait once more?" He warned that "if the Kuwaitis have forgotten that Iraq has already occupied their country then this is a clear flaw in their policy, especially when the language of and logic of the new Iraq [with regard to Kuwait] is more intense than that of the previous regime." Kuwaiti demands that Baghdad resolve all issues between the two states before Chapter VII restrictions can be removed "only reminds the Iraqis of the long series of mistakes committed by the Kuwaitis over past decades." For Iraqis, the mistakes include "developing Shuwaikh port, and [spending] millions of dollars to feed the Iraqi war machine during the Iraq-Iran war, according to the method of we provide the money, and you provide the troops." He concluded that Arab governments, particularly in the Gulf, "must be very careful, for Saddam has gone, but he has been replaced by one thousand Saddams."[20]

Iraq and the Arab States of the Lower Gulf: Distance Encourages Solidarity

Bahrain, Qatar, the United Arab Emirates, and Oman have felt little threat from Iraq historically and, with the possible exception of Oman, have preferred to see Baghdad as a Sunni Arab state linked to them by the mystical bonds of Arab solidarity. The occupation of Kuwait was an aberration, perhaps, and Iraq is still a needed presence, especially when Iran threatens. This sense of needing Iraq's Sunni Arabs has had an added dimension since the 1990s, with Sunni Arab ruling elites in Bahrain, for example, seeking to bolster their numbers by offering employment in police and security jobs and citizenship to Sunni Arabs from Iraq and Jordan. The lower Gulf has become strategically more important to Iraq, too. Many Iraqis—including supporters and opponents of the new government in Baghdad and exiled Ba'thist sympathizers—live in Bahrain, Qatar, and Abu Dhabi where they are allowed to raise money and recruit supporters.[21]

Bahrain's Shiite community is approximately 75 percent of the population, comprised of Arab and Persian origin families who have lived in

19. "Kuwait Reveals Its Ugly Face; Hatred and Grudges against Iraqis Not against Saddam," *Ishraqat*, June 4, 2009. The speaker may have been a member of the Sadrist faction, but the sentiment is not limited to Shiite extremists.

20. Tariq Alhomayed, "Iraqi Reaction: What's under Iraq's Carpet?" *Al-Sharq Al-Awsat*, June 5, 2009.

21. Author interviews in Bahrain and the United Arab Emirates, 2007–9.

Bahrain for generations. Historically, they have lacked political power and access to jobs in the government, military, and security services, including the Bahrain Defense Force. The 1979 Islamic Revolution in Iran and the rise to power of an elected government dominated by the Shiite majority in Iraq raised sectarian and national consciousness among Bahrain's Shi'a and, at the same time, both events shattered a sense of complacency among the island's Sunni elites. Bahrain can ill-afford to ignore Iraq, given the occasional outbursts from Iranian politicians that describe Bahrain as a province of Iran that was taken away. Bahrain ended negotiations with Iran for a natural gas import deal that had been signed during Iranian president Mahmoud Ahmadinejad's 2007 visit to Manama.[22]

The United Arab Emirates is Iraq's largest GCC trade partner and thus has a substantial role in its reconstruction. Abu Dhabi's sympathy for Iraq predates the Kuwait invasion and the Iraq-Iran War. The late Sheikh Zayid, one of the last of the "old-school" Arab nationalists, was quick to offer Saddam loans and diplomatic support in the name of Arab unity in the 1980s and call for forgiveness of Iraq's debt after the Kuwait debacle. In 2008, he announced forgiveness of $7 billion of Iraq's debt to Abu Dhabi and the reopening of the UAE embassy in Baghdad, making the UAE the first Arab country to return to Iraq.

Debt forgiveness has consistently been a request of Iraq's during its interactions with its "brothers" in the region. Only the United Arab Emirates has written off Iraq's debt. Kuwait has asked its Parliament to waive Iraq's debt, but with no success. Other Gulf states have made no efforts to forgive Iraqi debt, but also appear disinclined to push to collect it. The Department of State estimates that approximately $66.5 billion of Iraq's estimated $120.2 billion foreign debt has been forgiven, and that more than half of the outstanding debt is owed to Gulf states. The total estimated Iraqi debt does not include reparations to Iran for the 1980–88 war that were authorized by UN Security Council Resolution 598.[23]

Ties between Emiratis and Iraqis remain close, strengthened perhaps by the years of exile the Iraqis—both opponents of Saddam and now loyalists of Saddam—spent in Abu Dhabi and the other emirates. Iraqi business elites representing Sunni Arab, Shiite, and Kurdish interests and Gulf officials and investors meet in events sponsored by groups like the Emirates-

---

22. "Arab League Rejects Iran's Accusations, Threats against Bahrain," Kuwait News Agency, February 13, 2009. The most recent threat came from a senior official, Ali Nateq-Nouri. The secretary-general of the GCC accused the Iranian of "living beyond the boundaries of current history." See "Iran Says It Respects Sovereignty of Bahrain," *Arab News*, February, 20, 2009.

23. In 2008, Iraq owed the GCC states approximately $80 billion, including $24 billion to Kuwait, $4 billion to Qatar, and $7 billion to the UAE. In addition, Iraq still owed $40 billion to the Paris Club.

Iraq Business Forum and Dana Gas and Crescent Petroleum to seek investment by European and Gulf companies in Iraqi Kurdistan and other parts of Iraq with the hope of pumping Iraqi gas to Europe.[24]

Like Kuwait and Bahrain, the United Arab Emirates security concerns focus more on Iran, which has occupied the Tunbs and Abu Musa Islands since the Shah seized them in the 1970s, and on Saudi Arabia, with whom it has contested borders and secret agreements relating to their resolution.[25] Iraq defends Abu Dhabi's claim to the three islands in the Gulf and would certainly give its diplomatic backing to the United Arab Emirates in any dispute with Saudi Arabia.

The Iranian Threat

The second major threat to the Gulf states comes from Iran. Worry about Iranian intentions, warlike rhetoric, and threats to shut down the Strait of Hormuz shapes the strategic vision of the Gulf Arabs toward distant patrons and masks interest in any security thinking or policy toward Iraq. Iran's quest for regional leadership and nuclear ambitions (both civilian and military) raise a greater near-term risk of conflict in the Gulf. Loathe to provoke Iran by denying its right to civilian nuclear energy capability, the Gulf Arab states have only begun in recent years to express their unease with a nuclear-empowered Iran. They acknowledge Iran's right to develop civilian nuclear power. Indeed, several states—Saudi Arabia, Qatar, and the United Arab Emirates—are themselves considering construction of civilian nuclear power plants, all under Non-Proliferation Treaty obligations and International Atomic Energy Agency supervision.[26] The Gulf Arabs, however, now speak openly of their concerns about Iran developing nuclear weapons, insisting on full-cycle control of uranium enrichment, and intentions to construct as many as twenty more nuclear power plants strung out along the northern shore of the Gulf. They do not believe that Iran would use a nuclear weapon against them, so their fears of weaponization appear at this point to be second to fear of environmental damage from a Chernobyl-style accident or from a natural disaster, such as an earthquake at a nuclear plant built on or near a fault, and Iran's lack of

---

24. "UAE Firms to Send Iraq Gas to Europe," *Gulf News*, May 17, 2009, http://archive.gulfnews.com/articles/09/05/18/10314644.html.

25. Iran's media enjoy ridiculing the United Arab Emirates and the GCC by referring to the Tunbs and Abu Musa as "the always Iranian islands in the always Persian Gulf" and insist on referring to the GCC as the Persian Gulf Cooperation Council.

26. Other nations that have said they plan to construct civilian nuclear reactors or have sought technical assistance and advice from the International Atomic Energy Agency (IAEA), the Vienna-based United Nations nuclear watchdog agency, since 2007 include Egypt, Jordan, Syria, Turkey, and Yemen, as well as several North African nations. Bob Drogin and Borzou Daragahi, "Arabs Make Plans for Nuclear Power," *Los Angeles Times*, May 26, 2007.

responsibility or preparation for consequence management in the event of a nuclear "event."

Linked to their concern about Iran's nuclear aspirations and intentions is worry about what the United States and Israel might do to prevent Iran from achieving its goals. The Gulf governments worry that the United States will launch a war against Iran, or allow Israel to attack Iran, or negotiate security issues with Iran without consulting them. Should the United States launch military operations against Iran, it would be the fourth Gulf war in one generation. Gulf rulers would like the United States to consult them before making any initiatives—hostile or friendly—toward Iraq and Iran. Privately, however, many admit that they would feel compelled to support Washington but are uncertain about U.S. willingness to honor its commitments to their stability and security (read: their survival).

Qatar keeps close watch on developments in Iraq and Iran. In recent years, Qatar has begun taking an uncharacteristically active role in Arab and regional diplomacy, offering to help mediate intra-Arab disputes without waiting for Saudi approval. It worries about the consequences of sectarian unrest in Iraq for Gulf stability, but avoids taking stands on what is often described as "a domestic affair." Doha pays more attention to developments in Iran. Qatar is a leading oil exporter and the world's top exporter of liquefied natural gas. It shares a gas field with Iran and, unlike the northern GCC states, has normal diplomatic relations with Iran. In July 2009, the chief of staff of the Qatari Armed Forces held talks in Tehran with Iranian defense minister Mostafa Mohammad-Najjar. Qatar sought assurances of Iran's commitment to safeguarding the security of the Gulf and the transport of energy through the Strait of Hormuz. Iran was still reeling from the demonstrations following its June 2009 presidential election and rumors of a possible attack by Israel or the United States. The Iranian assured the Qatari that "sustainable security will be established in the region through collective cooperation."[27]

Oman often takes positions on political and regional security issues at odds with its GCC brothers. In the 1980s, when the Gulf Arabs and the United States were firmly anti-Iranian, Muscat kept open its ties with Baghdad and the Islamic Republic as it had with the Shah, and urged the GCC and Washington to open contacts with Tehran. Muscat today sees a role for itself in resolving regional security differences between the GCC states, Iraq and Iran. Oman's general focus is increasing its trade, investment, economic, energy, and infrastructure projects; as such, the country's interest in Iraq appears to be driven more by financial interests, with the

---

27. "Qatar, Iran Hold Defence Talks," *Peninsula*, July 9, 2009.

hope that a secure Iraq will prove to be a useful trading partner and source of investment for Oman.

Strategic Options for the Gulf Arabs

Events in the Gulf region since the Iranian Revolution, the eight-year Iraq-Iran War, and the Iraqi invasion of Kuwait should have taught Gulf leaders some bitter lessons about national self-interest and the need for strategic planning and collective defense. It is not always possible to avoid provoking a rising and powerful neighbor determined on territorial or ideological expansion. U.S. and European governments may not always have the best interests of the oil-rich Gulf Arabs as their first priority. Lavish sums spent on weapons systems enrich arms merchants but do not guarantee a country the capability to defend itself. A security strategy that did not work as hoped in 1990 or 2003 may not be appropriate for the next decade.

The smaller Gulf states have several challenges ahead. As the events labeled the Arab Spring demonstrated in early 2011, internal threats—growing domestic unrest over political and social marginalization of significant elements of the population; sectarian discrimination; overreliance on expatriate labor in a time of global recession, labor unrest, and investment losses; and the spread of violence and terrorism if Iraq and Yemen fail—are far more serious threats than external ones. Protesters in Bahrain, Saudi Arabia, and Oman took to the streets to complain about official corruption and demand an end to political exclusion and economic discrimination. Prominent Iraqi Shiite politicians and Iran's leaders offered to send aid to Bahrain's beleaguered Shi'a. The Gulf regimes responded with force, in hopes of avoiding regime collapse as happened in Tunisia and Egypt. Saudi Arabia and the United Arab Emirates deployed troops the Bahrain ostensibly to protect infrastructure.[28] In Kuwait, which had just concluded the trials of an alleged terrorist cell allegedly recruited by Iran, Shiite politicians protested the government's offer to join the Saudi and UAE force already in Bahrain.

Saudi Arabia was quick to blame Iran for inciting riots and encouraging the Gulf Shi'a to protest. The smaller states seem to agree, but they also live in uneasy alliance with Saudi Arabia, which tries to exercise its rights as Big Brother to dictate the actions and attitudes of the fragile five. In the short term, they must contend with Iran and its vision as the preeminent power in the Persian Gulf, its efforts to expand its influence to the Greater Middle East, and its nuclear ambitions. In the longer term, Iraq will once

---

28. The GCC announced 1,500 military personnel were sent to Bahrain, but other Gulf sources claimed they joined approximately 2,500 Saudi military personnel already in country.

again expect to play a larger role in Gulf affairs and it will remember past slights. The options all involve Iraq, Iran, and the United States.

Option 1: Engage Iran, Ignore Iraq

For the moment this seems to be the option preferred by the Gulf Arabs. From their perspective, the most effective course for them and for U.S. policy is to seek engagement with Iran, regardless of Iran's fickleness. Sanctions, which have been imposed on Iran since the 1979 takeover of the U.S. embassy in Tehran, have not modified Iranian support for terrorists, prevented its acquisition of advanced nuclear technology, or dissuaded it from threatening the Gulf states should they continue to support a U.S. military presence and policies in the region. Iran's leaders believe it is Iran's destiny to oversee Gulf security, represent and protect Shiite communities outside Iran, and lead the world's Muslims. Iranian leaders occasionally remind the small Gulf states of their vulnerabilities should they ignore Iranian guidelines. And Iran has a proposal for greater regional security that was delivered by President Mahmoud Ahmadinejad when he attended the GCC summit in 2008. This was the first appearance by an Iranian leader at a GCC meeting. According to the press, he spoke about a twelve-point plan for regional security, which apparently included an invitation for the Gulf states to replace U.S. security assurances and military presence with Iran's protection.

All the Gulf states maintain relations with Iran. In October 2008 Ahmadinejad visited the United Arab Emirates and signed a memorandum of understanding that outlined the development of a joint UAE-Iran committee to increase bilateral cooperation. The following July, UAE president Sheikh Khalifa Bin Zayed Al Nahyan presented the Iranian ambassador to the United Arab Emirates the Order of Independence for his work in promoting closer ties.[29] In November 2009 the prime minister of Kuwait, Sheikh Nasser al-Mohammad al-Ahmad al-Sabah, met with Ahmadinejad and other senior officials in Tehran to discuss boosting economic cooperation and bilateral ties, including "cooperation in connection to the resolution of the continental shelf issue," a possible reference to the disputed Arash gas field. This was the first visit to Tehran by a prime minister from Kuwait in more than thirty years. A senior Iranian official noted that his country objected to the presence of U.S. and other foreign troops in the region and stressed that Iran "is ready to contribute to the establishment of sustained peace and security in the Gulf along with other countries of

---

29. Ariel Farrar-Wellman and Robert Frasco, "United Arab Emirates-Iran Foreign Relations," *Irantracker*, July 21, 2010, www.irantracker.org/foreign-relations/united-arab-emirates-iran-foreign-relations.

the region."[30] And, Bahrain's foreign minister announced in May 2011 that Manama "had no intention of ending diplomatic ties with Tehran despite its continuous interference in the country's affairs."[31]

Option 2: Engage Iraq, Ignore Iran

This appears to be the Gulf Arabs' least favored option for the moment, even though Iraq in its current weak state poses little threat to the GCC states. So long as Baghdad is enmeshed in factional rivalries, parliamentary battles over election rules, constitutional reform, federal versus provincial authority, containing militias, and deciding who can be reconciled, it will not be able to threaten or seriously harangue its Gulf neighbors. More to the point, Iraq's military has made progress forming an effective national force, but it needs training, weapons, and a defined mission. Does it defend Iraq's borders against external aggression or will it be used by the state to protect it against the people of Iraq, as it was used by Saddam? It also needs to be independent of political manipulation and loyal to the state rather than the regime.

Increased cooperation with Iraq could accomplish for the small Gulf states what sanctions could not—a Baghdad willing to temper its actions and modify its behavior toward them. Keeping sanctions on Iraq may satisfy Kuwaitis still seeking to punish Iraq for Saddam's actions, but it is not likely to make Kuwait safe and secure from Iraqi anger and frustration. Kuwait's determination to exact full payment from Iraq is probably not shared in the lower Gulf, where the preference seems to be to ignore Iraq but tolerate its exiles. More importantly, sanctions will not work as they did in the 1990s to keep Saddam cowed. The U.S. dual-containment policy included embargoes on trade with and investment in Iraq and Iran under the misguided assumption that sanctions would modify the behavior of so-called rogue states. Sanctions, it was assumed, would force Saddam Hussein to surrender his weapons of mass destruction, forswear his support for international terrorists groups, and stop using terrorism against his own people. Iran was to stop trying to disrupt Middle East peace process efforts, stop supporting international terrorism, and stop seeking weapons of mass destruction. For the most part, sanctions failed to modify behavior in Baghdad and Tehran. In the case of Iraq, sanctions strengthened Saddam's control—his regime determined contracts, received kickbacks, and was in charge of distribution. Today, embittered Iraqis

---

30. "Iran, Kuwait Reaffirm Ties," *Kuwait Times*, November 22, 2009.
31. "Bahrain Has No Intention of Severing Ties with Iran," GMP20110510153001, *Manama Gulf Daily News Online* (in English), May 10, 2011.

blame Kuwait and the United States for their devastating impact on the country.

Iraq has been trying to normalize relations with the Gulf Arab states and wants to be recognized as an equal and relevant regional partner. In 2008 a spokesman for Prime Minister Maliki unveiled a proposal for regional economic and security partnership.[32] The ambitious plan, which has Iraq as its strategic center, calls for building roads between the Mediterranean and the Gulf, sharing water supplies, improving oil and gas transport, promoting joint economic projects, removing trade barriers, fighting terrorism, and defusing border disputes. The spokesman envisioned Turkey, Iran, Syria, Jordan, Saudi Arabia, and Kuwait as part of this architecture and said that Iraq would also be at the heart of a power grid linking Europe with the energy-rich Gulf states. The plan, he boasted, would "eliminate the seeds of hatred and mistrust" by bringing the region's ethnic and religious groups closer together. Iraq will have abandoned its past destabilizing role and moved toward a democratic system with an ethnic and sectarian makeup that reflects the region's diversity. Kurds would not be isolated, and Sunni Arab minorities in Iraq, Arab minorities in Turkey and Iran, and Shiite communities in Bahrain, Qatar, the United Arab Emirates, and Oman would not be marginalized. There has been no response from Iraq's neighbors.

Option 3: Seek Stronger Commitments from Consumers

The Gulf states have long used consumer power—their own—to engage more powerful states in their survival and well-being. Kuwait, the United Arab Emirates, and Qatar in particular use arms deals and investments to make friends and influence governments. They now seek to draw in consumers who are growing increasingly dependent on their oil and gas. Delegations from most European, African, and Asian states have joined China, India, and Japan in seeking more oil, gas, and investment from Riyadh, Doha, Abu Dhabi, Dubai, and Kuwait. What none have done, with the exception of France, is to commit any military contingents to a presence in the Gulf. France, Spain, and Germany have been talking with individual members of the GCC about security issues (France has deployed an 800-man naval contingent to Abu Dhabi) and construction projects, including building nuclear power plants and aircraft sales, but none seem willing to exchange security guarantees for ensured access to oil, investment, and arms sales. This includes China, India, and Japan, which now depend on

---

32. "Iraq Outlines Regional Plan for Security, Development," *Agence France-Presse*, December 10, 2008.

the Persian Gulf for more than half their energy needs but seem uninterested in contributing to Gulf security or protecting sea-lanes and access.

Arms sales are a major part of the GCC states' security strategy. France and Kuwait signed an agreement on strategic defense cooperation during the October 2009 visit of the French defense minister to Kuwait. According to press sources, the agreement pledged cooperation in training and joint exercises as well as the provision of state-of-the-art French arms to Kuwaiti forces.[33] Kuwait and the United Arab Emirates would like to purchase France's Rafale warplane and may also be interested in French helicopters and naval systems.[34] Other arms packages under consideration include a $20 billion U.S. package of weapons systems and logistical support to the United Arab Emirates, Kuwait, Oman, Qatar, and Bahrain announced by the George W. Bush administration in January 2008; this package includes aircraft, armor, naval missiles, Patriot air-defense missile batteries, and other systems specifically intended to bolster Arab defenses over ten years. The question remains, who is the enemy? Are these intended for use against a rearmed and cranky Iraq or against an expansionist Iran?

The Hard Truths about Gulf Security

Who will protect the Gulf Arabs from Iraq, Iran, and themselves? The GCC states control nearly half the world's known oil reserves, are major purchasers of advanced arms systems and technology, and are generous donors to many Arab and Islamic causes. Who will protect them from an assertive Iraq or when Tehran demands acceptance of its claims to be the dominant power in the Gulf and an active participant in matters dealing with the Greater Middle East? If the fragile Gulf states are to avoid risks to their security and seek opportunities for their defense, then a few precautions are in order:

---

33. Kuwait signed its first defense cooperation agreement with France in 1992, two years after the Iraq invasion. The Rafale is a twin-jet combat aircraft capable of carrying out a wide range of short- and long-range missions, including ground and sea attack, air defense and air superiority, reconnaissance, and high-accuracy strike and nuclear strike deterrence. So far, it is only available to French forces. "French-Kuwaiti Security Agreement Builds on Previous Accord," Kuwait News Agency, October 22, 2009; "Kuwait, France Sign New Defense Pact," *Kuwait Times*, October 24, 2009.

34. "UAE to Award Nuclear Deal in November," Reuters, October 23, 2009. A nuclear cooperation agreement between the United Arab Emirates and the United States in theory took effect on October 21, but the UAE government is still considering bids. With the pact enacted, the United Arab Emirates would have the formal diplomatic framework in place to consider a U.S.-Japanese consortium that is interested in the contract, as well as French and South Korean bidders. The United Arab Emirates anticipates its electricity requirements to rise to 40 gigawatts (GW) in 2020 from 15.5 GW in 2008.

- *Move cautiously to develop ties to Iran.* Those ties, for now and the foreseeable future, will probably be limited to cooperation on trade, commerce, police matters, and sharing of intelligence on drugs and narcotics trafficking. Given the revelations in 2010 of Iran recruiting terrorists in Kuwait and its encouragement of anti-government protestors in Bahrain, the Gulf states are not likely to conclude any significant security pact with Iran whose terms would include a demand for the withdrawal of U.S. military forces from the region. Gulf governments prefer to avoid antagonizing their larger and dangerous neighbors, but they also realize that U.S. commitments to their security and the U.S. presence, however invisible they may pretend it is, allow them the freedom to negotiate with former enemy Iran and, at some point in the future, current enemy Iraq.
- *Trust no one.* Baghdad will not be happy with Gulf efforts to exclude them from an active role in regional affairs. The Gulf governments worry about the consequences if Iraq returns to a state of civil war, anarchy, and chaos. They are also at risk if Iraq succeeds. All the Gulf governments share a mutual concern with Iraq: the factors that could destroy Iraq—religious and nationalist extremism—could destroy them, too. Iraq in the long term could resort once again to its former muscle-flexing practices—in ten to fifteen years, once a government in Baghdad has stabilized and enjoys control. Baghdad is shopping for arms—including aircraft, tanks, and high-tech weapons systems—acquisition of which will threaten the current nonbalance of power. Kuwait will need to look to its borders and the GCC to its alliances. The GCC states will not see a need for better, integrated security until a threat is imminent. Even then, their first reaction will be the same as it was in 1990—do nothing to provoke the bully. Given its large military, Iran with or without nuclear capabilities could become an existential threat rather than a theoretical one.
- *Promote cooperative relations with Iraq.* For the next ten to fifteen years Iraqis will need to concentrate on reinventing themselves, their identity, their political institutions, and their economic infrastructure. For that, they will need cooperation from their neighbors in stabilizing trade and development plans and maintaining secure borders. In the long-term Iraq could decide to reassert what it once viewed as its prerogative— defender of the Gulf with newly acquired advanced weapons systems. If it does, then Kuwait had better look to its borders and the GCC to its alliances.
- *Manage crises.* The Gulf states, Iraq, and Iran recognize each country's inherent right to take legitimate measures for self-defense, but ownership of nuclear power requires rules and restraints on everyone. These

governments share common problems—terrorism, religious and nationalist extremism, organized crime, arms smuggling, illegal immigration,
environmental pollution, drug trafficking, disease, poverty, lack of water
resources, and desertification. They lack a common norm of cooperation and have no effective pan-regional institutions or code of conduct
for interaction. Tailored subregional strategies and institutions may make
progress in improving regional security, cooperation, and productivity.
Focusing on subregions may be more productive than trying to recreate
the Arab League in a new building, declaring the region a nuclear-free
zone, or deploying a regionwide missile-defense system. Sometimes
smaller is better.

- *Broaden the security circle*. Engage other Arab states as well as European
and Asian consumers (China, Japan, and India) that depend on Gulf
energy resources but do little to protect them or to assist in regional
defense planning. This may have been the reasoning behind the GCC
announcement in May 2011 that it was considering bids by Jordan and
Morocco to join the organization.

In the face of a nuclear-armed Iran or a rearmed Iraq, the Gulf Arabs
are likely to seek an expanded U.S. commitment to protect and defend them
if a confrontation with an external power is imminent. They have made
clear, however, that they will not support use of their territory for pre-
emptive military strikes to lessen their problems with their neighbors.
Like the Europeans, they instinctively shrink from the use of armed force
to settle political problems. They will not join Iran in a security arrangement that would preclude a U.S presence in the Gulf, reflecting in part
their understanding that the U.S. military presence allows them to improve relations with Tehran now and Baghdad some day. At the same
time, the Gulf regimes are wary of closer ties to the United States, fearing
popular protest to the costs of the U.S. presence and dependence on the
United States for protection their governments should be able to provide.
For them, Iraq is the litmus test. If the United States leaves too soon, before
Iraq is stabilized, then how strong will Washington's commitments be to
the Gulf governments?

Saddam in the years between 1990 and 2003 assumed that the United
States maintained a large military force in the Gulf to monitor Iraq. Iranian leaders since the 1979 revolution have made a similar assumption—
that the United States was in the Gulf to watch them. Iraqis may develop
a similar paranoia in time. Iran has indicated to the GCC states that it
preferred American military forces be sent home and has offered to spread
its protective wing over the fragile states. The GCC response has been
transparency—talk about a lower profile and over-the-horizon positioning

for U.S. forces but, being risk averse, do not bend to requests from Tehran or Baghdad to change commitments with the United States or other external sources of security cooperation. Instead, the Gulf states will hope that Iraq and Iran's quest for friends in the Gulf, their own nonconfrontational diplomacy, and transparency in military relationships and operations will stave off Baghdad and Tehran. To prevent Iran from misinterpreting GCC-U.S. intentions and activities, they will encourage the United States to continue pursuit of engagement with Iran and expand on confidence-building measures, such as de-mining initiatives, an incidents-at-sea agreement, and joint rescue exercises, and, at some point, to gradually include both Iran and Iraq in regional security discussions. This would not amount to a security pact or membership in the GCC or some other NATO-style arrangement. But it could mean a new venue where tensions could be reduced without risk of military confrontation. Pan-regional solutions will not work—they are too broad in scope and too vague in purpose.

Conclusion

New governments, new weapons systems, and new alliances will not change the basic fragility of the small Arab states of the Gulf. They will never have large populations well versed in military science or technology that could compete with Iraq or Iran, nor are they likely to agree on a coordinated and coherent defense planning strategy that includes joint commands, combined forces, and interoperable equipment. The GCC states are consumers and not producers of security, and far away from "jointness" in military planning and strategic thinking. Their response to risk has been to seek stronger commitments to their security from the United States and European governments and to encourage greater cooperation with their new friends and customers in Asia—China, India, and Japan—such as through arms and oil sales. However, the extent of their discussions with European and Asian governments to date indicate that actual security cooperation may not have been raised and that none are interested in contributing to Gulf security or protecting sea-lanes and access to oil and gas.

The Gulf Arabs are showing heightened concern for their fragile environment. They fret about the increased risk of tanker traffic, lack of potable water, danger of air pollution from oil-well fires, and possible contamination from a nuclear "event" in the Gulf. They worry about terrorists infiltrating from Iraq and Iranian encouragement of local Shiite and restive Sunni communities to demand regime change. Despite their overarching dependence on expatriate labor, they seem to share a lack of interest in the human costs of keeping small rich populations happy. Despite all the talk of Arab solidarity and Arab nationalism as the solution to all Iraq's problems and all the Gulf's woes, there is too little regard for each other. The Gulf Arabs publicly urge the United States to get out of Iraq but only after establishing a secure and stable government there.

The United States' military presence in the Gulf will be required for some time; the desire to reduce the U.S. military footprint and the vulnerability of forward deployed forces needs to be balanced against the political deterrent value of a visible U.S. military presence in the Gulf. If friends and enemies no longer see U.S. forces and operations, they may conclude that the Gulf governments are once again vulnerable to intimidation or outright threat and that the United States is less likely to defend its interests and honor its security commitments in the region. In weighing risks and opportunities in future GCC-U.S. relations, several political realities need to be taken into account. First, Iraq is not perceived by the GCC states as a major and imminent threat to their security and most of them believe the United States needs to reshape its strategies to engage Iraq and Iran positively. Second, Palestine is important to the Gulf governments and citizens. Their views are shaped by the violence of the Israeli-Palestinian conflict, the intractability of Israeli and Palestinian leaders, and U.S. reluctance or inability to find a solution. Finally, regime change in Iran or Iraq may come smoothly or violently, but it will not alter a defense strategy based on acquiring a nuclear capability or securing territorial or border gains. More importantly, regime change in Iran or Iraq is unlikely to lead to major reversals in Tehran's or Baghdad's foreign and security policies.

6

Syria and the New Iraq

Between Rivalry and Rapprochement

Mona Yacoubian

In the aftermath of the U.S. invasion of Iraq and the fall of Saddam Hussein, Syria's relations with Iraq are caught between the historic animosities and distrust that have long plagued bilateral relations and a desire to reap the mutual benefits that each side would surely accrue should they establish stronger ties. Syrian interests vis-à-vis Iraq are rooted in the two strategic imperatives that inform all Syrian policies: regime survival and the projection of regional power. Syrian-Iraqi ties are beset by contradictions and misunderstandings that arise from the context of each country's domestic circumstances as well as a long history of shared animosity. To characterize the Syrian-Iraqi relationship as "conflicted" would be a supreme understatement. Moreover, Iraq's continual state of flux will further complicate efforts at stabilization and reconciliation both inside Iraq as well as with its neighbors—including Syria. In addition, the 2011 "Arab Spring," which led to unprecedented unrest in Syria, adds yet another layer of uncertainty and complexity. As noted in Phebe Marr and Sam Parker's chapter, "In the short term (three to five years), it is the changes, rather than the continuities, that will most define the relationship between Iraq and its neighbors."

Syrian-Iraqi ties have been on a roller coaster since the 2003 U.S. invasion, marked by deep tensions followed by unprecedented warming that was abruptly reversed following a series of Baghdad truck bombings at the end of 2009. The dramatic decline in Syrian-Iraqi ties, particularly on the heels of significant progress on many fronts, is illustrative of the perils that plague the bilateral relationship and that will likely continue to complicate regional efforts at shoring up Iraq's stability. While Iraq's current atmosphere of flux and significant change holds the promise of new opportunities for the two countries to cooperate, it is also fraught with uncertainty and threats that already have derailed the nascent rapprochement. Much will depend on developments inside Iraq, particularly the status of reconciliation efforts as well as efforts to resolve tensions in the Kurdish north. Progress toward ethnic and sectarian reconciliation inside Iraq and security improvements will likely have a positive effect on Syrian-Iraqi relations, while a continued deterioration in the security situation, a failure to sustain Sunni participation in the political process, and deepening tensions with the Kurds could further undermine Syrian-Iraqi ties. Moreover, deep uncertainty inside Syria as the Bashar al-Assad regime contends with significant unrest adds yet another "X factor" to the bilateral equation.

A Relations Roller Coaster

A chief opponent of the U.S. operation, Syrian president Bashar al-Assad, allowed his country to serve as the primary launching pad for jihadists and other extremists bent on foiling U.S. plans. Following the election of Prime Minister Nuri al-Maliki, who had lived in Damascus for several years while in exile, ties began to warm. In November 2006, the countries renewed diplomatic relations following a twenty-five-year rupture. The relationship soared with a nearly unprecedented rapprochement in 2008 and early 2009 only to plummet following the August 19, 2009, truck bombings in Baghdad that targeted the foreign affairs and finance ministries and killed more than one hundred civilians.[1] On the eve of the bombings, the two countries, together with the United States, were on the verge of launching a tripartite commission to monitor the Syrian-Iraqi border and cooperate on security related issues. This development would have represented a significant step toward enhancing regional security arrangements and establishing a long-term security framework for Iraq and its neighbors.

Indeed, Syrian-Iraqi relations witnessed a marked improvement in the eighteen months prior to their precipitous decline. In 2007, the countries signed a five-year defense cooperation agreement that featured pledges to

---

1. Two additional multiple truck bombings in Baghdad—on October 25, 2009, and December 8, 2009—resulted in massive casualties and further strained Iraqi-Syrian relations.

combat terrorism and to step up border controls. Numerous high-level visits also took place. In January 2007, Iraqi president Jalal Talabani visited Damascus, the first visit by an Iraqi president to Syria in thirty years. Iraqi prime minister Maliki visited Syria twice, and his Syrian counterpart, Prime Minister Muhammad Naji al-Otari, traveled to Baghdad. In late 2008 and early 2009, the countries exchanged ambassadors for the first time since 1979 when Saddam Hussein took power. The Iraqis deemed Prime Minister Otari's visit in April 2009, when some twenty trade deals were discussed, a watershed event, and the Syrians voiced hope of tripling bilateral trade, estimated at $800 million in 2009.[2]

The bilateral improvement took the form of cooperation in numerous spheres. A new freight rail line between the Syrian cities of Tartus and Latakia on the Mediterranean and the Iraqi city of Basra on the Persian Gulf opened in June 2009. The two countries also agreed to repair the damaged Kirkuk–Banias oil pipeline and discussed the possibility of constructing a natural gas pipeline from Iraq's Akkas fields to Syria. Discussions also focused on security cooperation, as Baghdad remained intent on consolidating the gains reflected by a significant drop in violence during the preceding year.

Instead, bilateral relations fell into a tailspin. The bombings provoked a rapid and harsh response from Iraqi prime minister Maliki, who immediately accused Syria of harboring the attacks' masterminds and demanded that Damascus hand over two ex-Ba'thists whom Iraq believes are linked to the attack. With Syria refusing to extradite any suspects without concrete evidence, Baghdad recalled its ambassador. Damascus then followed suit. Iraq has continued to reiterate its long-standing demand for the extradition of 179 former Ba'thists who have sought haven in Syria. The prime minister repeated the demand in a meeting with Syrian president Bashar al-Assad on the eve of the August 19 bombings.

For their part, the Syrians greeted the rapid downgrade in ties with a combination of bafflement and anger. Surprised and puzzled by the vehemence of Prime Minister Maliki's response, Damascus hardened its position, showing little inclination to cooperate with Iraqi demands. The episode also led to the abrupt termination of Syrian-U.S. security cooperation on Iraq, freezing any movement on launching the tripartite security commission. Forging deeper security cooperation with Syria would probably have done more to help improve security inside Iraq.

---

2. Julien Barnes-Dacey, "Syria Looks to Iraq for Economic Boost," *Wall Street Journal*, June 1, 2009.

A Long History of Animosity and Mistrust

In many ways, stress in the Syrian-Iraqi relationship comes as no surprise and merely represents a perpetuation of the status quo. The history of Syrian-Iraqi relations is littered with episodes of mutual attempts at regime overthrow, bitter rivalries, and the provision of safe haven for each other's oppositionists. The stakes in these disputes between the two countries have always been high—depicted as nothing less than existential. Together, they lay the foundations for a bilateral relationship that is characterized by deep distrust and hostility that transcend different regimes and personalities. At the same time, periods of mutual cooperation throughout their history are also noteworthy. These episodes typically arose from the perception of a mutual threat—usually Israel—and were usually short-lived, with the relationship typically reverting to its "default" setting—animosity and mistrust.

Syria's ties with Iraq have been strained since well before Saddam Hussein came to power in 1979. Indeed, Iraq aided and abetted numerous conspiracies in Syria during a thirty-year turbulent period of revolving coups before Hafez al-Assad became president in 1970.[3] Beginning in 1949, Baghdad's Syria policy sought to cultivate potential allies who might agree to a union with Iraq and to undermine Iraqi opponents. Iraq played a role in the deposing of Syrian president Husni al-Za'im in August 1949 and in the overthrow of Colonel Adib Shishakli in February 1954, part of a long-standing pattern of meddling in Syrian affairs. Moreover, Baghdad paid off Syrian politicians and newspaper editors and contributed to Syrian exile groups in Lebanon and elsewhere in a patronage scheme designed to build alliances and project Iraqi influence.[4]

The roots of the Syrian-Iraqi Ba'thist rivalry date to 1963 when Syria and Iraq became seats of rival branches of the Ba'th party—still ruling in Syria today and deposed with Saddam Hussein in Iraq in 2003. The animosities deepened when the Ba'th Party split in 1966. Each country's Ba'th Party believed itself to be the rightful heir of the original Ba'th founded in 1940 by Syrian intellectuals Michel Aflaq and Saleh Bitar. The fissure that opened between the two countries at this time resonated for decades, defining the entrenched rift dividing the two countries. Strains between the competing Ba'thists became particularly tense in 1968 when Iraq provided sanctuary to old-guard Ba'thists who had been expelled from Syria

---

3. For more detail on Iraq's role in fostering coups and dissent inside Syria, see Patrick Seale, *The Struggle for Syria* (New Haven, CT: Yale University Press, 1987).

4. Ibid., 266. Seale notes that the Iraqi military attaché in Damascus was the primary conduit of Iraqi patronage. These and other details emerged from a series of trials that took place in both Damascus and Baghdad following various coups.

two years prior[5]—an interesting twist considering Iraq's anger at Syria for doing much the same after 2003. In this tumultuous period, both sides also sponsored coup plots and assassination attempts.

The 1979 rise of Iraq's Saddam Hussein followed by his 1980 invasion of Iran cemented this Ba'thist rivalry and plunged Syrian-Iraqi relations to their depths. Tensions between the two countries ratcheted up even further. Indeed, the 1980s marked a true low point as Syria opted to side with Persian Iran rather than Arab Iraq in the eight-year-long war. "Rivalry between the Ba'th regimes of Damascus and Baghdad had deep ideological, historical, political, and personal roots. It had intensified during the 1980s over Syria's support of Iran in the latter's long-drawn-out war with Iraq (1980–8). Iraq, for its part, extended aid and succor to opponents of the Syrian regime, chief among them the Muslim Brotherhood in 1976–1982."[6]

Strains between Syria and Iraq were reflected in Syria's hosting of anti-Saddam Ba'thist splinters seeking safe haven from Baghdad. Syria also hosted members of Iraq's Shiite Da'wa Party, including a number of Iraqi Shiite politicians who rose to prominence in post-Saddam Iraq, such as former prime minister Ibrahim al-Ja'fari and Prime Minister Nuri al-Maliki. For decades, Iraqi oppositionists of all political stripes resided in Syria, holding opposition conferences and plotting against Saddam's regime. (Many remained in Syria until Saddam was overthrown in 2003.) Deep-seated resentment of Saddam Hussein stood as the common theme uniting them and their Syrian hosts.

Following the end of the Iran-Iraq War in 1988, Iraq's postwar bluster culminated in its August 1990 decision to invade Kuwait. Syria, still stinging from Arab world isolation due to its siding with Iran in the war, exploited the dual opportunity to regain its standing among the Arabs and open a channel of rapprochement with the West, specifically the United States. Damascus joined the multilateral coalition aligned against Iraq, dispatching 10,000 troops and 300 tanks to Saudi Arabia to aid in the First Gulf War effort. In the years after Iraq's ejection from Kuwait, both the United States and the Gulf Arab countries amply rewarded Syria's decision to contribute troops. Not surprisingly, its relationship with Iraq remained broken—eviscerated by decades of animosity and mutual hostility.

The long-standing rivalry between Syria and Iraq laid the seeds for many of the concerns reflected on both sides today. Both sides have long

---

5. John Devlin, *Syria: Modern State in an Ancient Land* (Boulder, CO: Westview Press, 1983), 108–109.

6. Eyal Zisser, *Asad's Legacy: Syria in Transition* (New York: New York University Press, 2001), 53.

aspired to the mantle of Arab world leadership. Throughout the modern era, each country has underscored its self-ascribed power and influence in the region. Each has long vied for Arab nationalist credentials and has sought to portray itself as the primary force for resistance against Israel.

For Syria, the perception of threats to regime survival emanating from Baghdad has long characterized its animosity toward Iraq. Certainly, Saddam's decision to support the Muslim Brotherhood, the most threatening opposition to Hafez al-Assad's rule, provoked deep anger in Damascus and served as a potent reminder of Iraq's decades-old habit of meddling in Syrian affairs. Iraq's earlier track record of supporting successive coup plotters was not forgotten and surely continued to resonate among the Syrian leadership.

Meanwhile, for Iraq, Syria's decision to side with Iran, Iraq's bitter rival in a long and destructive war, was equally traumatic. From Baghdad's vantage point, a "brother Arab" state opting to support Persian, Shiite Iran was nothing short of treasonous. When Iraq emerged intact from the war, "the Iraqis did not conceal their desire for vengeance . . . against Syria for supporting Iran in the conflict."[7] The Iraqis hardened their stance against Damascus, waiting for Syria to make the first move toward reconciliation. Iraqi foreign minister Tariq Aziz reportedly said, "As Syria was the one to act against Iraq during the last eight years, it is [Syria] who must explain its policy. Such reconciliation is impossible under the current circumstances."[8] Syria's decision to then contribute troops to the multilateral effort arrayed against Iraq only deepened animosity and the mutual distrust.

Despite the deep distrust and animosity dividing Syria and Iraq, bilateral relations have occasionally experienced periods of rapprochement. These periods of warming usually arise due to perceptions of a common threat, typically Israel. As early as November 1948, just six months after Israel's founding, the newly formed Syrian People's Party called for union with Iraq in order to counter the Israeli threat.[9] In 1951, following a brief renewal of hostilities between Syria and Israel over Lake Hula, Iraq mobilized antiaircraft batteries and provided troops, culminating in a parade through the streets of Damascus.[10] During the October 1973 War, Iraq sent troops to back Syrian Army forces battling Israel.

Later, following the signing of the 1978 Camp David Peace Treaty between Egypt and Israel, Syria and Iraq formed a unified alliance rejecting

---

7. Zisser, *Asad's Legacy*, 53.

8. Ibid.

9. Seale, *The Struggle for Syria*, 30.

10. Ibid., 106–108.

the treaty, signing a "Charter for Joint National Action." According to a declassified CIA assessment, "The Camp David Accords shocked the Iraqis into action to end their bitter feud with Syria."[11] For the Syrians' part, "With Egypt neutralized and a large part of the Syrian army in Lebanon, Syria's military position vis-à-vis Israel is untenable."[12] Most cooperation took place in the military sphere where the countries exchanged senior military staff and senior Iraqi army officers toured areas of potential shared deployment in the Golan. Iraq may also have prepositioned spare parts and ammunition in Syria. The union, however, was short-lived, falling apart with Saddam Hussein's ascension to power the next year.[13]

In other instances, the two countries have exploited areas of mutual economic interest. Beginning in 1998, Syria initiated a limited, economic opening with Iraq, reopening its border with Iraq and the long-shuttered Kirkuk–Banias oil pipeline. As had been the case throughout Syria's tumultuous history with Iraq, this foray into bilateral warming was motivated by mutual self-interest and the perception of a shared threat. Both Syria and Iraq stood to benefit immensely from their agreement to smuggle and resell embargoed Iraqi oil, following the 1995 United Nations Oil for Food Program that allowed Iraq to sell limited amounts of oil for food and other humanitarian needs. Syrian smuggling of Iraqi oil grew significantly over the next several years. At its height in December 2002, nearly 200,000 barrels of Iraqi oil flowed through two pipelines, allowing Syria to increase its oil imports by 50 percent (buying Iraqi oil at the concessionary price of $10–15 per barrel while exporting its own oil at prime market prices) and reap a significant financial windfall.[14] On the eve of the 2003 U.S. invasion, Syrian-Iraqi bilateral trade was estimated to be $2 billion.[15]

This episode of Syrian-Iraqi bilateral cooperation also sprang from regional developments, namely Turkey's blossoming relationship with Israel and Turkey's declaration of a "security zone" in northern Iraq in 1995.[16] Both countries were concerned by Turkey's intentions, particularly in light of its strengthening relations with Israel. As in the post-Saddam era, Damascus was equally fearful that Iraq could be carved up, with unfriendly powers reaping the benefits. "They feared a Turkish takeover of the area,

---

11. CIA, "Iraqi-Syrian Rapprochement," National Foreign Assessment Center, May 30, 1979, www.foia.cia.gov/browse_docs.asp.

12. Ibid.

13. Zisser, *Asad's Legacy*, 54.

14. Michael Evans, "Syrian Oil Pipeline Helps Iraq Evade UN Oil Sanctions," *Times*, December 16, 2002, www.timesonline.co.uk/tol/news/world/article802549.ece.

15. Barnes-Dacey, "Syria Looks to Iraq for Economic Boost."

16. For more detail on this warming, see Zisser, *Asad's Legacy*, 86–87.

followed by the dismantling of the Iraqi state, all with American or Israeli backing."[17]

Hostility and rivalry then are the norm between Syria and Iraq, with or without the presence of Saddam Hussein. While opportunities have arisen for greater bilateral cooperation in the past, they have typically been defined by perceptions of a mutual threat rather than recognition of mutual interests. As such, these past opportunities were quickly subsumed by the fears, recrimination, and distrust that characterize Syrian-Iraqi relations. Damascus's decision to host pro-Saddam Iraqi Ba'thists, such as Revolutionary Command Council deputy chairman Izzat Ibrahim al-Douri, illustrates this trend, underscoring Syria's seeming imperative to keep Baghdad off balance.

In this case, while the irony of Syria hosting its former mortal enemy and one of Saddam's closest advisers is not lost, Damascus was also motivated by a desire to undermine the United States' project in Iraq, particularly given its concern that Syria could be the next target for regime change. The U.S. withdrawal from Iraq could certainly alter this calculus for Damascus should it determine that the price of hosting ex-Ba'thists such as Douri and others does not merit any perceived benefits. In a classic Damascene bargaining tactic, sheltering Iraqi Ba'thists is likely a bargaining chip to be played in the course of broader negotiations, with the United States, Iraq, or both.

Syrian Interests and Threat Perceptions in Iraq

Syria's interests and threat perceptions vis-à-vis Iraq originate in the two primordial interests that define Syrian strategy and policies: first and foremost, regime survival, and second, the desire to protect and promote Syria's self-described centrality and influence in the region. For Damascus, these two critical interests—survival and regional primacy—are intimately linked and mutually reinforcing. Consolidating its power at home allows the Syrian regime to project its influence more effectively in the region, which in turn strengthens the regime's levers of power domestically.

Likewise, any threat to one necessarily impinges on the inviolability of the other. Certainly, actions designed to undermine, let alone overthrow, the regime—whether domestic or external—will necessarily limit its ability to project influence in the region. Similarly, shifts in the regional order that counter Syria's influence could easily be construed as a threat to the regime's hold on power, particularly if these changes result in a new regional constellation that leaves Syria surrounded by potential adversaries.

---

17. Zisser, *Asad's Legacy*, 86.

These two core priorities inform Syria's multifaceted and evolving interests in Iraq and illuminate the reasons behind policies that at times seem inherently contradictory. In particular, Syria's decisions to turn on and off the jihadist "pipeline," despite clear threats of "blowback" on Syria, can be best understood in this context. Calibrating the flow of militants and money across its border allows Damascus to apply pressure when needed against the Iraqi regime while also providing Syria with an important card to play against the United States. By the same token, Syria's decision to take in an estimated one million Iraqi refugees at great expense, straining the country's already weakened infrastructure, hews to a strategy that seeks to promote Syria as a country with strong Arab nationalist ideals. It allows Damascus "bragging rights" within the Arab world and the broader international community, provides Syria with yet another strategic card, and potentially could attract significant international aid, although these monies have yet to flow into Syria. Essentially, Syria's interests in Iraq today can be distilled into three key strategic objectives.

First, Damascus seeks a stable and cohesive Iraq with a strong, nonsectarian central government that it is favorable, or at least not hostile, to Syria. Chaos, partition, or the breakup of Iraq, resulting from widespread sectarian violence, would constitute a "worst-case" scenario for Syria. In particular, the Syrians remain deeply concerned by the possibility of an independent Kurdistan being carved out of Iraq because of the precedent it would set for Syria's repressed Kurdish population. Syria fears that strong Kurdish nationalist forces in Iraq could mobilize Syrian Kurds against the regime. Indeed, Kurdish president Masoud Barzani underscored Kurdish rights in Syria during a January 2010 discussion at the Brookings Institution in Washington, D.C.: "The official position of the KRG is that we are against any inhuman conduct or behavior with the Kurds wherever they might be. And we support the rights of the Kurdish people whether they are in Syria, in Turkey or in Iraq."[18] While far less likely, a separate Iran-dominated Shiite enclave in Basra and southern Iraq would constitute another threat to Damascus. More broadly, Damascus is also threatened by heightened sectarian violence in Iraq given Syria's potentially volatile mix of sects and ethnic groups, not to mention the Syrian Alawi regime's minority status in a Sunni-majority country.[19] While the Syrian Sunni merchant class has not joined the protests roiling Syria, the Assad regime's vulnerability as a

---

18. Masoud Barzani, "Assessing Iraq's Future: The Path to the March Elections and Beyond" (speech, Saban Center's Statesman's Forum with H.E. Masoud Barzani, President of the Kurdistan Region of Iraq, Brookings Institution, Washington, DC, January 27, 2010).

19. An estimated 74 percent of Syrians are Sunni Muslim, while roughly 12 percent of Syrians hail from other Muslim sects such as the Alawi and the Druze, according to the CIA, "The World Factbook," 2009, https://www.cia.gov/library/publications/the-world-factbook/.

minority regime has likely been heightened by the domestic unrest. While a Shiite-dominated (and sectarian) government in Baghdad does not necessarily pose a threat to Damascus, Sunni political exclusion provoking a return to peak levels of sectarian violence would be a cause for concern. Mindful of its own Sunni population that harbors grievances against the minority Alawi regime, Syria is wary of potential blowback of Sunni jihadist violence in Iraq. Moreover, for Damascus, the prospect of being sandwiched between two sectarian models of governance, in Iraq and neighboring Lebanon, raises worrisome prospects of sectarian spillover in Syria.

Second, Syria is interested in building strong trade and economic ties with Iraq to help bolster the sluggish Syrian economy. As Damascus struggles to modernize and privatize its economy, transforming it from a centralized, state-controlled enterprise into a market economy, building trade and economic ties with its neighbors will be essential. Beginning in 2008, Syria—with its dwindling oil supplies and burgeoning consumption—became a net importer of oil. Syria's loss of oil revenues and dried-up Gulf aid (once an important source of revenue, although foreign investment from the Gulf plays an important role in the Syrian economy) and diminished agricultural output (typically 20 percent of GDP) due to a searing drought impelled Damascus to reform its economy and to seek greater integration into the regional and ultimately global economy. Described as "an implicit quid pro quo for diplomatic engagement,"[20] improved Syrian-Iraqi economic ties can play an important role for Syria in its global economic strategy. Syria remains interested in purchasing Iraqi oil exports, particularly at concessionary prices. Over time, Iraq could serve as a market for Syrian goods. More importantly, Damascus seeks to gain significant revenues by serving as the key conduit for Iraqi oil, gas, and goods to the Mediterranean and beyond. Prior to the downturn in relations, Syrian officials described an optimistic future with a possible free-trade zone, encompassing Syria, Turkey, Iraq, and Lebanon, that would serve as a crucial outlet to Europe and the basis of strong economic and commercial ties between Syria and Iraq.[21] In a July 2009 National Public Radio interview at the height of Syrian optimism over trade relations with Iraq, Syrian deputy foreign minister Faisal Mekdad elaborated, "What we and our Iraqi brothers have in mind [is that] anything Iraq needs to import from the world will go through [Syria]."[22]

---

20. International Crisis Group (ICG), "Reshuffling the Cards? (II): Syria's New Hand," Middle East Report no. 93 (Brussels: ICG, December 16, 2009), 15.

21. Author's interview with a Syrian government official, Washington, DC, July 17, 2009.

22. Faisal Mekdad, in an interview with Deborah Amos, National Public Radio, July 16, 2009.

Third, Damascus wants to minimize "blowback" from Iraq. Primarily, Syria is interested in minimizing the negative impact on internal security generated by returning jihadists—now well trained and with significant combat experience under their belts—as well as shielding Syria from spillover sectarianism and any additional refugee flows should violence escalate again in Iraq. Jihadist blowback remains an enduring concern fed by fears that Iraq's Sunni insurgency could spread to Syria. Indeed, Damascus is no doubt aware that its double-edged manipulation of jihadist traffic into Iraq could backfire. A September 2008 suicide car bombing in Damascus near the Sayyida Zeinab shrine, a Shiite neighborhood where many Iraqi refugees have settled, underscored the potential danger. The attack, which left seventeen dead, was the first mass casualty terrorist incident in Damascus in nearly twenty years. A July 2009 post on the jihadist Web site Al-Falluja.com calls on jihadists to focus their efforts on Syria, which, since fall 2005, has escalated its campaign against jihadists following the end of "an unannounced agreement to stop mutual hostilities."[23] If the Sunni insurgency regains momentum in Iraq, Damascus fears that these elements could incite extremist violence in Syria. Certainly, the Syrian regime would seek to prevent a repeat of the Sunni extremist violence that threatened the government in the 1980s.

Similarly, Damascus seeks to insulate itself from Iraq's ethnic and separatist tensions, with regard to its Kurdish minority. While the regime's concerns about Sunni extremism are rooted in the fears of an Alawi-minority governing a Sunni majority, Damascus also fears stoking Kurdish separatism in Syria. In 2004, emboldened by the U.S. invasion of Iraq and resurgent Kurdish nationalism, Syria's own restive Kurdish population, estimated at approximately 1.5 million, clashed with Syrian security forces in the eastern Syrian city of Qamishli. The violence marked the worst Kurdish-inspired unrest in decades. Smaller-scale protests occurred the following year, and Syrian repression of its Kurdish minority has intensified over the past several years.[24] In a failed attempt to arrest the 2011 domestic unrest, the Syrian government opted to grant citizenship to a portion of Syria's Kurdish population in April 2011. Sporadic unrest continued after the announcement in some Kurdish cities in eastern Syria.

Finally, with its resources stretched, Syria seeks to prevent the flow of additional refugees should violence spike in Iraq. Syrian officials remain

---

23. Murad Batal al-Shishani, "Jihadis Turn Their Eyes to Syria as a Post-Iraq Theater of Operations," *TerrorismMonitor* 7, no. 26 (August 20, 2009), 3–4.

24. See "Group Denial: Repression of Kurdish Political and Cultural Rights in Syria," Human Rights Watch, November 26, 2009, and Radwan Ziadeh, "The Kurds in Syria: Fueling Separatist Movements in the Region?" Special Report no. 220 (Washington, DC: United States Institute of Peace Press, April 2009).

concerned by the stresses induced and the tensions exacerbated by hosting this refugee population—both within the Iraqi population itself and among Syria's heterogeneous population. Additional inflows of refugees, in response to heightened Iraqi violence, could force a breaking point, both with respect to stretching Syrian infrastructure beyond its capacity and to stoking simmering resentments among the Syrian people.

At the same time, Syria's interests and threat perceptions in Iraq are not static but are constantly evolving to reflect changing circumstances in Iraq. These interests can be traced through three distinct periods: first, the invasion and immediate postinvasion atmosphere, from 2003 through 2005; second, Iraq's descent into sectarian civil war, from 2006 through 2007; and third, the U.S. surge and postsurge troop withdrawal, from 2008 until the present. Syrian threat perceptions during the first period focused on concerns that the United States would turn its powerful military on Syria. Damascus was thus motivated to sabotage U.S. efforts in Iraq to the greatest extent possible. During the second period, Syrian threat perceptions shifted to concerns about spillover violence and ethnic tensions from Iraq's sectarian chaos undermining Syrian stability. Syrian interests reflected these concerns as Damascus recalibrated its policies by beginning to stave the flow of insurgents and by voicing its concerns regarding Iraq's territorial integrity. Following the security improvements inside Iraq that coincided with the U.S. surge and the announced U.S. troop withdrawal by the end of 2011, Syrian threat perceptions in Iraq continued to evolve. With the U.S. withdrawal already under way and domestic Iraqi actors struggling to consolidate security gains and promote national reconciliation, Syrian interests in Iraq have converged toward those of the United States—seeking a stable, cohesive, nonsectarian Iraq that develops strong economic and trade ties with Syria amid a stable and secure regional environment.

The U.S. invasion of Iraq in 2003 was "catastrophic" from the Syrians' perspective.[25] Syria was deeply opposed to the invasion from the start and grew increasingly fearful that Damascus would be the next target in the U.S. crosshairs. Indeed, in the months just after the invasion, a number of Bush administration officials ratcheted up their rhetoric, suggesting that Syria was ripe for regime change. Beyond its concerns regarding regime change, Damascus also perceived the major U.S. military presence on its eastern flank as a significant threat to the regional order and Syria's perceived sense of primacy in the region. These two threats—to the Syrian regime and its place in the regional order—were mutually reinforcing and provoked a strong Syrian response.

---

25. Author's interview with a senior Syrian official, July 17, 2009.

Indeed, "Damascus interpreted the U.S. invasion and occupation of Iraq as a threat to Syria's geopolitical environment and consequently regime security." Syrian president Assad, in an interview he gave to the Arabic-language *as-Safir* newspaper on March 27, 2003, noted, "This is not a storm, for a storm passes." Instead, the invasion marked a U.S.-Israeli "plan . . . to reorganize the region." As noted, "Whether the plan was to divide the region into sectarian states—the Israeli option according to Bashar—or other types of groupings congenial to U.S. interests, Damascus interpreted the invasion and subsequent occupation of Iraq as a direct threat to its security environment."[26]

Tensions between Syria and the United States escalated significantly in the following months as Syria brazenly allowed its territory to serve as a key transit point for foreign jihadists and ex-Ba'thists to join Iraq's growing insurgency. Busloads of militants—many arriving through the Damascus airport—were reportedly ferried to the border and onward into Iraq. Although facilitating the jihadists' entry into Iraq meant that Damascus was effectively supporting its sworn enemies,[27] Syria's manipulation of the militant "pipeline" became an effective tool for Damascus to wield as it sought to stymie the U.S. military effort in Iraq.

Citing its Arab nationalist ideals, Syria would not institute visa requirements for Arab citizens entering Syria. Damascus also provided safe haven to former Iraqi Ba'thists who fled Iraq after the invasion. From Syria, they were able to hold conferences and organize against the U.S. occupation of Iraq. Today, there are estimates that as many as 400,000 Iraqis with ties to the Saddam Hussein regime reside in Syria.[28] Syria's calculations were based on a desire to see American forces pinned down in Iraq, thereby hemorrhaging U.S. blood and treasure. Helping to ensure that the United States was kept off balance in Iraq would serve the dual aims of insulating the Syrian regime against the threat of overthrow by the United States *and* inhibiting the American project in Iraq, which sought to redefine the regional order in a way that would be antithetical to Syrian regional interests.

In 2006–7, as the situation inside Iraq deteriorated and Iraq descended into a sectarian civil war, Syrian interests and threat perceptions vis-à-vis Iraq began to shift. The potential dissolution of Iraq, including the creation

---

26. Bassel F. Salloukh, "Demystifying Syrian Foreign Policy under Bashar," in *Demystifying Syria*, ed. Fred H. Lawson (London: Saqi Books, 2009), 159–179.

27. Salafi jihadists subscribe to a retrograde Islamist ideology that deems secular governments such as the Syrian regime to be apostate and therefore targeted for overthrow (particularly since Syrian president Assad is Alawi—an offshoot of Shi'a Islam, considered heretical by hard-line Sunni elements).

28. Andrew Lee Butters, "Can Former Iraqi Baathists in Syria Ever Go Home?" *Time*, September 27, 2009.

of an independent Kurdistan in the north, coupled with signs of militant jihadists "blowback" in Syria and fears of the spillover of both ethnic and sectarian tensions, led Damascus to alter its calculations. Preserving Iraqi cohesion and protecting Syria from any fallout due to Iraq's chaos became a preeminent concern. Syria restored diplomatic relations with Iraq and started to stave the flow of jihadists by stepping up border controls. By the summer 2007, the flow of militants from Syria into Iraq reportedly decreased by half or two-thirds, according to General David Petraeus, who was the senior U.S. commander in Iraq at the time.[29] The Syrians also reportedly arrested nearly 2,000 suspected jihadists.

The dire situation inside Iraq also led to a massive refugee crisis beginning in 2005.[30] In line with its tradition of hosting Arab citizens, Syria opened its doors to Iraqi refugees, receiving far more than any other country, including neighboring Jordan, which implemented strict regulations restricting the refugee flow. Iraqi refugee flows into Syria ballooned during the peak of Iraq's sectarian violence in 2006–7. While the numbers have stabilized, the number of Iraqi refugees returning permanently to Iraq remains low. Estimates of Iraqi refugees in Syria range between several hundred thousand and 1.5 million depending on the source. The United Nations High Commissioner for Refugees (UNHCR) has registered 1 million refugees, although some counter that not all refugees have registered with the UN agency. For its part, the Syrian government places the number at 1.2 million refugees, while some Western observers place the number far lower.[31] Hosting the refugees is estimated to cost the Syrian government approximately $1 billion per year.[32] Although Syria provides the refugees with access to health services and education, their circumstances have grown increasingly desperate over the years due to their dwindling savings as well as the decrepit state of Syria's public service infrastructure. Many refugees live in crowded and unsanitary conditions with poor medical care, inadequate schooling, and a lack of job opportunities. These conditions have provoked growing frustration among the refugees—particularly the youth—as well as with their Syrian hosts, raising the potential for political instability in the coming years. Few believe that the refugees will be able to return to Iraq any time soon,

---

29. Mona Yacoubian and Scott Lasensky, *Dealing with Damascus: Seeking a Greater Return on U.S.-Syria Relations*, Council Special Report no. 33 (New York: Council on Foreign Relations, June 2008).

30. ICG, "Failed Responsibility: Iraqi Refugees in Syria, Jordan and Lebanon," Middle East Report no. 77 (Brussels: ICG, July 10, 2008), 1.

31. Ibid., 3.

32. Roula Khalaf and Anna Fifield, "An Assured Assad," *Financial Times*, May 10, 2009.

particularly among the Christian Iraqis whom many believe will stay in Syria permanently.[33]

In the current period, Syrian interests and threat perceptions have evolved to reflect a different calculus that considers key factors such as the U.S. military withdrawal from Iraq and efforts inside Iraq to consolidate security gains via political reconciliation. Syria's objectives in Iraq now coincide more closely to those of the United States. Damascus sees the potential of a "new Iraq" where Syria is no longer threatened by a significant U.S. troop presence and where Syria can enjoy the benefits of strong political and economic ties. Specifically, Syrian officials at the highest level, including President Assad himself, have asserted their desire for a stable, cohesive Iraq with a strong central government and nationalist rather than sectarian identity.[34] Syrian officials have noted that Iraq's territorial integrity is of "paramount importance," citing in particular concerns about the potential for a breakaway, independent Kurdistan.[35] Syrian officials have also underscored that "the absolute need to preserve Iraq's unity [has] come to dominate and shape our policy."[36]

Damascus has also grown somewhat leery of Iran's influence in Iraq. While the thirty-year Syrian-Iranian alliance remains strong, Syrian officials, both publicly and privately, have expressed fears that Iran's presence in Iraq can become overwhelming. In particular, they cite both separatist sentiment in Iraq's Shiite southern region and Iran's preference for a sectarian rather than nationalist central government in Baghdad. While Syrian resources and influence in Iraq pale in comparison to Iran, Iraq increasingly appears to hold the potential of being an arena of competition rather than cooperation between Syria and Iran. As Syrian academic Sami Moubayed noted, "Syria and Iran do not agree wholeheartedly on how a post-U.S. Iraq should look. . . . Iran wants to maintain Muqtada al-Sadr's Shiite Mahdi Army and the Badr Brigade, the armed wing of the Iran-backed Supreme Iraqi Islamic Council, while Syria wants a militia-free Iraq, be these armed groups Sunni, Shiite, or Kurd."[37]

Just as changes in Iraq appear to have drawn Syrian interests in a stable, cohesive Iraq closer to those of the United States, Iraq's evolving circumstances could also signal the possibility of another Syrian-Iraqi rapprochement. Damascus's interest in a unified Iraq where sectarian violence gives

33. "Iraq, Its Neighbors and the Obama Administration: Syrian and Saudi Perspectives" (working paper, United States Institute of Peace, Washington, DC, February 3, 2009).

34. Ibid.

35. Author's interview with a Syrian government official, July 17, 2009.

36. Quoted in ICG, "Failed Responsibility," 18.

37. Sami Moubayed, "Syria Reaches Out to 'Friend' Iraq," *Asia Times*, April 24, 2009.

way to political reconciliation could dovetail with Iraqi government interests. Likewise, Syria's dire need for economic growth and investment coupled with Iraq's desires to expand and build upon its hydrocarbon-based
economy could fuel bilateral cooperation. To date, Syria and Iraq have not
been able to translate the existence of these overlapping interests into the
foundation for a strong and well-grounded bilateral relationship. Moreover, the long history of their troubled ties provides little hope that they
can sustain cooperative relations. Nonetheless, the atmosphere of sweeping change that pervades Iraq might alter the equation and give rise to an
unanticipated warming in relations with Syria.

Syrian Vectors of Influence in Iraq

Syria's strategic influence in Iraq is relatively limited when compared with
that of Iraq's other neighbors, particularly Iran, Turkey, and Saudi Arabia.
Certainly, Syria's political and economic ties do not carry the historic heft
or the financial significance that Iran brings to the arena. On the contrary,
Syria must ply its influence in the shadow of the deep and long-standing
animosity and distrust that has pervaded bilateral relations. Unlike Iran,
Syria's familiarity with Iraq is far more limited, placing its understanding
of the complexities of Iraqi politics and tribal dynamics on a relatively
steep learning curve.

For the most part, Syria's vectors of influence are "offshore" and are
based on Damascus's capacity to influence events via levers, both positive
and negative, that it pulls from home. Foremost among these are Syria's
role in hosting ex-Ba'thists and its nominal control over the "jihadist" spigot.
Taken together, these levers allow Damascus important, albeit negative,
influence over Iraq. At times, Syria has proven itself capable of reducing
militant traffic by undertaking more assiduous control over the border.
These restrictions have coincided with Syrian fears that the Sunni insurgency in Iraq was threatening its cohesion. At other times, Damascus
appears willing to turn a "blind eye" to jihadists when ratcheting up the
pressure on Iraq or the United States suits its purposes. In 2009, U.S. officials, including General Petraeus, noted their concerns that the jihadist
pipeline had been "reactivated."[38] While militant traffic reportedly dropped
to an all-time low by December 2008, these officials highlighted a notable
increase in jihadists crossing from Syria beginning in the spring of 2009.
While not game changing, Syria's decision to block or facilitate the flow
of arms and fighters into Iraq has an important impact on Iraqi security

---

38. Karen DeYoung, "Terrorist Traffic via Syria Inching Up," *Washington Post*, May 11, 2009.

and overall stability and by extension, on prospects for fostering political reconciliation.

Syria's decision to offer safe haven to a number of senior ex-Ba'thist officials constitutes another card the Syrians have opted to play in Iraq. While couched in terms of Syria's long-standing role as host to Arabs of all stripes, Damascus's willingness to protect more than 150 ex-Ba'thists whose extradition is demanded by Baghdad has had a deleterious effect on Iraqi-Syrian relations. Some observers claim that Syria could easily round up a number of the well-known oppositionists and curtail their activities if not hand them over to Baghdad outright. Damascus is also aware that holding them provides a powerful bargaining chip, not to be relinquished easily. Meanwhile, some Iraqi Ba'thists in Syria have reportedly cemented strong business and social ties with their Syrian hosts, further entrenching their presence.[39] Indeed, Syria appears unwilling to hand over the former Ba'thists unless it receives something significant in exchange. A complicating wrinkle is that some of the ex-Ba'thists in Syria have reportedly voiced their desires to return to Iraq given the appropriate security guarantees and the freedom to participate in the political process. Their fate is intimately linked to the progress of Iraq's political reconciliation, a goal favored by U.S. and Syrian officials alike.[40]

Playing host to an estimated one million Iraqi refugees provides Syria with yet another "offshore" vector, albeit a positive one. Syria's decision to take in the Iraqi refugees allowed Iraq a crucial safety valve for huge segments of its population who were fleeing violence and ethnic cleansing. Syria's willingness to allow these refugees to stay—barring an unexpected and sustained improvement in Iraq's security environment, they are not expected to return any time soon—allows Baghdad important breathing space as it pursues sporadic efforts at political reconciliation. While Damascus has not held up the threat of forced repatriation, it certainly emphasizes its role as an altruistic host to these refugees when portraying itself as a positive force in Iraq.

Syria's vectors of influence *inside* Iraq are far more limited. Syria's economic presence inside Iraq is minimal; however, Damascus does wield political influence across a broad spectrum of players. Indeed, Syria has purposefully courted a number of actors among all the key constituencies in Iraq—Shiite, Sunni, and Kurd, in the hopes of exerting influence over political developments in Iraq and ensuring Syrian interests. Syria's strategy

---

39. "Reshuffling the Cards? (I): Syria's Evolving Strategy," Middle East Report no. 92 (Brussels: ICG, December 14, 2009), 27, www.crisisgroup.org.
40. Butters, "Can Former Iraqi Baathists in Syria Ever Go Home?"

has been to diversify its contacts in order to ensure that all its bases are covered across the Iraqi political landscape.

Concerning the Shiite community, Syria played host to a number of prominent Shiite politicians during Saddam's era, including Prime Minister Maliki. The Syrian government retains ties to a number of these politicians. Syria has also ensured that it brokers relations with Shiite politicians from different camps, hosting Iraqi Shiite cleric Muqtada al-Sadr in July 2009, for example, while also engaging with secular Shiite politician Ayad Allawi in a bid to broaden its influence across the Shiite spectrum.

The Syrians have also worked to cultivate contacts across the Sunni community. Syrian strategy vis-à-vis Iraq's Sunnis has focused on all segments of the Sunni community: tribes, Sunni politicians, the Awakening Councils, and elements of the insurgency, as well as former Ba'thists residing in Syria. In some instances, Damascus has leveraged long-standing, cross-border tribal ties. For example, Syria's ambassador to Iraq, Nawaf Fares, hails from a prominent, mixed Syrian-Iraqi tribe, and Damascus believes he can interface with the Sunni Awakening Councils and influence them in a positive direction, toward political reconciliation and away from the insurgency.[41]

The Syrians have also cultivated strong relations with Kurdish leaders such as Iraqi president Talabani. Talabani resided in Syria in the 1970s during his exile from Iraq and the Syrians likely seek to benefit from his ties to Syria. Indeed, Talabani has noted his "special relationship" with Damascus, underscoring that he "owe(d) a national, personal and moral debt to the honorable Al-Assad family. I cannot forget the help and support given to us by President Hafez al-Assad. . . . I am proud of this relationship and I understand its motives."[42]

Taken together, these connections across Iraq's various communities allow Syria to work various angles of the "Iraq file." By building bridges to all communities, Syria believes it can play a critical role in aiding Iraqi political reconciliation. The Syrians like to distinguish themselves from Iraq's other neighbors, which Damascus claims cannot leverage their influence both within and across Iraq's diverse communities in the same way that Syria can. Syrian analyst Sami Moubayed notes, "The Saudis certainly do not have Muqtada's ear, and the Iranians have no such influence with heavyweight Sunnis like Vice-President Tarek al-Hashemi or parliament Speaker Iyad al-Samarrai."[43]

41. Moubayed, "Syria Reaches Out to 'Friend' Iraq."
42. Jalal Talabani, in an interview with *Asharq al-Awsat*, January 3, 2010.
43. Sami Moubayed, "Maliki Sees the Light in Damascus," *Asia Times*, August 20, 2009.

Compatibility with U.S. Interests

Syrian interests in Iraq have increasingly converged with those of the United States. Indeed, of the various issues that divide the United States and Syria, Iraq, in many ways, seems most "ripe" for resolution. Like the United States, Syria has a strong interest in Iraq's stability and in preserving its unity. The Syrians have also expressed their desire to encourage political reconciliation in Iraq, another key objective of the United States. Moreover, with the U.S. troop withdrawal from Iraq, Syria no longer perceives the United States presence in Iraq to be a threat. By 2012, when U.S. troops are slated to have withdrawn from Iraq, the United States and Syria will both share an interest in ensuring that a stable, nonsectarian Iraq is left behind. Indeed, as noted by Syrian deputy foreign minister Feisal Mekdad, "Now with a new administration, when we have assurances that the United States will withdraw from Iraq by 2011, then we do believe that full cooperation between Syria and the United States, in different fields, not only security issues, will definitely be welcomed."[44]

Despite this convergence, Syria and the United States continue to be divided over key differences with respect to Iraq. Most importantly, the United States blames Syria for not doing enough to secure its borders and stave the flow of foreign fighters into Iraq. Tentative progress had been made in this area following two visits to Syria by a senior U.S. military delegation in the summer 2009. Headed by Major General Michael Moeller of the U.S. Central Command (CENTCOM), the delegation was on the verge of successfully negotiating the creation of a tripartite commission, together with Iraq, to cooperate on security matters. The initiative—which would have strengthened border controls through trilateral cooperation—was derailed following the August 19 car bombing that torpedoed Syrian-Iraqi relations. Prior to the downturn, the Syrians had reportedly arrested more than 1,700 jihadists, clamped down on border-security procedures, and started to rein in former Ba'thists operating from Syria.[45]

The aborted effort to launch a tripartite commission gives rise to both pessimism and hope with respect to Syria's cooperation as the United States seeks to withdraw from Iraq and the degree to which differences can be reconciled. The rapidity with which the venture unraveled underscores the tensions and fragility of Syrian-Iraqi ties, as well as the vulnerability of U.S. interests to those tensions. The fluid and uncertain nature of developments in Iraq suggests that this dynamic will not abate anytime soon. Indeed, Iraq's security situation could continue to deteriorate, particularly

---

44. Jay Solomon and Julien Barnes-Dacey, "Damascus Agrees to Help Monitor Iraqi Border," *Wall Street Journal*, August 19, 2009.
45. Ibid.

in the absence of genuine, sustained political reconciliation. Syrian-Iraqi relations will likely be buffeted by these difficulties, inhibiting a rapprochement that could help stabilize Iraq and facilitate an easier U.S. withdrawal.

Nonetheless, Syria's willingness to cooperate with the United States on security issues, as evidenced by measures taken in the summer of 2009 in anticipation of the tripartite commission's establishment, suggests that Damascus realizes its long-term interests in supporting a stable, nonsectarian Iraq coincide with those of the United States. Security cooperation would serve both countries' strategic interests, underscoring the possibility that Damascus would still be willing to play a constructive role in ensuring an orderly U.S. withdrawal from Iraq.

7

Coming to Terms

Jordan's Embrace of Post-Saddam Iraq

Scott B. Lasensky

King Abdullah of Jordan decided well before the 2003 U.S. invasion of Iraq that he had little alternative other than to cooperate with Washington in ousting Saddam Hussein. After the war, Jordan, the only neighbor with close ties to both Iraq and the United States during the Saddam era, had little choice other than to come to terms with Iraq's post-Saddam political order, which has been dominated by Saddam's long-persecuted political opponents. Given Jordan's long-standing economic ties with Iraq and its strategic dependence on Washington, the kingdom's maneuverability vis-à-vis Iraq has been tightly constrained. Despite lingering resentment among many Iraqis over Amman's close ties with Saddam, Jordan moved ahead of its Arab peers early on in reaching out to Baghdad and recognizing the new status quo. While its more powerful Arab neighbors demurred, or stood on the sidelines, the Jordanian regime eventually embraced Iraq's post-Saddam leadership. Jordan needs positive relations with Iraq, plain and simple, which is fundamentally why

The author takes full and sole responsibility for the content of this chapter, which draws on an earlier report on the same subject, "Jordan and Iraq: Between Cooperation and Crisis," Special Report no. 178 (Washington, DC: United States Institute of Peace Press, December 2006). The author also wishes to thank several colleagues who reviewed various drafts of this chapter, including the other contributors to this volume, Laurie Brand, Wael Alzayat, Mustafa Hamarneh, Joseph Lataille, Leslie Thompson, Hassan Barari, and Edward Gnehm.

the kingdom adapted so quickly to the post-Saddam environment, and why King Abdullah himself soon ceased his early alarmism about resurgent Shiite political power.

Jordan's intrinsic vulnerabilities—a hostile regional setting, a weak economy, social fissures, and a lack of natural resources—fueled early concerns about Iraq's post-Saddam chaos spilling over to Jordan and upsetting what is, even in the best of times, a delicate domestic balance. Hundreds of thousands of Iraqi refugees, an upsurge in terrorism in Jordan, the surge in Shi'a Islamist political power, and the loss of Saddam-era oil perks and special trade benefits all combined to raise fears of a new era of instability in Jordan. A restive, underemployed population with strong sympathies for the Iraqi insurgency added to fears that the net impact of the U.S. invasion and occupation could lead to trouble for the Hashemites. But Jordan managed to contain the threats by tightening its relationship with Washington and pivoting toward Baghdad's new leaders, once again proving its ability to adapt to a changing strategic environment. While it lacks the power to shape the regional context, Jordan has proven time and again that it can withstand momentous regional shifts. In the case of post-Saddam Iraq, the kingdom avoided its worst-case fears of an economic meltdown, even enjoying a real-estate and investment boon.

Although maintaining good relations with whomever rules in Baghdad signals continuity in Jordanian foreign policy, the post-Saddam era has altered Jordan's broader, regional threat perceptions—as it has Saudi Arabia's and the Gulf States' (see the chapters by Toby Jones and Judith Yaphe)—putting Iran closer to its borders and raising basic questions about Iraq's traditional role in the Arab political order. Given the outsized role Iraq has played in Jordan's economy over the past twenty-five years, particularly in the energy, consumer goods, and transportation sectors, it remains in Jordan's interest to maintain a strong, working relationship with Iraq—regardless of who is in power. Jordan's ideal scenario would be a unified and secular Iraq, where the Sunni Arab community is protected and invested in the political order. Jordan would prefer to see an Iraq that remains an ally of Washington and that offers Jordan continued energy and economic privileges. With few choices, and little influence, Jordan can adapt to an Iraq that is far from ideal. As long as Iraq remains nominally united, terrorism does not spillover into Jordan, trade and transport channels remain open, and Iraq does not threaten Jordan's peace with Israel, the kingdom's most basic interests can be addressed.

Unlike some of Iraq's other neighbors, Jordan's relationship is relatively uncomplicated. It has no territorial disputes with Iraq, no cross-border population, no conflict over natural resources, and no threat of separatism, and it seeks no special influence over a particular region or political group. Jordan's principle liability is lingering bitterness among the new Iraqi leadership over the kingdom's close embrace of Saddam, but even this resentment has not stood in the way of cooperation.

The American presence in Iraq presented a paradox for Jordan: the kingdom became accustomed to the United States acting as a guarantor of Iraq's stability, but at the same time Jordan's population wanted to usher the Americans out of Iraq—highlighting a profound and growing credibility gap between the ruling elite and the public. This credibility gap feeds into Jordanian attitudes about U.S. policy, which rank among the least favorable in the Arab and Muslim world. The regime has managed this problem of legitimacy by gaining additional American aid, masking the true extent of its strategic cooperation with the United States, and by highlighting anxiety about Iran. The credibility problem has also been limited due to Iraq's own instability, which has presented a model Jordanians do not wish to emulate, regardless of their opposition to U.S. intervention. In fact, by 2009 the king was confident enough to dismiss the Parliament and delay new elections for a year, a move that led Freedom House to lower its assessment of the country to "not free." Numerous political parties, led by Islamists, boycotted the October 2010 elections, arguing that the Parliament was a captive institution and that the elections were effectively meaningless.

The suppression of dissent and the rollback of political reform has not gone completely unnoticed in Washington; it is one reason why the United States is sometimes restrained in what it asks of Jordan. It may also explain why, at times, Jordanian leaders publicly accentuate their disagreements with the United States.

But on the question of Iraq, strong U.S.-Jordanian cooperation has coexisted alongside wide divergences on a range of day-to-day policy questions, not to mention periodic tensions and suspicions between Amman and Baghdad. Areas of divergence and tension between Amman and Washington relate principally to the Palestinian question and the marginalization of Sunnis in Iraq. These differences have been frequently aired in public, though less so as the kingdom developed a closer working relationship with the government of Nuri al-Maliki after 2006.

The remainder of this chapter provides a detailed examination of (1) Jordan's interests and threat perceptions; (2) its influence in Iraq; and (3) the intersection of its Iraq policy with U.S. interests.

Jordan's Interests and Threat Perceptions

Jordan's interests in Iraq center on three broad concerns: strategic vulner-abilities, the delicate balance of political forces at home, and economic and energy security. These three sources of anxiety, external vulnerability and a divided society, have both been aggravated by the U.S. intervention in Iraq.

Spillover from Iraq

Jordan's future is tied to Iraq's. Jordan wants to see Iraq with a strong cen-tral government where no sectarian group is marginalized, particularly the Sunni Arabs. The kingdom fears the emergence of separate or quasi-independent regions, assuming this would lead to more instability and even less control by Iraqis over their borders. The November 2005 triple suicide bombings in Amman, and the Aqaba missile attack that preceded it, demonstrated how vulnerable the kingdom is to instability across its borders.[1] The planning and execution of both the hotel bombings, which killed dozens, and the Aqaba attack that targeted a U.S. naval vessel bore Iraqi fingerprints. The flood of Iraqi refugees in 2005 and 2006 was an-other stark example of the "spillover" threat.

Even with the June 2006 killing of Abu Musab al-Zarqawi (himself a Jordanian), who was responsible for numerous attacks against Jordan, a weak Iraqi state poses threats that are unlikely to dissipate until Baghdad is able to exercise effective control at home and over its borders. On this score, Jordan's fears are also America's concerns. Previous plots have been aimed at both Jordanian and American targets in the kingdom. The 2002 assas-sination of U.S. diplomat Lawrence Foley in Amman was intended as a strike against both countries.

Unlike the case with some other neighbors, there are no past or present unresolved territorial questions between Jordan and Iraq. Nor does the kingdom seek influence over a particular region or political group in Iraq. "The preservation of [Iraq's] unity and stability is an obligation of all the neighbors," said former Jordanian foreign minister Marwan Muasher, adding that democracy will not bring stability to Iraq unless it is "coupled

---

1. Jordan is no stranger to terrorism. The kingdom has uncovered numerous plans for spectacular attacks, like the millennium plot and the 2004 plan to blow up Jordan's intelligence headquarters; see Desmond Butler and Judith Miller, "Police in Jordan Kill 4 It Says Plotted against It and the U.S." *New York Times*, April 21, 2004. In 2003, Jordan suffered a devastating attack on its embassy in Amman, suspected to be the work of Jordanian Abu Musab al-Zarqawi, the leader of al-Qaida in Iraq, who was killed in a U.S. air raid north of Baghdad in June 2006. In 2002, U.S. diplomat Lawrence Foley was assassinated in Amman.

with respect for minority rights."[2] Jordan fears instability and violence to its east. This may explain King Abdullah's comment in mid-2004 that post-Saddam Iraq could use a strongman. "I would say that the profile [of a leader for post-Saddam Iraq] would be somebody from inside, somebody who's very strong . . . somebody with a military background who has experience of being a tough guy."[3] Since the January 2005 election, the king has not repeated this position in public, but Iraq's 2006–7 civil war reinforced the view among Jordanians.

Iranian influence in Iraq is another top worry for Jordan: anxiety about Iran is common both within official circles and among critics of the government. This fear relates to the broader Arab-Iranian and Sunni-Shiite divides in the region, Jordan's own fears about political Islam, Iran's post-1979 attempts to export its Islamic revolution, and Iran's continued support for Palestinian rejectionist groups, like Hamas, that pose a challenge to Jordan's peace with Israel.

Anxiety about Iran may explain the king's oft-quoted warning of a new crescent of Shiite influence that could destabilize the region and alter the balance of power. Said Abdullah, "Even Saudi Arabia is not immune . . . [from] the possibility of a Shiite-Sunni conflict . . . out of the borders of Iraq."[4] Abdullah has reportedly raised the specter of a widening arc of Shi'a power in discussions with American leaders, though he has toned down such rhetoric in public after it elicited hostile reactions from Iraqi leaders and from Iran. Before the U.S. invasion, said Jordanian writer Tariq Masarwah, "United Iraq was the only thing that prevented the infiltration of the Iranian sectarianism."[5] Anxiety about Iran is a popular preoccupation, fueled by a regime that prefers to highlight external threats, rather than focus on internal challenges, like unemployment and the rising cost of living.

As is often the case for Jordan, it can make do with less than hoped for. In practice, Jordan can—and has—come to terms with an Iraq that falls far short of Amman's ideal scenario. Its minimal interests boil down to preventing Iraq from again becoming an exporter of instability, keeping

---

2. Marwan Muasher, transcript of remarks at the Brookings Institution's Saban Center for Middle East Policy forum on "A View from Jordan: Iraq, the Peace Process, and Arab Reform," Washington, DC, September 30, 2004, www.brookings.edu/fp/saban/events/muasher20040930.pdf, 9.

3. Alan Cowell, "Old Iraq Army Could Provide a Leader, Jordan's King Says," *New York Times*, May 18, 2004.

4. See Robin Wright and Peter Baker, "Iraq, Jordan See Threat to Election from Iran; Leaders Warn against Forming Religious States," *Washington Post*, December 8, 2004.

5. Tariq Masarwah, "They Are Not Refugees," *Al-Rai*, July 10, 2007, translated in *BBC Monitoring Middle East*.

trade ties open, and making sure Iraq does not actively challenge Jordan's peace with Israel.

Domestic Politics: Keeping the Peace at Home

Jordan's interest in a stable Iraq relates not only to traditional national security concerns but also to internal dynamics. Jordan, perennially anxious about instability and turbulence on its borders, also needs to avoid a situation where events in Iraq might upset the delicate balance of political, social, and economic forces at home. Because of its high Palestinian population, and the related fault line between "East Bank" Jordanians and Palestinians, Jordan has had to contend with a large, restive internal constituency that opposed the removal of Saddam and that wanted to "see the Americans suffer" in Iraq, in the words of a former adviser to the late King Hussein.[6] In many respects, the Palestinian factor—both the situation west of the Jordan River and the role of Palestinians within Jordan—looms larger than Iraq. The same can be said for Islamism in Jordan. The Hamas victory in the 2006 Palestinian elections resonated far more strongly in Jordanian politics than did Iraqi Islamist politics. To be sure, from a security perspective the Jordanian regime worries about Zarqawi-style Salafist radicalism emanating from Iraq, but politically Hamas poses a much greater challenge—to Jordan's peace with Israel and to the balance between secular and religious forces at home. The same is true of the East Bankers who, despite their declining numbers, often hold sway in the constantly shifting internal balance of power. Early 2011 protests—sparked by events in Egypt and across the Arab world—and unusually blunt criticism by old-line East Bankers led King Abdullah to dismiss the government and make a series of concessions to tribal elites and Islamists.

In response to unrest and opposition activity directed at both foreign and domestic policy, King Abdullah has taken tough measures at home. Following public protests in March 2003, the government banned most demonstrations. Moreover, the Jordanian government has tightened limits on the media and has leaned on them not to report on U.S. military activities in Jordan. In late 2004, the government also clamped down on the Islamic Action Front (IAF), the largest Islamist party in Parliament, arresting a number of prominent leaders.[7] Tensions with the IAF have continued to escalate. In August 2006, IAF parliamentarians were jailed for "inciting sectarianism" by visiting Zarqawi's family in Jordan after his

---

6. Author's interview with a former general in the Jordanian military and adviser to King Hussein, Amman, September 13, 2004.

7. Scott Wilson, "Jordan Acts to Curb a Rising Chorus of Critics," *Washington Post*, September 30, 2004. The government even cracked down on parliamentarians and Islamists who offered words of praise for Zarqawi after his death.

death and for referring to him as a "martyr." The IAF threatened to boycott sessions of Parliament if the MPs were not pardoned.[8]

By 2011, the king seemed better positioned than most Arab leaders to deflect the challenge sparked by mass protest movements across the region and in Jordan, but the balance of forces at home remains precarious.

For several years, the government has also tried to change the law governing professional associations and restrict their ability to express political views. The associations have become centers of anti-American sentiment and protest against normalization with Israel. The new policies were condemned both by groups outside Jordan, like Human Rights Watch, and by opposition parties at home. IAF leader Hamzah Mansur said it amounted to an "assassination" of the associations.[9] It was a clear attempt to constrain public space at a time when Jordanians felt the overall pace of political reform had moved backward.[10]

Jordan is a Sunni Arab state, and one issue on which both the king and the public are united appears to be "Sunni solidarity." The one group in Iraq toward which most Jordanians feel some affinity is the Arab Sunnis; it is both an enduring source of identity and a legacy of the Saddam years when Arab Sunnis controlled Iraq and maintained extensive links in Jordan. The king has used the Sunni card to bolster support at home and also to improve Jordan's standing in the Arab world.

Energy, Trade, and the Economy

Fuel price increases in 2005, a direct result of the war, were a major source of public dissatisfaction with the government of then–prime minister Adnan Badran. But so far, Jordan's ability to secure alternative energy guarantees, the trade and real estate boom that followed the fall of Saddam Hussein, and increased restraints on internal dissent have prevented any serious domestic upheavals. Still, Jordanians worry about the steadily increasing cost of fuel and whether the benefits of serving as a "gateway" to Iraq can be sustained over the long term. Should real domestic unrest bubble to the surface, it is more likely to be in response to economic factors rather than foreign policy decisions, as with the bread riots in 1989 and 1996.

---

8. "Jordan's Largest Political Party Boycotts Lower House Sessions," *Deutsche Press-Agentur*, August 21, 2006.

9. "Jordan: Draft Bill Would Muzzle Civil Society," Human Rights Watch, April 7, 2005. See also Stephen Glain, "Letter from Jordan: Kingdom of Corruption," *Nation*, May 30, 2005; and Samer Abu Libdeh and David Keys, "Terror Attacks Highlight Case for Reform in Jordan," Washington Institute for Near East Policy, PolicyWatch no. 1053, November 18, 2005, www.washingtoninstitute.org/templateC05.php?CID=2404.

10. See Rami Khouri, "Democratic Jordan: Enticing but Still Not a Done Deal," *Beirut Daily Star*, May 25, 2005.

Oil has always been an important consideration in Jordan's relations with Iraq. Since the 1980s, not only was Iraq one of the largest players in Jordan's economy, but Saddam single-handedly guaranteed most of Jordan's energy needs at below-market prices. Oil lay at the heart of Jordan's late 1990s trade boom with Iraq. At the time, the Clinton administration turned a blind eye, seeing it as an unavoidable trade-off in order to maintain the larger international sanctions regime. Although Jordanians detested Saddam's brutality toward his own people, Baghdad was a generous benefactor.

In a bid for greater influence with Amman, Iraq sold oil to Jordan at below-market prices after the UN oil-for-food program was established in Iraq. In 2000, with prices around $30 a barrel, Jordan received Iraqi oil at $9.50 a barrel. Moreover, Iraq allowed Jordan, a country without domestic energy resources, to pay for the subsidized oil with consumer goods. Through the UN program, Iraq was able to steer preferential contracts to Jordan, and some Jordanian firms were essentially given monopolies. Exports to Iraq reached $420 million in 2001, nearly a quarter of Jordan's exports.[11] The system amounted to an annual grant, in real terms, of approximately $400 million to $600 million a year.[12] According to some estimates, the benefit was even higher—$500 million to $1 billion annually.[13]

In the post-Saddam era, Jordan has been able to secure its oil needs on the open market and from Saudi Arabia, Kuwait, and the United Arab Emirates—quite a turn of events considering the chilly relations after the 1990–91 Gulf War. In the immediate aftermath of the U.S. invasion, Saudi Arabia remained the principal guarantor of Jordan's oil needs, supplying 50,000 barrels per day as a grant. But this was not a long-term solution.

The future of Jordan's oil supplies is the subject of debate among Jordanians. Some acknowledge that the Saddam-era benefits are a thing of the past. Jordan should not expect a future Iraqi government to restore the Saddam-era "deals." Moreover, it would be unrealistic to expect that the ongoing subsidies from the Gulf neighbors will continue indefinitely. "[T]his is not sustainable," Muasher has said regarding the high economic growth rates accruing from oil subsidies; pressed on the subject, he conceded that "we need to move to a situation where we can do it on our own."[14]

---

11. See Hassan Fattah, "Amman Dispatch: After the Fall," *New Republic*, May 19, 2003, 12.

12. See David Schenker, *Dancing with Saddam: The Strategic Tango of Jordanian-Iraqi Relations* (Washington, DC: Washington Institute for Near East Policy, 2003), 3–41.

13. Fattah, "Amman Dispatch," 12.

14. Muasher, transcript, 29 and 21.

Yet although some Jordanians say the country will have to adjust to market forces, others see preferential energy benefits as an entitlement. In August 2006, Jordanian prime minister Marouf Bakhit visited Baghdad and secured a two-year Iraqi commitment to supply 10,000 barrels of oil per day at a slightly discounted price. But the situation in Iraq prevented implementation. Later, in 2008, during a visit to Amman, Prime Minister Maliki extended the deal for another three years. With rising world energy prices, pressure is mounting on the government to further reduce fuel subsidies. Jordan experienced large current account deficits largely from this "one-two punch" of high energy prices and diminishing energy assistance. By comparison, Jordan's position is the reverse of another small neighbor that has cooperated on post-Saddam Iraq—Kuwait. Increasingly, oil wealth has allowed Kuwait to weather the storm of the war and its aftermath.

So far, Jordan's worst-case fears about energy security have not materialized. Similarly, early concerns about the country's economic position have since faded. In the three years following the war, Jordan has enjoyed robust growth. Not only has Jordanian trade with Iraq remained strong, but also much of the Iraqi-Jordanian commercial relationship has now shifted to Jordan's private sector.[15] Jordan has even managed to keep down the costs incurred by hosting so many Iraqi refugees.

According to one report, more than 60 percent of UNHCR's Iraqi refugee budget passes directly to the Jordanian government—a form of "trickle-down development."[16] Furthermore, the "gateway" role that Jordan has played has done much to compensate for the drop in tourism and loss of the oil-for-food deal. (Ironically, the "gateway" benefits—to some degree—are tied to continuing instability in Iraq.) Some Jordanian businesses have also expanded into neighboring states.[17] The "Iraq effect" is also creating a boom in Jordanian real estate, as Iraqis look for a safe haven and as more and more multinationals and nongovernmental organizations base their Iraq operations out of Jordan. Even the used car market has been surging since the war. The kingdom's relaxed rules on financial transactions have also led to a surge in Iraqi assets in Jordan's growing

---

15. According to the *Economist Intelligence Unit*, 16 percent of all Jordanian exports go to Iraq, second only to the United States (24 percent); "Jordan: 2006 Country Report," *Economist Intelligence Unit*, June 2006.

16. Nicholas Seeley, "In Jordan, Aid for Iraqi Refugees Is Often Redirected," *Christian Science Monitor*, July 2, 2008.

17. One area in which Jordan holds a comparative advantage over its Arab neighbors is banking and financial services. Jordan's Housing Bank for Trade and Finance has already moved into Syria and Iraq; other financial firms are not far behind. See Rupert Wright, "Jordan Makes Best of It Despite Regional Turmoil," *Financial Times*, January 1, 2004.

banking sector, though the lack of transparency worries Iraqi and American authorities.

Jordan's Interests: Unchanged and Newfound

For the most part, Jordan's interests vis-à-vis Iraq have not changed substantially over time. Jordan's need for support from major powers, its obsession with stability (internal and external), a rejection of Islamist politics, energy insecurity, the Palestinian question, and the kingdom's systemic economic vulnerabilities remain as they were before 2003. Moreover, Jordan's reliance on a strategic relationship with the United States is unchanged. Unlike the case with other neighbors, such as Syria, as Mona Yacoubian explains in her chapter, the use of U.S. military force to overthrow Saddam Hussein did not lead Jordanian leaders to worry that it could happen to them.

But in two arenas, terrorism and Sunni politics, Jordan's interests have been upended. In the past, challenges posed by Iraq stemmed from Baghdad's strength. But in the post-Saddam era, as Phebe Marr and Sam Parker argue in their chapter on Iraq, it is Iraq's newfound weakness that poses a threat. To the extent that Jordanian and Iraqi elites once shared a complementary worldview—pro-modernization, secular Arab, anti-Iran—their perspectives no longer coincide. The fault line over Iran, the area of greatest divergence, is partially mitigated by Iraq's Arab identity. Still, the shifting balance has raised new anxieties for Jordan that are unlikely to fade anytime soon.

Given recent steps to curtail political activity, as well as the king's effective control over Parliament (particularly on foreign policy, budget, and electoral issues), does the building of democratic institutions and increased contestation in Iraq increase pressure on the Hashemites to cede control and support greater political reform? The democracy factor is undoubtedly a source of some concern, but more so over the long term. If Iraq stabilizes, Jordanians are likely to push the monarchy for a greater role in decision making. But in the short term, the regime and the public are more concerned with stability than the ballot box.

Constraints on Foreign Policy Objectives

Post-Saddam Iraq has placed constraints on Jordan's other foreign policy objectives, the most glaring being the Palestinian question. The situation in Iraq has steadily increased pressure on the Jordanian government to improve relations between Israel and the Palestinians. "The Jordanian government calculated that there was significant potential benefit to Jordan in supporting the U.S. [behind the scenes] in the Iraq War," said a former U.S. diplomat, "because if you can get the U.S. to participate in the peace process, that relieves tensions in Jordan and thus bolsters Jordanian stability."[18]

After the war began, the kingdom was effective in urging the United States to move forward with a new peace initiative—the George W. Bush administration's "road map for peace"—which bore some Jordanian fingerprints. Then, Yasser Arafat's death, an informal Israeli-Palestinian ceasefire, and the Israeli withdrawal from Gaza gave Jordan some breathing room, enough to return its ambassador to Tel Aviv (withdrawn since 2000). But Israeli-Palestinian relations remain profoundly unstable. The election of Hamas in January 2006 has made Jordan uneasy, and as Israeli unilateralism further displaces the road map, Jordan's position has been undermined. Jordan tried to revive the Arab League initiative in early 2005 but failed to gather support. The December 2008 Israeli war in Gaza put Jordan's Palestinian peace "deficit" on full display.

Jordan's Influence in Iraq: Positive, but Modest

Unlike many of Iraq's other neighbors, Jordan can claim little if any influence on developments in Iraq. Turkey has had a military presence in northern Iraq and has long been a vital gateway for Iraqi oil exports. Iran has close ties with key figures in the new Iraqi leadership and an extensive network of ties throughout the Shiite community. Kuwait and Saudi Arabia were for many years major financial backers of Iraq, for which the debt issue gives them some leverage over the post-Saddam leadership (as Yaphe and Jones discuss in their chapters). Moreover, Saudi Arabia has the financial wherewithal to fund clients in Iraq in a bid for influence, while Iraq has influence with its fellow Arab oil producers, and vice versa. As Mona Yacoubian argues in her chapter, Syria has several channels of influence, given its hosting of Iraqi oppositionists, its pipeline and commercial routes to the Mediterranean, its water resources, and its long border.

But Jordan—lacking military power, economic prowess, or ideological ambitions—is not in a position to exert great influence over events in Iraq. In fact, if one considers the period before Saddam's fall, the more interesting question is gauging Iraqi influence in Jordan—which Saddam actively pursued through government-to-government assistance, privileged trade protocols, and attempts to buy influence with the Jordanian media and civil society.[19] Still, Jordan's influence is not totally absent. The kingdom serves as a "gateway" to Iraq, a role it began during the Iran-Iraq War and

---

18. Author's interviews with a former senior U.S. diplomat, Washington, DC, September 2, 2004, and May 24, 2005.

19. See Schenker, *Dancing with Saddam*, particularly chapter 3.

maintained throughout the 1990–2003 sanctions period (principally via its Red Sea port of Aqaba and the land route).[20] Amman and Aqaba are key pass-through points for a good deal of traffic going in and out of Iraq. Government officials, aid workers, contractors, and businesspeople—Iraqi and non-Iraqi—have come to rely on Jordan's position as a stable and reliable gateway. Should this be closed down, it would prove costly not only for Jordan, but also for Iraq.

In the security realm, Jordan has played host to a major international training facility for Iraqi police recruits. The kingdom also ran training programs and exchanges for several thousand officers in the reconstituted Iraqi Army. But given the enormity of Iraq's security needs, the Jordanian programs—which average just a few weeks—had limited impact on the ground.[21]

In terms of U.S. military planning, the kingdom's contributions have been valuable but not decisive. "Jordan went from marginal to semi-important with the disappearance of the Turkish front," said one former senior U.S. official.[22] The extent to which U.S. military forces have been operating out of Jordan is a closely guarded secret, and the Jordanian media is pressured not to report on the U.S. troop presence. During the war, the government acknowledged the presence of a small number of U.S. troops, ostensibly to operate Patriot antimissile batteries (a defensive measure). Independent estimates put the true figure at around 5,000 U.S. and coalition forces in Jordan at the time of the war.[23] As U.S. military planners sought to keep Saddam Hussein guessing about invasion routes, Jordan again played a valuable role. Fearing a major U.S. invasion force from Jordan, Saddam reportedly overruled some of his own generals and allocated defenses toward blunting an invasion from the west.[24]

Military and Economic Ties, Shared History

Jordan has not provided direct or indirect support to paramilitary groups in Iraq, nor does the Jordanian military operate in Iraq. Jordan has provided

---

20. Jordan was a staunch supporter of Iraq during the Iran-Iraq War. Support for Iraq also fueled Jordan's economic boom during the 1980s.

21. For a critique of the training program, see Paula Broadwell, "Iraq's Doomed Police Training," *Boston Globe*, August 30, 2005.

22. Author's interviews with a former senior U.S. diplomat, Washington, DC, May 24, 2005.

23. See William M. Arkin, *Code Names: Deciphering U.S. Military Plans, Programs, and Operations in the 9/11 World* (Hanover, NH: Steerforth Press, 2005); see also William M. Arkin, "Keeping Secrets in Jordan," *Washington Post*, November 18, 2005.

24. See Michael R. Gordon and Bernard E. Trainor, *Cobra II: The Inside Story of the Invasion and Occupation of Iraq* (New York: Pantheon, 2006), 345–347. According to his own account, General Raad Hamdani warned Saddam Hussein and high-level leaders that a U.S. attack from the south was imminent, yet he was overruled. Saddam and his advisers were convinced the attack from the south was a feint and the real attack was coming from the west.

assistance to train Iraqi security forces in Jordan, but it has stated repeatedly that it will not send police or peacekeeping forces—unless requested by the Iraqi government or as part of a joint Arab force. The kingdom also sold defense equipment to the new Iraqi security forces. Jordan's intelligence service, widely considered the most professional in the Arab world, reportedly operates throughout Iraq.[25]

Jordan and Iraq do have a long history of military cooperation in the period before 1990, particularly in the context of the Arab-Israeli conflict. Iraqis fought alongside Jordanians in the 1948 and 1967 wars, and Iraq positioned aircraft in Jordan for safekeeping during its war with Iran.[26] Although there are Jordanians participating in the insurgency, Zarqawi having been the most prominent, none appear to be doing so with the acquiescence of the Jordanian government.[27] Moreover, the number of Jordanian militants in Iraq is relatively low.[28]

For more than two decades, Jordan and Iraq have enjoyed close economic relations. During the years of UN sanctions, mutual dependence reached its peak, but the balance of economic influence rested more with Iraq than Jordan. Although not a short distance, the Baghdad–Amman and Baghdad–Aqaba land routes became well-worn beginning with the Iraq-Iran War. The two countries have discussed major upgrades to roads and pipelines, but planning has repeatedly been delayed. Jordan's international airport remains a critical air link for Iraq. Theoretically, Jordan could close these land and air routes in order to pressure Baghdad, but in light of Jordan's own political and economic vulnerabilities, such a scenario seems remote. In terms of experience on the ground, Jordanian businesses have an advantage over some other neighbors, having been active throughout the turbulent Saddam years.

Jordan and Iraq have similar postcolonial histories, but these historical connections afford little if any influence in the post-Saddam era. In fact, Baghdad's Hashemite heritage could be a political liability for Jordan. Both states had their borders defined by the British, who installed Hashemite ruling families in Amman and Baghdad after World War I. While the Hashemites retained power in Jordan, they could not hold on in Iraq,

25. Jordanian intelligence reportedly shared information with the United States that led to the killing of Abu Musab al-Zarqawi in June 2006. See Borzou Daragahi and Josh Meyer, "'We Knew Him': Jordanian Spies Infiltrated Iraq to Find Zarqawi," *Los Angeles Times*, June 13, 2006.

26. Kenneth M. Pollack, *Arabs at War: Military Effectiveness, 1948–1991* (Lincoln: University of Nebraska Press, 2002), 150, 186, 314, 346–348; see also Schenker, *Dancing with Saddam*.

27. See Middle East Media Research Institute (MEMRI), "Al-Hayat Inquiry: The City of Al-Zarqaa in Jordan—Breeding Ground of Jordan's Salafi Jihad Movement," Special Dispatch Series no. 848 (Washington, DC: MEMRI, January 17, 2005).

28. See International Crisis Group (ICG), *Jordan's 9/11: Dealing with Jihadi Islamism*, Middle East Report no. 47 (Amman/Brussels: ICG, November 23, 2005), 13–14.

where a violent coup wiped out the royal family in 1958—just a few months after signing a confederation agreement with Jordan.[29] Despite this colonial connection, historically the two countries have not been closely linked, with Jordan oriented toward Palestine and the Levant. After the fall of Saddam, gossip swirled around the idea of reviving the Hashemite connection. But most Jordanians dismiss a priori any notion that Hashemites will ever again play a role in Iraq's political future.[30]

Cross-border and Expatriate Links

Some Jordanians point to cross-border tribal and family connections with the Sunnis of western Iraq, citing these links as a source of influence, but this appears more imagined than real. Granted, there is a strong measure of Sunni solidarity between Jordan and the Iraqi Sunni community, but this falls short of the entrenched cross-border ties between the Kurds of Syria, Turkey, Iran, and Iraq; Iranian and Iraqi Shi'a; or even the cross-border, tribal ties between Syria and Iraq, where the border is considerably longer and ties between populations are more deeply rooted. Moreover, even if Jordan could claim strong links, its ties with Washington would be a liability. "The strategic nature of American-Jordanian relations," writes a Jordanian analyst, "has not helped Amman win the confidence and support of broad sectors of Sunni Arabs dispersed among extremist fundamentalist and nationalist movements."[31] Jordan may have ties with various strata of the Iraqi Sunni community, but it seems to enjoy little influence when it comes to mediating between Iraqi factions.

Jordan enjoys some indirect influence in Iraq by hosting a large and ever-changing expatriate Iraqi community. Following the 1991 Gulf War and the subsequent UN sanctions, regime Iraqi refugees (referred to as "guests" in Jordan) swelled to some 300,000–350,000, including members of Saddam Hussein's family.[32] In the aftermath of the U.S.-led invasion in

---

29. See Adnan Abu Odeh, *Jordanians, Palestinians, and the Hashemite Kingdom in the Middle East Peace Process* (Washington, DC: United States Institute of Peace Press, 1999), 84–86; and Robert B. Satloff, *From Abdullah to Hussein: Jordan in Transition* (New York: Oxford University Press, 1994), 19–40.

30. Despite a few murmurs, there was little discussion in Jordan of a Hashemite assuming a direct political role in Iraq. The strongest claimant by bloodline to the Iraqi Hashemite throne is Prince Raad, a Jordanian member of the royal family who, at one point, supported the U.S.-led invasion of Iraq. A much more prominent claimant, Sharif Ali bin Ali Hussein, was long active in the Iraqi-exile opposition; he ran in the January 2005 Iraqi elections on the constitutional monarchy slate but failed to gain any seats in the parliament. See Nicholas Pelham, "Royal House Hopes to Bridge Iraqi Divisions," *Financial Times*, April 14, 2003; and Jeffrey Gettleman, "The King Is Dead (Has Been for 46 Years) but Two Iraqis Hope: Long Live the King!" *New York Times*, January 28, 2005.

31. Oraib al-Rantawi, "Fearing Iraq's Instability, Jordan Seeks Its Unity," *Daily Star,* Tuesday, December 27, 2005.

32. Jordan has a long history of providing safe haven for Iraqi exiles, including survivors of Iraq's Hashemite royal family. In the mid-1990s, Saddam Hussein's two sons-in-law, Hussein Kamel al-

2003, the number of Iraqis in Jordan rose dramatically. In the immediate post-Saddam period, various estimates put the figure anywhere between 450,000 and 800,000. At the high point, which appears to have been in 2006, the UN High Commissioner for Refugees put the figure at 700,000, though it fell substantially in the years that followed as some refugees moved on to more affordable destinations, like Syria, or returned to Iraq. Other estimates put the figure much lower. A 2007 study by a prominent Norwegian research center suggested there were only 450,000 to 500,000 Iraqis in Jordan.[33] The Iraqi expatriate community is one way in which Jordan has tried to build bridges between Iraqi ethnic communities on both sides of the border and to encourage Iraqi Sunnis to participate in the Iraqi political process. But the expatriate issue is also a source of tension: Iraqi leaders worry about a "brain drain," and Jordanian officials worry about a growing source of Islamist militancy. Moreover, the Maliki government wanted to extradite Saddam's eldest daughter, Raghad, who is accused of bankrolling the insurgency. Jordan refused.

Compatibility of Jordanian and U.S. Interests— Past, Present, and Future

In a reversal of the 1990–91 split over Iraq, Jordan's approach to the post-Saddam era has been highly compatible with U.S. interests. Under almost any scenario, this compatibility is likely to endure. First, there is Jordan's strategic partnership with Washington. Jordan is a state beset with deep vulnerabilities in both its economy and its geostrategic position in the regional balance of power. The West, and the United States specifically, has long been a prominent part of Jordan's strategy for addressing its endemic vulnerabilities. Jordan was able to maintain its strategic relationship with Washington and also preserve its close ties with Saddam Hussein, but it was the United States—not Saddam Hussein's Iraq—that enjoyed an unprecedented place of privilege in Jordan's national security strategy. Since the mid-1990s, following the peace treaty with Israel, Jordan has made a determined effort to upgrade its ties with Washington and build a

---

Majid and Saddam Kamel al-Majid, defected to Jordan and were granted asylum by King Hussein. But the two later returned to Iraq and were assassinated. At the time of the U.S. invasion in March 2003, Saddam Hussein's daughters fled to Jordan. With King Abdullah's consent, they continue to reside in Amman. Raghad, the eldest daughter, took a high-profile role in her father's Amman-based legal defense team; see Randa Habib, "Jordan Stands by Saddam's Daughter Despite Iraq Extradition Call," *Agence France-Presse*, July 3, 2006. Both daughters are reportedly living quite comfortably.

33. "Iraqis in Jordan 2007: Their Number and Characteristics," released by FAFO, Norway, www .fafo.no/ais/middeast/jordan/IJ.pdf. Some Jordanian experts interviewed by the author believe the true figure is even lower than the FAFO figures, which were obtained in collaboration with the Jordanian government—which, according to some, has an interest in maintaining high estimates.

strategic framework based on close cooperation in security and trade—a relationship whereby Jordan relies on Washington to guarantee its security.[34]

Viewing Jordan as a reliable and friendly government is nothing new in Washington, but what is new is the determination of Jordan's present leader to make a strategic relationship with the United States a centerpiece of the country's foreign policy. King Abdullah managed Jordan's Iraq policy in such a way that reinforced Jordan's strategic alliance with Washington, much as he did on counterterrorism post-9/11.[35] Abdullah also wants Jordan to hold a privileged place in Washington and is sensitive to the relative position of other Arab states, such as Egypt, that are also closely aligned with the United States. Over time, this sensitivity could also include Iraq, should it develop into another key regional partner for Washington, alongside Israel and Saudi Arabia.

Second, Jordanian leaders took a lesson from history: the costs of opposing U.S. action in the 1991 Gulf War were unacceptable in retrospect. The next time around, not only did Jordan seek guarantees from the United States and its regional allies to offset the impact of the U.S. invasion and occupation, but it also considered the positions of regional benefactors and investors, such as Kuwait, which it could not afford to alienate.

Third, there is the Palestinian dimension. The Palestinian issue looms much larger than Iraq in Jordanian politics. Already under constraints imposed by the collapse of the Oslo Peace Process in 2000 and the surging violence between Israelis and Palestinians that followed, Jordan believed U.S. actions in Iraq would be joined by positive movement on the Palestinian question. Although this was not the primary calculation that produced Jordanian cooperation, it was an important element in Amman's thinking. Once Saddam was ousted, Jordanian leaders lobbied the United States very hard for more dramatic steps on the peace process. Former U.S. National Security Council analyst Flynt Leverett described King Abdullah's position on the eve of the war as follows: "We are going to support you in Iraq, we assume you are going to take military action, we will do everything we can to support you. But we need more cover on the Palestinian issue, we need a road map."[36]

---

34. The full extent of U.S.-Jordanian cooperation is not made public. For further details, see Arkin, "Keeping Secrets in Jordan."

35. U.S.-Jordanian cooperation on counterterrorism matters is far-reaching. There are many reports that Jordan participated in the CIA's rendition program. According to a report by Amnesty International, Jordanian security agents have tortured U.S. terror subjects to obtain confessions; see Amnesty International, Jordan, "'Your Confessions Are Ready for You to Sign': Detention and Torture of Political Suspects," MDE 16/005/2006, Amnesty International, July 2006.

36. See the Public Broadcasting Service documentary *Elusive Peace: Israel and the Arabs*, originally aired October 10–24, 2005 (released on DVD January 2006).

Fourth, Jordan's cooperation is also tied to Washington's use of positive economic and military inducements. This strategy is not new: more than a decade ago, in the aftermath of the Israeli-Jordanian peace treaty, the Clinton administration convinced Congress to cancel hundreds of millions of dollars of Jordanian debt. Arab-Israeli peace, together with counterterrorism priorities, led to a steep rise in annual foreign aid to Jordan. Then, after 9/11, the U.S.-Jordan Free Trade Agreement—signed under Clinton but held up in the Senate—was quickly ratified. Bilateral trade has boomed. In addition, as the United States went to war against Saddam in early 2003, Washington put forward an expansive new aid package for Jordan. Unlike Turkey, a democracy, which also received U.S. aid pledges, there was effectively no debate in Jordan about whether to cooperate with the United States. In 2003, U.S. aid to Jordan hit a high-water mark. Aid alone was not responsible for Jordan's cooperation, but it did provide the Bush administration with a tangible way to signal support to the kingdom and reassured Abdullah at a moment when he was anxious about the potential economic dislocations of war. Since Saddam Hussein's ouster, bilateral foreign aid to Jordan has remained at high levels, averaging about $500 million annually.

As Jordan pursues what is an unpopular policy at home, foreign aid has allowed the king to make the case that he is putting "Jordan First"—a slogan favored by the Hashemites. Using foreign aid to bolster regime stability is a long-standing Jordanian strategy.[37] Increased U.S. aid is the tangible manifestation of America's commitment to the stability and well-being of Jordan. It is also a sign of Jordan's relative importance to U.S. strategic goals in the region, from Arab-Israeli peacemaking to counterterrorism to rebuilding Iraq. Thus it is little surprise that aid to Jordan has risen so dramatically since 2001.

Jordan's cooperation on Iraq has also been reinforced by the course of events. Despite all the instability brought on by war, Jordan has been able to maintain high growth rates (between 3 percent and 6 percent). In other words, Jordan has a vested economic interest in post-Saddam Iraq. The threat of terrorism continues to loom large, but Jordan has managed to do remarkably well economically since the fall of Saddam. The fact that Jordan's worst-case scenarios—interrupted energy supplies, a surge in unemployment, economic meltdown—did not materialize has helped to reinforce the decision to cooperate with Washington.

---

37. See Laurie Brand, *Jordan's Inter-Arab Relations: The Political Economy of Alliance Making* (New York: Columbia University Press, 1994); and Markus Bouillon, "Walking the Tightrope: Jordanian Foreign Policy from the Gulf Crisis to the Peace Process and Beyond," in *Jordan in Transition*, ed. George Joffe (New York: Palgrave, 2002), 1–22.

Jordan-Iraqi Relations: Future Sources of Tension

Spillover of Violence and Terrorism

Jordan, lacking economic or strategic power, is uniquely vulnerable to instability in Iraq. The November 2005 Amman suicide bombings, as well as earlier plots and attacks, highlighted a combination of flashpoints, including the large and fluid Iraqi exile community, lax Iraqi border control, violent opposition to the U.S. occupation, and opposition to Jordan's strategic relationship with Washington. Following the U.S. "surge" in 2007–8, it appears Jordan's security improved along with Iraq's. Even if Jordan's highly regarded intelligence services continue to perform effectively, even the best counterterrorism capability is no substitute for a functional Iraqi state that can patrol its borders effectively and maintain public order. Nor can it compensate for the destabilizing effects of a long-term U.S. military presence, which could be a magnet for Iraqi insurgents. In many respects, Jordan is caught between its fundamental reliance on U.S. security guarantees and the negative externalities caused by America's military presence in Iraq.

Sunni Marginalization and the Role of Iran

Jordan worries about the marginalization of Iraq's Sunni community and the possibility that Iraq is drifting deeper into Iran's orbit. The first alarm was sounded early after the fall of Saddam, when Jordan opposed the widespread, U.S.-supported de-Ba'thification campaign. As a result, the kingdom has tried to play a bridge-building role: "We are working to try to reach out to the Sunni community in Iraq and to convince them that they are part and parcel of the future of Iraq," King Abdullah said in mid-2005.[38] At the diplomatic level, the kingdom supported the Arab League's reconciliation initiative and encouraged Sunnis to join the political process—albeit with modest results so far. But Jordan's fear of growing Iranian influence and a concomitant rise in Shiite power in Iraq is unlikely to disappear. Jordan's concern, reflective of a broader concern in the Arab world, could become a source of tension with Iraq.

Lingering Mistrust

Lingering mistrust between Jordan and Iraq could resurface, as it did so dramatically in the first years following Saddam's ouster. Given the close Hashemite-Saddam relationship, and the fact that Iraq's new leadership is drawn heavily from Shi'a exiles persecuted by Saddam, the potential for a

---

38. King Abdullah, interview by Lally Weymouth in "In the End, 'Iraq Will Succeed,'" *Washington Post*, May 22, 2005.

rift is not surprising. King Abdullah's early warning about an emerging Shiite "crescent" was not well received by members of the United Iraqi Alliance, who swept the 2005 election and led Iraq's first permanent, post-Saddam government. Moreover, given that some insurgents are themselves Jordanian, a belief has developed among some Iraqi Shi'a that the Jordanian government is complicit in exporting insurgents.[39] At worst, Shiite public opinion in Iraq considered Jordan complicit in exporting Zarqawi-style radicalism; and at best, Iraq's new political elite felt Amman has been too permissive toward support for the insurgency.

The most dramatic incident to stoke the Iraqi-Jordanian crisis of confidence was the February 2005 bombing in Hilla, Iraq. The attack, reportedly carried out by a Jordanian, killed more than 120 Iraqis, mainly Shi'a. An obituary published in Jordan hailed the alleged bomber—Raed al-Banna, a Jordanian—as a "martyr." The Banna case led to an outcry in Iraq, with Shiite leaders leveling harsh criticisms against Jordan. For months, accusations were hurled at Amman. "We are sorry to say that until now, a high number of the figures of the [former] regime and those who supervise terrorist groups are based in Jordan," said Laith Kubba, spokesman for interim Iraqi prime minister Ibrahim al-Ja'fari.[40]

After the Hilla bombing, demonstrators attacked the Jordanian embassy in Baghdad. The Iraqi demonstrations, followed by the withdrawal of ambassadors and mutual recriminations, signaled a steep decline in relations. The late Shiite leader Abd al-Aziz al-Hakim said Jordan was exporting "terrorists" to Iraq. It was weeks before formal diplomatic relations returned to normal.[41] The Amman bombings later that year fueled mistrust in the other direction, given that the bombers were Iraqi. For the most part, the early breach was repaired. The heart of the bilateral relationship—trade, transport, security training, and the "gateway"—even at the worst of times was largely untouched by the breach over Hilla and the Amman hotel bombings. Visits by Iraqi president Jalal Talabani and other senior Iraqis,

---

39. See MEMRI, "Al-Hayat Inquiry." For more background on Jordanians and the Iraqi insurgency, see James Glanz, "In Jordanian Case, Hints of Iraq Jihad Networks," *New York Times*, July 29, 2005; Nir Rosen, "Iraq's Jordanian Jihadis," *New York Times Magazine*, February 19, 2006; and Nir Rosen, "Thinking Like a Jihadist: Iraq's Jordanian Connection," *World Policy Journal* 23, no. 1 (Spring 2006): 1–16.

40. Kubba quote in "Iraq Wants Jordan to Extradite Ex-Regime Figures Behind Insurgency," *Agence France-Presse*, August 21, 2005.

41. See Dexter Filkins, "Tortuous Trail: From a Bombing in Iraq to Fury at a Family in Jordan," *New York Times*, March 15, 2005; Steve Negus, "Iraq Spat Deepens as Jordan Evacuates Embassy," *Financial Times*, March 22, 2005; Nimrod Raphaeli, "Iraqi-Jordanian Tension over the Most Lethal Suicide Bombing in Iraq," Middle East Research Institute, March 29, 2005, www.intelligence.org.il/eng/memri/apr_a_05.htm; and Rawya Rageh, "Iraq, Jordan at Odds over Border Security," Associated Press, March 21, 2005. The editor of the Jordanian paper that broke the story was forced to resign.

which have been reciprocated on the Jordanian side (unlike most Arab neighbors), have healed some of the wounds.

Economics: Sustainable Growth, Transparency, and Debt

Trade and economic matters generate positive cooperation between Jordan and Iraq, but they are also a source of discord. Iraq relies on trade and transport routes via Jordan, bilateral trade is robust, and Jordan is a convenient safe haven for Iraqis to park their assets—illicit or otherwise. Stories of Iraqis using cash to purchase multimillion-dollar properties in Amman are all too common. But the financial ledger is murky, the lack of transparency is noticeable. At least in terms of Saddam-era assets, Jordan has generally complied with U.S. and Iraqi requests to trace and return assets. Even though Jordan enjoys certain added economic benefits as a result of instability in Iraq, these benefits are unsustainable and potentially damaging to the Jordanian economy over the long term. The run-up in real estate is the best example of this mixed blessing; the real estate boom is having a vastly disparate impact on the Jordanian economy and contributing to an ever-widening income gap.

The pre-2003 economic balance sheet is also a source of discord. Jordan claims it is owed close to $1 billion in Iraqi commercial debt. The kingdom has worked tirelessly to ensure that its debt is not lumped into the larger multilateral debt process—Jordanian officials call the debt "exceptional" and say it should be handled on a separate ledger. They also complain that the United States is not fully supporting Amman in securing these funds. The kingdom has also lobbied creditor nations to reduce Iraqi debt by offering more reconstruction contracts to neighbors like Jordan.[42] But the debt issue is complex. For example, without the Saddam-era concessions the balance sheet might look very different. If Jordan is intent on pressing the issue, the United States and other debtor nations could press Jordan to be more forthcoming in opening up the kingdom's Saddam-era ledgers.[43]

The Israeli-Palestinian Conflict

As noted earlier, U.S. actions in Iraq have further increased pressure on the Jordanian government to improve the situation in the Palestinian territories—which has also created some tension with the United States. Although Amman was pleased with the 2003 U.S. endorsement of the road

---

42. See "Jordan Calls for Reconstruction Contracts to Lessen Iraq Debt," *Agence France-Presse*, September 13, 2004.

43. The debt issue was reportedly raised during Prime Minister Bakhit's 2006 visit to Baghdad and Prime Minister Maliki's 2008 visit to Jordan. A Jordanian official suggested to the author that one way to resolve the issue would be to "swap" the Iraqi commercial debt with the frozen assets of Iraq's al-Rafidayn Bank held by Jordan, which, like the debt, totals approximately $1 billion.

map for peace plan—for which Jordanians claim some credit—the glaring lack of progress is a growing sore point for Amman. If the Aqaba Summit in June 2003—where President Bush presided and pledged to "ride herd" over the parties—was a high point for Jordan, the April 2004 Bush-Sharon exchange of letters, the 2006 Israel-Hizballah war, and the 2008 Israeli war in Gaza were low points.[44] Jordanian officials point with some pride to the May 2004 U.S. letter of assurances to King Abdullah, but what is heard more often is despair over unending Israeli-Palestinian conflict and the failure of mediation efforts. Jordanian optimism was renewed following the election of President Barack Obama, but faded quickly as Obama's initial efforts stalled.

Conclusion

Despite widespread support within the foreign policy community, Jordan still has its critics—those who argue that Jordan is on the wrong side of the equation.[45] "Abdullah works against U.S. interests in Iraq and elsewhere while pretending otherwise," wrote Jim Hoagland in the *Washington Post*.[46] This critique goes further, particularly on governance: "In short, Jordan has degenerated into the kind of despotic kleptocracy the Bush administration [said] it will no longer tolerate," said former *Wall Street Journal* Middle East correspondent Stephen Glain. "But tolerate it the White House does."[47] For those whose primary prism is governance and transparency, whether neoconservatives or liberals, disappointment with the kingdom is inevitable. But a broader analysis, taking into account strategic concerns and stability, suggests that Jordan continues to play a generally positive role. Specifically, on the question of Iraq, Jordan has made positive, if modest, contributions to stabilizing its neighbor to the east and engaging in

---

44. See David Sanger, "Middle East Mediator: Big New Test for Bush," *New York Times*, June 5, 2003. The Bush administration's "road map for peace" can be found at www.state.gov/r/pa/ei/rls/22520.htm, and the Bush-Sharon correspondence can be found at www.mfa.gov.il/MFA/Peace+Process/Reference+Documents/Exchange+of+letters+Sharon-Bush+14-Apr-2004.htm.

45. See Jim Hoagland, "Playing Both Sides in Jordan," *Washington Post*, March 27, 2005; Glain, "Letter from Jordan"; and Jon Leyne, "Jordan Fears Loss of U.S. Favor," *BBC News*, April 25, 2005, http://news.bbc.co.uk/1/hi/world/middle_east/4472833.stm.

46. Hoagland, "Playing Both Sides in Jordan."

47. Glain, "Letter from Jordan." Criticism of the kingdom's spotty record on political reform surfaced again after the king dismissed Parliament in late 2009, and ahead of the November 2010 elections. Anne Mariel Peters captured much of the critical sentiment among liberals in the United States: "The United States is playing a double game in Jordan. On the one hand, it has dumped millions into activities promoting liberalism and best-practice electoral processes, calling them democracy promotion. On the other hand, it does not seem willing or able to pressure a reliable friend and ally to transfer sovereignty to the Jordanian people, and continues to provide the Hashemite regime with aid that encourages policymaking behind closed doors." "Jordan: Just What Exactly Are We Promoting," Middle East Channel, *FP.com*, October 12, 2010, http://mideast.foreignpolicy.com/posts/2010/10/12/jordan_just _what_exactly_are_we_promoting.

meaningful ways with the post-Saddam political class. Without Jordan, the United States would have faced a much more difficult situation in Iraq and in the region. The kingdom, more vulnerable than the other neighbors, has every interest in continuing to cooperate with the United States and Iraq—and in a strengthened, and stable post-Saddam political order. Among Iraq's neighbors, Jordan may not be pivotal, but neither is it peripheral.

Jordanian-American cooperation on Iraq is likely to remain strong and Jordan will continue to play a positive, if modest, role. In terms of its sheer weight—that is, population, military capabilities, and economic power—Jordan is not in a position to play a pivotal role in Iraq. But looking at raw power is just one measure. There are less obvious, harder-to-quantify ways in which Jordan will continue to be important to the future of the new Iraq. The kingdom has provided a reliable gateway through which the international community operates in Iraq. Jordan's political support, especially in regional forums, is important to the United States.

For much of the time since the fall of Saddam Hussein, Jordan has been the only Arab state to engage with Iraq. Beyond Baghdad, Jordan remains one of America's most reliable partners on a wide range of issues, from counterterrorism and Arab-Israeli peacemaking to military and intelligence cooperation—much of it deliberately kept out of the spotlight. Granted, Jordan's poor record on political reform stands out and poses a continuing dilemma for Washington—as do the records of other autocratic regimes with which the United States cooperates. The question of balancing America's interests in both governance and stability—brought into sharp relief by the 2011 "Arab Spring" that upended politics in many Arab countries—is no less urgent for Barack Obama than it was for George W. Bush, and it raises issues that extend well beyond the difficult, albeit limited, question of Iraq and its neighbors.

III

Iraq, Arab Politics, and the Regional Order

Lessons Learned

8

The New Iraq and Arab Political Reform

Drawing New Boundaries (and Reinforcing Old Ones)

Hesham Sallam

Long before the advent of the "Arab Spring," the promise of democracy in the new Iraq raised the hopes of advocates of transformative political change in the Middle East. Many opinion shapers inside Washington, most notably former U.S. president George W. Bush, wagered that the new Iraq would serve as a successful model for democratic change in the rest of the region. In a historic November 6, 2003, speech that inaugurated what later became known as the United States' "freedom agenda," President Bush promised that "Iraqi democracy will succeed—and that success will send forth the news, from Damascus to Tehran—that freedom can be the future of every nation. The establishment of a free Iraq at the heart of the Middle East will be a watershed event in the global democratic revolution."[1] With more than seven years passing since the date of that speech, this chapter assesses the impact of the Iraqi nation-building experiment on political reform in the rest of the region. Besides deepening this volume's assessment of post-2003 Iraq's impact on its neighbors, these trends hold some provisional theoretical lessons on

The author would like to thank Ziad Abu-Rish, Daniel Brumberg, Muriam Davis, Larry Diamond, Bayann Hamid, Steven Heydemann, Daniel Hopkins, Toby Jones, Daniel Nexon, and Leslie Thompson for their valuable comments on earlier versions of this essay. All errors and omissions are the responsibility of the author.

1. "President Bush Discusses Freedom in Iraq and Middle East," WhiteHouse.gov, November 6, 2003, http://georgewbush-whitehouse.archives.gov/news/releases/2003/11/20031106-2.htw.

how external and regional shocks can undermine or enhance regime stability.[2]

The analysis shows that on the one hand, regionwide opposition to the occupation of Iraq helped invigorate political dissent in traditionally closed political arenas throughout the Arab world. Anti–Iraq War activism provided many opposition groups throughout the region with valuable opportunities to organize cohesively and advance demands for political change, as illustrated by the Egyptian Movement for Change, commonly known as "Kifaya" (Arabic for "enough"). As a cause that appealed to diverse ideological trends in the Arab world, whether Islamist, liberal, Arab nationalist, or leftist, concern about the U.S.-led occupation of Iraq offered ideologically fragmented oppositions with a platform for joint political action. At the same time Iraq's troubled "democratic experiment," specifically the sectarian differences it precipitated, the Iranian influence it reinforced, and the threat of U.S. hegemony it symbolized, aided partisans of the status quo. Ruling regimes and their allies appealed to images of destruction, chaos, and sectarian violence in Iraq to discredit demands for transformative political change domestically. While the history of this nation-building experiment is still being written, the balance sheet of Iraq's impact on political reform in the Arab region seems to have fallen in favor of ruling regimes. In early 2011, these regimes began facing new and imminent challenges to their rule, as evidenced by the proliferation of uprisings throughout the region, which led to the ouster of Hosni Mubarak of Egypt and Zine Abdine Ben Ali of Tunisia. Preliminary evidence, however, indicates that these challenges were largely grounded in mass discontent relating to socioeconomic grievances and the failure of state-led political reform initiatives. As much as some observers would like to trace the so-called Arab Spring to Bush's promise of democracy spreading from Iraq to the rest of the region,[3] the "Iraqi democratic experiment" is nowhere to be seen in the ongoing backlash against Arab authoritarianism. Regardless of whether they will be able to withstand the challenge of the Arab Spring, most

---

2. There is a rich literature addressing the effects of external diffusion on regime type. See, for example, Daniel Brinks and Michael Coppedge, "Diffusion Is No Illusion: Neighbor Emulation in the Third Wave of Democracy," *Comparative Political Studies* 39, no. 4 (2006): 463–489; Kristian Skrede Gleditsch and Michael D. Ward, "Diffusion and the International Context of Democratization," *International Organization* 60, no. 4 (2006): 911–933; Steven Levitsky and Lucan A. Way, "International Linkage and Democratization," *Journal of Democracy* 16, no. 3 (2005): 20–34; Jeffrey Kopstein and David A. Reilly, "Geographic Diffusion and the Transformation of the Postcommunist World," *World Politics* 53, no. 1 (2000): 1–37; Samuel P. Huntington, *The Third Wave: Democratization in the Late Twentieth Century* (Norman: University of Oklahoma Press, 1991); and Harvey Starr, "Democratic Dominoes: Diffusion Approaches to the Spread of Democracy in the International System," *Journal of Conflict Resolution* 35, no. 2 (1991): 356–381.

3. See for example, Charles Krauthammer, "From Baghdad to Benghazi," *National Review Online*, March 4, 2011, www.nationalreview.com/articles/261278/baghdad-benghazi-charles-krauthammer.

Arab autocrats have been successful in turning the new Iraq from a threat to their continued monopoly over political power to a lifeline that has reinforced their capacity to diffuse and fragment domestic challenges to their rule.[4]

The rest of this chapter describes two distinct ways through which Iraq's nation-building experiment impacted political reform in the Arab world. The first trend involves Iraq's strengthening of sectarian cleavages across the Sunni-Shiite divide in nearby countries. This development has arguably undermined opposition cohesion and claims for greater political rights, while propping up autocrats' divide-and-rule tactics, as the case of Bahrain illustrates. The second trend pertains to how opposition to U.S. policies in Iraq created common ground between ideologically diverse opposition groups and facilitated their cooperation on issues of political reform. The anti-imperialist bent of these coalitions, however, made them vulnerable to attacks by autocrats and their allies, as the case of Egypt illustrates. Finally, the concluding section offers some tentative insights into the prospects for a regionwide democratizing effect emanating from Iraq in the future.

Iraq and the Strengthening of Arab Sectarian Divides

Growing sectarian tensions in the Iraqi political arena contributed to the hardening of political cleavages across the Sunni-Shiite divide in many parts of the Arab world, particularly the Gulf region. Many Arab opinion shapers and observers deem tensions across this divide as one of the biggest problems facing the Arab world today.[5]

There is some evidence that the recent growth in Shiite political activism throughout the region is linked, at least in part, to the political gains achieved by self-proclaimed Shiite groups in post-2003 Iraq.[6] For example, Hassan al-Saffar, a prominent Shiite political figure in Saudi Arabia, cited the electoral gains achieved by Iraqi Shi'a in the January 2005 parliamentary election to encourage their Saudi counterparts to vote

---

4. This is consistent with Steven Heydemann's notion of "authoritarian learning." See Steven Heydemann, "Upgrading Authoritarianism in the Arab World," Saban Center Analysis Paper no. 13 (Washington, DC: Brookings Institution, 2007).

5. Anthony Shadid, "Across Arab World, a Widening Rift," *Washington Post*, February 12, 2007, www.washingtonpost.com/wp-dyn/content/article/2007/02/11/AR2007021101328.html.

6. For example, Vali Nasr observes, "The Shi'a cultural revival in Iraq has broad implications not only for the future political development of Iraq, but also for future sectarian developments in the greater Middle East, tipping the balance of power in favor of the Shi'a. The cultural and religious ties that bind Shi'a populations from Lebanon to Pakistan are once again of political significance; after two decades of suppression at the hands of Sunni regimes, the Shi'a are again demanding greater rights and their place in the political arena." See Vali Nasr, "Regional Implications of Shi'a Revival in Iraq," *Washington Quarterly* 27, no. 3 (2004): 7–24.

in the kingdom's municipal election that same year.[7] The Iraqi experience may have demonstrated to Shi'a in Saudi Arabia that "they, like the Shi'a of Iraq, deserve more political opportunity."[8] In response to growth in Shiite political activism in recent years, the Saudi government lifted a ban on Ashura observances, began giving permission to build more Shiite mosques, and appointed five Shiite representatives to serve on the Shura Council. In Kuwait, Shiite representation in the National Assembly increased in successive parliamentary elections and nearly doubled in 2009 to nine seats.[9] Examples of Shiite political activism that emerged following the ascendancy of Shiite groups in the new Iraq are not limited just to the Gulf region. Shiite demands for greater political representation in Lebanon grew dramatically in recent years. Even in faraway Egypt, where Sunni-Shiite political divides are largely unheard of, reports broke out in August 2005 that the country's Shi'a were attempting to form a political party.[10]

While it is tempting to attribute these developments entirely to the diffusion of Iraq's "Shiite revival," it is difficult to assess fully the extent to which the new Iraq influenced decisions by Shiite activists elsewhere to heighten their demands for greater political rights. After all, many of these demands are long-standing, and the argument that they emerged only in response to internal developments in Iraq overlooks the agency of Shiite political communities throughout the region. At the same time, the claim that developments similar to those experienced by the new Iraq are causing Shi'a in the Arab world to step up their activism, as debatable as it may be, played a major role in shaping public debates and perceptions regarding political reform in the rest of the region. The perceived links between events inside Iraq and demands for political representation by Shi'a elsewhere hardened the view that Shi'a throughout the region are emulating the "Iraqi model" by using elections to achieve a pro-Iranian sectarian dominance. Thus, it is unsurprising that Arab autocrats and their supporters have often asserted in recent years that the new Iraq mirrored the growing influence of an ambitious Iran that is seeking to advance its schemes for regional hegemony by backing Shiite groups in Arab countries. In April 2006, former president Hosni Mubarak of Egypt raised doubts about the loyalty of Arab Shi'a, stating in an interview with Al-Arabiya television: "Definitely Iran

---

7. Vali Nasr, "When the Shiites Rise," *Foreign Affairs* 85, no. 4 (2006): 58–74.

8. Toby Jones, "The Iraq Effect in Saudi Arabia," *Middle East Report* no. 237 (2005): 20–25.

9. Mohammed Abdulrahman, "Four Women in New Kuwait Parliament," Radio Nederland Wereldomroep, May 18, 2009, http://static.rnw.nl/migratie/www.radionetherlands.nl/currentaffairs/region/middleeast/090518-women-kuwait-parliament-redirected.

10. "Sh'at misr yotaleboon ta'sis hizb siyasy" [Egypt's Shi'a demand the formation of a political party], *Alarabiya.net*, September 19, 2005, www.alarabiya.net/Articles/2005/09/19/16932.htm.

has influence over the Shi'a. Shi'a are 65 per cent of the Iraqis. . . . Most of the Shi'a are loyal to Iran, and not to the countries they are living in."[11] Similarly, King Abdullah II of Jordan warned in December 2004 of the emergence of a "Shiite crescent" extending from Iran into Iraq, Syria, and Lebanon in the wake of the political ascendance of pro-Iranian Shiite politicians in Iraq.[12]

A similar discourse has taken hold among various Arab opinion shapers. Salman al-'Auda, a prominent Islamic preacher in Saudi Arabia, expressed concerns in October 2006 over Iranian interventions in Iraq's affairs, and over reports of alleged conversions of Sunnis to Shiism in Arab countries.[13] Sheikh Yousef al-Qaradawi, a highly influential Egyptian Islamic preacher based in Qatar, often claims that the new Iraq is a hub for the violent persecution of Sunni Muslims: "Thousands have been killed in Iraq since the Americans entered the country and Sunnis are the ones suffering most in Iraq. There is an ethnic cleansing going on."[14] In 2008, Qaradawi was the center of pan-Arab media attention, as he renewed his warnings of growing Shiite influence throughout the region via Iraq. He said, "If we let Shi'a penetrate Sunni societies, the situation will not be pleasant, as evidenced by the instability they are causing in Lebanon and Iraq."[15] The use of the post-2003 Iraqi experience to warn Sunni Arab communities of the dangers of Shiite political ascendance is also seen in Lebanon, particularly after Hizballah's war with Israel in the summer of 2006. A Lebanese Sunni preacher crudely articulates this sentiment: "I am not calling on [Sunnis] to take on arms, although precautions for protection and self-defense are warranted. We do not want to be slaughtered like sheep . . . just like our brethren in Iraq."[16]

These same trends are highly pronounced in post-2003 Bahrain, where the war in Iraq reinforced sectarian divisions in the kingdom's political arena. Although sectarian tensions across the Sunni-Shiite divide are anything

11. "Mubarak's Shi'a Remarks Stir Anger," *Aljazeera.net*, April 10, 2006, http://english.aljazeera.net/NR/exeres/144CACBB-05C5-4C9B-BF19-DE575E636C62.htm.

12. "Arab Leaders Watch in Fear as Shi'a Emancipation Draws Near," *Guardian*, January 27, 2005, www.guardian.co.uk/Iraq/Story/0,2763,1399370,00.html.

13. He stated: "Given the presence of Shi'a political groups in Iraq after the conflict between Hizballah and Israel in Lebanon, many Sunnis have conceived some kind of allegiance" to Shiism, which can "be exploited with money or job offers to encourage people to switch from Sunni Islam to Shi'a Islam." See "Saudi Cleric Alarmed by Possible Sunni Conversions to Shi'a Islam," *Asianews.it*, October 24, 2006, www.asianews.it/view.php?l=en&art=7565.

14. "Al Qaradawi Blames Iran for Sectarian Strife," *Gulfnews*, January 21, 2007, http://archive.gulfnews.com/articles/07/01/21/10098391.html.

15. "Al-Qaradawi bayn al-tahreed did al-shi'at wa al-fehm al-khati' li al-tashayu'" [Al-Qaradawi between inciting against Shi'a and the incorrect understanding for shiism], *Annabaa.org*, September 30, 2008, www.annabaa.org/nbanews/71/813.htm.

16. Quoted in "Wa aydan al-ta'ifiyya al-suniyya" [And also Sunni sectarianism], *Alarabiya.net*, December 12, 2006, www.alarabiya.net/views/2006/12/12/29839.html.

but new to Bahrain, the compelling narrative that the electoral success of Iraq's Shi'a (for better or for worse) has encouraged their Bahraini counterparts to intensify their quest for greater political rights played a major role in shaping post-2003 Bahraini politics. A Shiite political activist from Bahrain told *Al-Jazeera* in February 2005, if Shi'a come to power in Iraq, "this would be a positive development for Bahraini Shi'a and will give them confidence in their quest for political rights."[17]

The lead-up to the 2006 parliamentary election solidified the perceived parallels between Bahrain and the new Iraq. After boycotting the 2002 election on grounds that the current constitutional framework does not grant the elected legislative chamber any effective powers vis-à-vis a dominant executive, Wefaq, one of the most prominent Shiite political groups in Bahrain, decided to contest the 2006 election. Observers question why the group decided to break the boycott even though the regime had largely failed to address its original grievances. This has often led to allegations that Bahraini Shi'a are taking cues from Iraq- and Iran-based Shiite religious leaders who are choreographing a regionwide campaign to prop up the power of their allies among Shiite opposition groups in the Arab world.[18] During the prelude to the vote, supporters of the status quo in Bahrain appealed to images of sectarian violence in Iraq as a way of encouraging Sunni participation in the election. "Wake up Sunnis! Don't be naive or your fate will be like the Iraqi Sunnis, who lost their rights and their lives," read one of many sectarian-colored text messages sent to thousands of Bahrainis ahead of the vote.[19] This was not dissimilar to the strategy that the government and its allies followed in 2011 in an attempt to discredit an antiregime uprising that called for greater political rights. In order to justify the extreme use of violence against demonstrators and to discredit

---

17. "Mkhaouf khalijiyya min hekouma shi'iyya fi al-'iraq" [Fears in the Gulf of a Shiite government in Iraq], *Aljazeera.net*, January 29, 2005, www.aljazeera.net/News/archive/archive?ArchiveId =104705.

18. For example, news reports came out in the fall of 2005 that anti-Wefaq activists put up signs in the streets alleging that "foreign elements," including Shiite religious leaders based in Iran, encouraged Wefaq's leaders to participate in the 2006 election. "Al-bahreen: jam'iyat alwefaq tanfi hedouth inshiqaq bayn a'da'aha" [Bahrain: Al-Wefaq society denies that a split has arisen among its members], *Asharq Al-Awsat*, September 3, 2005. These allegations gained momentum after Iraq-based Grand Ayatollah Ali Al-Sistani released a statement encouraging Bahraini Shi'a to break the boycott and participate in the election. See "The International Herald Tribune: Bahrain Expects Huge Voter Turnout after Divisive Election Campaign," Bahrain Center for Human Rights, www .bchr.net/en/node/768.

19. This same perception was articulated by a member of the Sunni Muslim Brotherhood: "Since the American involvement in Iraq, and the very obvious presence of Iranian fingerprints in Iraq as well, the Shia population here has created problems. . . . This has made us as Sunni feel that something is coming to Bahrain, especially with the so-called victory of Sayyed Hassan Nasrallah in the Lebanon war. The Sunni are seeking protection from their leadership because they feel threatened." See "Sectarian Tension Overshadows Bahrain Election," *Financial Times*, November 26, 2006, www.ft.com/cms/s/0/564d27e4-7b61-11db-bf9b-0000779e2340.html.

their demands domestically and internationally, proregime figures portrayed the uprising as an Iran-instigated sectarian movement.[20]

Iraq was also at the center of many fractures within an increasingly
polarized Bahraini opposition. Cooperation between Shiite and Arab
nationalist activists was markedly weakened by the sectarian-colored differences over the situation in the new Iraq.[21] In early 2005, Mahmoud
al-Qassab, a ranking member of the Nationalist Democratic Rally Society,
an Arab-nationalist group, wrote an article in *Al-Khaleej Al-Arabi* implic-
itly criticizing Grand Ayatollah Ali al-Sistani for collaborating with the
U.S.-led occupation of Iraq. Shiite members of the opposition who were
traditionally allied with Qassab's group strongly condemned his article, demanding an apology for his comments. Shiite political activists that same
month expressed anger at an article by another Arab nationalist figure,
Samira Rajab, in which she described Sistani as a "general for the American
occupation." A ranking member of Wefaq told *Al-Hayat* that his party,
which was still officially engaged in an alliance with the Nationalist Democratic Rally Society at the time, condemned any attack against Shiite *marji'yya*
(religious authority) and its commitment to its principles is "above any
political alliances."[22]

The emergence of sectarian conflict in Iraq deepened the sectarian divide
within the Bahraini political field. Salafi political figures used allegations of
Sunni persecution in Iraq to undermine the legitimacy of the political demands set forth by Bahraini Shi'a and to question their motives. The salafis'
general rhetoric echoes the government's recurrent warning that "without
the monarchy, Bahrain would go the way of Iraq and Lebanon."[23] A similar
strain was felt in the relationship between Shiite groups like Wefaq and
former allies among Arab nationalists and leftists who were dismayed at
what they perceived as the tacit support of Iraqi Shi'a for the U.S.-led occupation. These differences allowed the regime to continue to benefit from
sectarian divisions in Bahrain's political field, thereby broadening support
for the political status quo due to fear of the Iraq scenario in Bahrain.

---

20. Matthew Cassel, "Silencing Bahrain's Journalists," *Aljazeera English*, May 31, 2011, http://
english.aljazeera.net/indepth/features/2011/05/20115318046839411.html.

21. A similar trend is observed in Saudi Arabia where developments inside Iraq imposed strains on
cooperation between the Kingdom's Shiite and non-Shiite reform activists. See Frederic Wehrey
et al., *The Iraq Effect: The Middle East after the Iraq War* (Santa Monica, CA: RAND, 2010), 81.

22. "Albahreen: mawqef al-sistani min ehtellal al'iraq yohaded binshiqaq altahalof alroba'I" [Bah-
rain: Al-Sistani's position on the occupation of Iraq threatens the fissure of the four-member alli-
ance], *Al-Hayat*, February 21, 2005, www.daralhayat.com/arab_news/gulf_news/02-2005/Item
-20050220-313faa96-c0a8-10ed-001c-22ff97f5a60c/story.html.

23. Statement attributed to a Bahraini official quoted in Fred Wherey, "Elections and Managing
Sectarianism," *Arab Reform Bulletin*, August 13, 2008, www.carnegieendowment.org/arb/?fa=
show&article=20642.

The rise of a new Iraq, however, was not exclusively a source of division and disunity for political activists throughout the region. In some cases, the Iraq War played a unifying role and contributed to coalition building among ideologically disparate groups.

Iraq and Opposition Alliances in the Arab World

An Unusual Point of Consensus

The fragmentation of political opposition across the Islamist–non-Islamist divide to the advantage of ruling incumbents is widely observed in the Arab world.[24] Fears of an Islamist electoral sweep à la 1991 Algeria, coupled with the repercussions such a victory might have for the limited civil liberties protected by the current political order, help maintain the tacit support of secular-leaning opposition groups to incumbent regimes.[25] The U.S.-led invasion of Iraq and the anger it instigated on the Arab street partly mitigated these divisions, creating areas of common concern among ideologically fragmented political opposition communities. Beginning in 2003, opposition to U.S. actions in Iraq became an important policy issue on which traditionally fragmented opposition actors in Jordan could agree.[26] In Yemen, opposition to U.S. policy in the region, particularly Iraq, is one of the issues uniting members of the Joint Meeting Parties (JMP), an opposition alliance encompassing Islamists and non-Islamist groups.[27] In Egypt, post-2003 antiwar political activism invigorated channels of dialogue between Islamist and non-Islamist actors, thereby paving the way for reform-oriented cross-ideological coalitions such as Kifaya.

Iraq was the perfect rallying point for many Arab opposition efforts. The situation in Iraq stirred the passions of Arab public opinion and

---

24. For a discussion of opposition fragmentation and authoritarian divide-and-rule strategies in the Arab world, see Ellen Lust-Okar, *Structuring Conflict in the Arab World: Incumbents, Opponents, and Institutions* (New York: Cambridge University Press, 2005). For recent debates on authoritarian durability in the Arab world, see Oliver Schlumberger, ed., *Debating Arab Authoritarianism: Dynamics and Durability in Nondemocratic Regimes* (Stanford, CA: Stanford University Press, 2007); and Heydemann, "Upgrading Authoritarianism in the Arab World."

25. For a discussion of patterns of conflict between Islamists and secularists in Egypt, see Dina Shehata, *Islamists and Secularists in Egypt: Opposition, Conflict and Cooperation* (London: Routledge, 2009).

26. See Janine A. Clark, "The Conditions of Islamist Moderation: Unpacking Cross-ideological Cooperation in Jordan," *International Journal of Middle East Studies* no. 38 (2006): 539–560; and "Al-mu'arada al-urduniyya tatalaqa darba min al-hekouma wa darabat min al-share" [The Jordanian opposition receives a punch from the government and punches from the street], *Alarabiya.net*, December 2, 2004, www.alarabiya.net/articles/2004/12/02/8418.html.

27. See Iris Glosemeyer and Hesham Sallam, "The JMP Alliance: New Political Pragmatism in Yemen?" in *Conflict, Identity and Reform in the Muslim World: Challenges for U.S. Engagement*, ed. Daniel Brumberg and Dina Shehata (Washington, DC: United States Institute of Peace Press, 2009).

mobilized the masses in protest of U.S. policies and the support they receive from Arab autocrats and, more importantly, it was one of few policy issues on which a diverse set of political groups could agree. By appealing to a wide range of ideological sensibilities, Iraq was an ideal cause for unifying the opposition. Opposition groups upholding secular Arab nationalist norms feared that the entry of U.S. troops into Baghdad hammered the final nail in the coffin of Arab unity. Marxist and left-leaning activists saw U.S. intervention as yet another imperialist scheme by international capitalist forces to seize the region's oil wealth. Islamists saw the occupation as an imminent threat against Islamic values and principles; this was a view that the perceived marginalization of Sunni Iraqis under the post-Saddam political order crystallized.

The convergence of the various threats that the new Iraq embodied to each of these groups of actors played a major role in enhancing opposition cohesion—at least temporarily. It is no coincidence that the common narrative that various oppositions employ to justify unusual partnerships between political Islam and the secular Arab left is almost identical: our nation is surrounded by multiple threats; resisting these threats requires us to change the political status quo, and this goal cannot be achieved absent a unified joint political action. The declaration of principles of Yemen's JMP invokes this same narrative. The opening paragraphs of the document say that the JMP seeks to "strengthen the democratic political system, and reinforce its ability to confront the challenges and threats that surround our homeland, and our Arab and Islamic nations."[28] The JMP's political platform, released in the lead-up to the 2006 presidential election, pledged a more active Yemeni role in "defending the causes of our Arab and Islamic nations, especially Palestine and Iraq." A similar narrative is set forth by the Egyptian Kifaya's founding principles.

Before long, however, many Arab autocrats also started appropriating the "Iraq cause" in their own discourse and began employing it to undermine the credibility of opposition coalitions. Ironically, the anti-American agenda on which these groups built their strategies trapped them in the same contradiction that haunts many Arab autocrats—namely, the contradiction between proclaiming the role of the nation's protector from Western interference while simultaneously supporting the interests of this same "foreign enemy." On the one hand, these cross-ideological coalitions justified their existence by invoking the mission of protecting the "nation" from the creeping threats posed by American hegemony in the region. Yet

---

28. "Nas ittifaq almabadi' bayn ahzab alleqa' almushtarak" [Text of decalaration of principles between the Joint Meeting Parties], *Aljazeera.net*, March 10, 2004, www.aljazeera.net/NR/exeres/886D14D3-01B0-4978-8C7A-FF3117CCC896.htm.

on the other hand, their demands for serious political change ultimately converged with the same demands that the United States made via its democracy-promotion initiatives. Highlighting these contradictions was the winning strategy that many Arab autocrats employed in order to put their opponents on the defensive and damage their credibility. Suddenly, the dissatisfaction of Arab public opinion with the war in Iraq turned from being a weapon for opposition groups into a source of weakness. For example, in condemning an alleged relationship between the JMP and the U.S. embassy in Sanaa, an ally to Yemeni president Ali Abdallah Saleh compared the JMP to the prewar Iraqi opposition that "conspired with the U.S. against its own people."[29] A similar pattern is seen in Morocco, where allies of the palace often characterize U.S. support for democratic reform and opposition groups as Iraq-style foreign meddling. In response to such allegations, one member of the Parti de la Justice et du Développement (PJD) denied that he had ever met with U.S. government officials, declaring: "I'm not in favor of meeting Americans who are on official missions. They are killing Muslim people. . . . If they say they are going to leave Iraq, I don't have any problem with meeting them."[30] The instability and chaos seen in occupied Iraq have clearly provided Arab autocrats breathing room they did not enjoy on the eve of the U.S. invasion.[31]

In sum, Iraq played a central role in enhancing intraopposition cooperation across the Islamist-secular divide, a cleavage that has traditionally strengthened Arab autocrats' divide-and-rule strategies. Iraq provided a cause that appealed to the agendas of Arab nationalist, Islamist, and leftist opposition political activists to a degree that other joint domestic concerns have often failed to achieve. In some cases these antiwar partnerships reinforced cross-ideological democratic reform coalitions. However, like most antiregime opposition initiatives that built on Iraq War–related activism, these groups became prisoners to their own rhetoric and discourse. It was not long before regimes and their supporters used public outrage at U.S. policies in the region, particularly in Iraq, to exploit the internal contradictions from which these groups suffered. The convergence between U.S.

---

29. "Shabbah almushtarak bil mo'arda al'iraqiyya qabl alharb . . . (alba'th tatmasak bilra'ees le wilaya kadema" [Likening Al-Mushtarak to prewar Iraqi opposition, the Ba'th is committed to another term to the president], *Almotamar.net*, April 20, 2006, www.almotamar.net/news/30208 .htm.

30. Ilhem Rachidi, "Dealing with 'Moderate' Islam," *Atimes.com*, July 15, 2005, www.atimes.com/ atimes/Front_Page/GG15Aa03.html.

31. In a *Foreign Policy* special issue titled "Who Wins in Iraq," Marina Ottaway summarizes this trend: "the failure of U.S. policy in Iraq has provided autocratic regimes in the Middle East a reprieve from the pressure to democratize." See Ottaway, "Who Wins in Iraq?: Arab Dictators," *Foreign Policy* (March/April 2007), www.foreignpolicy.com/story/cms.php?story_id=3710.

democracy promotion policies and the reform agendas these groups have adopted exposed them to the jabs of the regime's anti-imperialist rhetoric. The example of Egypt's Kifaya is a case in point.

Kifaya but Now "Enough"

Officially founded in 2004 by an ideologically diverse coalition of political activists, for years Kifaya had been one of the main vehicles for coordinating the efforts of Egyptian opposition groups in their demands for democratic change.[32] Observers of Egyptian politics describe Kifaya, which claims a membership of at least 20,000,[33] as the first serious organized nonviolent opposition that openly called for the replacement of then incumbent president Hosni Mubarak, Egypt's longest-serving ruler since Muhammed Ali.[34] After its founding Kifaya organized numerous media campaigns and public rallies to protest Mubarak's decision to run for a sixth presidential term and his (alleged) plans to pass power on to his son, hence its famous motto: "No for Mubarak, no for extension [of his term], no for inheritance." In response to the opposition's demands, as well as to growing American pressures for reform, Mubarak announced in February 2005 that the government would propose a constitutional amendment that would allow for Egypt's first multiparty presidential election.[35] Later that same year, Kifaya became a key player in coordinating opposition efforts during the legislative election.

Many observers have attributed the rise of Kifaya to post-9/11 U.S. pressures for democratic reform in the region.[36] They are right in that U.S. policies played a huge role in paving the way for Kifaya's emergence. However, credit should not go to Washington's freedom agenda but rather to the 2003 U.S.-led invasion of Iraq. Referring to how anti-American sentiments in the wake of the Iraq War invigorated political activism in Egypt, one Arab blogger notes: "The Arab spring is happening because of Bush's policies. . . .

---

32. For more on Kifaya's history, see Ahmed Bahaa Eddin Shabaan, *Kifaya al-madi wa al-mutaqbal* [Kifaya—Past and present] (Cairo: Kefaya Printings, 2006).

33. As claimed by Mohammed Saeed Idriss, member of Kifaya's coordination committee in an interview with *Al-Jazeera* in 2006. For transcripts of the interview, see "Ma wara' al-khabbar—azmat kifaya al-dakhiliyya" [Behind the story—Kifaya's internal crisis]," *Aljazeera.net*, December 12, 2006, www.aljazeera.net/NR/exeres/ED3EEF37-1CF2-45B5-BF47-D13FE10CDA9F.htm.

34. "Kifaya: Asking the Right Questions," *Baheyya.blogspot.com*, April 30, 2005, http://baheyya .blogspot.com/2005/04/kifaya-asking-right-questions.html.

35. Nadia Oweidat et al., *The Kefaya Movement: A Case Study of a Grassroots Reform Initiative* (Santa Monica, CA: Rand, National Defense Research Institute, 2008), 46.

36. In reference to U.S. democracy promotion efforts, one *Washington Post* editorial in January 2005 read, "Hoping that Mr. Bush is serious, Egyptian opposition movements have formed a coalition [Kifaya] to call for fundamental reforms." See "'Enough' in Egypt," *Washington Post*, January 18, 2005, www.washingtonpost.com/wp-dyn/articles/A16727-2005Jan17.html.

But it's not the way they think about it. It's the other way around."[37] It was
the Iraq War, and not the freedom agenda per se, that created the political
space for mass demonstrations—a phenomenon that was largely absent
from the Egyptian domestic scene for decades.[38] Given the anger that dominated Egyptian public opinion at that time, the Mubarak regime calculated it would not actively confront anti–Iraq War political activism.[39] The
opposition was well aware that the Egyptian regime, eager to distance itself from exceedingly unpopular U.S. policies, was willing to tolerate antiwar public expressions.[40] In other words, the war carved out some safe
space for dissent in the Egyptian political arena, and opposition activists
were determined to take advantage of that space and to drive the "Iraq
bandwagon" as far as they could. It comes as no surprise, therefore, that
among the Egyptian opposition, it was the traditionally marginalized
political organizations including the Labor, Al-Karama, and Al-Wasat
Parties that took a front-seat role in supporting the activities of antiwar
groups. Kifaya was conceived within this growing traffic of exchange among
political activists as a result of the war.

Kifaya's founding is usually dated to the first official statement it released
in November 2004. However, this initiative effectively took off a year earlier in November 2003, the same month U.S. president George W. Bush
publicly announced America's commitment to supporting democratic
change throughout the world, particularly in the Middle East. It was that
same month that the movement's would-be founders gathered at the house
of an Islamist political activist, Abul Ela Madi, for an *iftar*,[41] ironically not
to celebrate the American project in the Middle East but to resist it. Kifaya
cofounder Ahmad Bahaa Eddin Shabaan notes in his firsthand account of
the movement's founding that participants at that meeting were concerned

---

37. "Egypt Shuts Door on Dissent as U.S. Officials Back Away," *Washington Post*, March 19, 2007,
www.washingtonpost.com/wp-dyn/content/article/2007/03/18/AR2007031801196.html.

38. Mona El-Ghobashy says that the invasion of Iraq provoked "the largest street protests since the
January 1977 'bread riots'. . . . The war accelerated a significant trend among elite and masses alike
to directly challenge Mubarak, such as a March [2003] statement signed by prominent intellectuals
disagreeing with Mubarak's view that Saddam Hussein alone was to blame for the impending invasion of Iraq." See El-Ghobashy, "Egypt's Summer of Discontent," *Middle East Report Online*, September 18, 2003, www.merip.org/mero/mero091803.html.

39. For example, in February 2003 the government licensed an antiwar rally organized by labor
unions and opposition groups, including the banned Muslim Brotherhood, and attended by at least
80,000 people. See "Threats and Responses: Demonstrations; Thousands of Egyptians Fill Cairo
Stadium for a Protest against a U.S. War in Iraq," *New York Times*, February 28, 2003, http://query
.nytimes.com/gst/fullpage.html?res=9D02EFDB133CF93BA15751C0A9659C8B63.

40. As *Cairo Times* editor Paul Schemm writes: "The regime recognizes the need to provide a state-
sanctioned outlet for the growing rage over the U.S.-led assault upon Iraq." See Schemm, "Egypt
Struggle to Control Anti-war Protests," *Middle East Report Online*, March 31, 2003, www.merip.org/
mero/mero033103.html.

41. *Iftar* is the first meal following a day of fasting during the Islamic holy month of Ramadan.

about where "Egypt is going" in the face of a volatile regional and international environment. In his own words, Shabaan summarizes the concerns that brought these figures together that evening:

> *American imperialism has occupied Iraq and humiliated its people.* . . . Threats of aggression were swirling around Syria, Sudan, Egypt, and Saudi Arabia, as well as other Arab countries. At a time when oppressive political elites control the nation's wealth and fate, in such a way that has turned the whole Arab nation into a large prison degrading the citizen's dignity and thus marginalizing the Arab masses in all power balances in the region, those very same elites bow at the feet of the U.S. and Zionism.[42]

According to Shabaan, the group agreed that effective resistance of these external threats would not be possible absent real domestic political changes that could allow Arab peoples to remove from power America's allies among the region's club of autocrats. Democratic change, the logic goes, could give way to a more enlightened leadership committed to defending the interests and territorial integrity of the "nation," in ways that would be impossible under the existing incumbent regimes, which had failed miserably in defending the country's interests, as Shabaan contends. Egyptian political scientist Manar Shorbagy explains: "To these actors, political freedoms have become the key to effective resistance to the occupation of both Palestine and Iraq."[43] This same perspective was conveyed by Kifaya's founding statement. Released in November 2004 and titled "A Statement to the *Ummah* [Nation]: Confronting the American-Zionist Invasion and Foreign Intervention through Comprehensive Political Reform and Transfer of Power," the statement identified two goals with which the movement was concerned. Democratic change was listed as number two and was described as a prerequisite for achieving the first goal. The first goal, which framed the discussion in the entire document, is addressing the gravest threats facing the "nation":

> The **gravest threats and challenges confronting our nation is in the American invasion and occupation of Iraq**, the persistent Zionist aggression against the Palestinian people, and the projects of redrawing the map of our Arab nation, the latest of which was the Greater Middle East proposal that threatens our nationalism and targets our identity and, therefore, requires the mobilization of all efforts for a comprehensive political, cultural, and civilizational opposition to protect Arab existence in its confrontation with the American-Zionist project.[44]

This excerpt (which, interestingly, resonates highly with Yemen's JMP's founding principles quoted earlier) reinforces the point that U.S. efforts in

---

42. See Shabaan, *Kifaya al-madi wa al-mutaqbal*. Translation of this excerpt from Manar Shorbagy, "Understanding Kefaya: The New Politics in Egypt," *Arab Studies Quarterly* 29, no. 1 (2007): 39–60.
43. Ibid.
44. Ibid.

Iraq were central to the rationalization of this group's call for democratic change. Kifaya's statement of March 14, 2005, captures this notion:
"Domestic political despotism and the foreign imperialist aggression
are two sides to the same coin, and it is not possible to resist one without
the other."[45] Thus, fear of U.S. regional hegemony had consistently framed
the movement's calls for democratic change in all its statements and activities. In October 2006, when the U.S. Senate passed an unbinding
resolution that called for dividing Iraq along ethnic lines, Kifaya responded with organized street demonstrations. In a statement titled "Dividing Iraq Is the Prelude to Dividing the Arab Region," Kifaya strongly
condemned the Senate's resolution and claimed that "dividing Arab countries on religious or ethnic basis is one of the goals of the American project in the region."[46]

Not only was the Iraq issue key to Kifaya's rationalization for calling for
democratic change, but it was also essential to bringing together an ideologically diverse group of individual activists. Kifaya's cofounders included
political figures from all across the Egyptian ideological spectrum, including leaders from the Islamist-oriented Al-Wasat and Labor Parties, and
the left-leaning Al-Karama, and the movement remains a rare example of
intraopposition cooperation across the Islamist-secular divide in modern
Egyptian history.[47] The Iraq War and its perceived negative implications
for Egypt and the rest of the Arab and Muslim worlds provided this group
of activists a common ground for joint political action. There was something unique about the "Iraq issue" that catered to the ideological sensibilities of these various actors and allowed them to overcome the ideological
differences that have fragmented the opposition throughout previous decades. For Islamists the invasion of a fellow Muslim country signified an
attack aimed at undermining Islamic values. For Nasserists and Arab nationalists, the war presented yet another American attempt to divide and
conquer the Arab world. For Egyptian Marxists, the war was a conspiracy
orchestrated by global capitalist forces to steal Iraq's oil wealth. The over-
lap between these various narratives and perceptions rationalized to the
leaders and supporters of each of these political trends cooperation with
groups that proclaim ideologically opposing agendas. This reality is mirrored

---

45. Shabaan, *Kifaya al-madi wa al-mutaqbal*, 68.

46. "Almo'aradda almisriyya tantaqed qarar taqseem al-'iraq wa modhahara mahdouda bi al-azhar
deddoh" [Egyptian opposition criticizies Iraq division resolution and a limited demonstration at
al-azhar against it], *Al-Marsad Al-I'lami Al-Iraqi Bil Qahera*, October 6, 2008, http://iraqegypt
.blogspot.com/2007/10/blog-post.html.

47. For more on the history of Islamist/non-Islamist cooperation in Egypt, see Shehata, *Islamists and
Secularists in Egypt.*

in the ambiguities in Kifaya's statements about who exactly is targeted by the alleged threats of American hegemony. Kifaya often claims that U.S. policies in the region, particularly in Iraq, are a threat to the *ummah*. However, there is no indication as to how this *ummah* is defined: Does it include all Muslims throughout the world whether Arab or not, as Islamists would say? Does it refer only to the "Arab nation," as Arab nationalists would claim? Or is it meant as shorthand for the Egyptian people, as many liberal Egyptian activists would assert? This ambiguity is by no means unintentional. The vagueness with which this term is vested allows Kifaya's agenda to travel across ideological barriers and to appeal to a diverse group of supporters. Iraq and the threats that emanated from the war provided Kifaya with the glue that kept it intact (at least temporarily) despite the many failed attempts to wage cross-ideological opposition alliances in recent decades.[48]

As much as Iraq was a source of strength for groups like Kifaya in that it facilitated the formation of cross-ideological partnerships within the opposition, at the same time Iraq was major source of weakness for them. The fact that Kifaya adopted resistance to U.S. hegemony in the region as the main cause framing its agenda made it vulnerable to the jabs of the Mubarak regime and its supporters. Before Mubarak's demise, proregime commentators questioned how a movement that proclaims an anti-imperialist stance in its positions on Iraq and Palestine still manages to converge with U.S. policies in its calls for democratic change.[49] "Any relationship with any foreign power, but especially the Americans, is the kiss of death. We don't need this kiss," says Kifaya cofounder Abul Ela Madi.[50] Focusing on this particular vulnerability, state-controlled media helped reinforce rumors that Kifaya was receiving support from the CIA.[51] Vocal proregime opinion shapers charged that Kifaya was a mere executor of American schemes to destabilize Egypt.[52] In an interview with *Le Figaro*, Mubarak himself accused Kifaya of "exploiting international conditions to put pressure on the regime and gain strength from abroad" and expressed "suspicions about its sources of funding."[53] Within this media war between Kifaya and the regime, Iraq War became a central theme. Mohammed

---

48. For more on these attempts, see Abdel Gaffar Shukr, *al-Tahalufat al-Siyasiyya wa al-'Amal al-Mushtarak fi Misr, 1976–1993* [Political alliances and joint action in Egypt, 1976–1993] (Cairo: Markaz al-Buhuth al-Arabiyya, 1994).

49. For examples of these attacks, see Shabaan, *Kifaya al-madi wa al-mutaqbal.*

50. "Egypt Shuts Door on Dissent as U.S. Officials Back Away."

51. Oweidat et al., *The Kefaya Movement.*

52. Shabaan, *Kifaya al-madi wa al-mutaqbal*, 154

53. Oweidat et al., *The Kefaya Movement*, 32.

Gamal Arafa of *Islam-Online* news service recounts how this trend played itself out in one of Kifaya's demonstrations in Cairo. While Kifaya's supporters yelled slogans condemning the war in Iraq and the regime's complicity in supporting this effort, according to Arafa, counterdemonstrators organized by the ruling party responded with slogans that described Kifaya as U.S. agents, likening them to the prewar Iraqi opposition that collaborated with the American-led occupation. Proregime slogans reveal a great deal about the former ruling party's strategy in exploiting anti-American sentiments to undermine Kifaya and the rest of the opposition: "No to America. No to the poisonous freedom"; "Yes to Mubarak, no to the traitors and foreign agents"; "No to every coward Egyptian who collaborates with the Americans"; "Yes to Mubarak"; "Enough dependency, enough foreign agency, the Egyptian people are not for sale"; "Yes for Mubarak and no to foreign funding."[54] There is evidence that the regime's anti-Kifaya media campaign was somewhat successful in weakening the group's internal cohesion. For example, Kifaya cofounder George Ishaq had to step down as coordinator of the movement, apparently in response to state-sponsored media allegations that he had attended a U.S.-sponsored conference alongside Israeli participants, a move that reportedly heightened internal tensions within the movement and alienated its nationalist elements.[55]

There is no doubt that Kifaya struggled to withstand these recurrent internal divisions, which pro-Mubarak pundits reinforced by questioning the movement's anti-American credentials and linking it to U.S. efforts to support democratic reform in the Middle East.[56] Nonetheless, in the long-run Kifaya helped pave the way to a new form of contentious political activism in Egypt that, years later, played a major role in the uprising that led to Mubarak's downfall in 2011. Mubarak's demise can in part be attributed to Egypt's youth protest movements' success in linking calls for political change to widespread bread-and-butter needs of Egyptians, as opposed to pan-Arab causes, like Iraq, which dominated antiregime contentious activism between 2003 and 2006. In fact, the limited role that pan-Arab issues played in justifying calls for the January 25 uprising arguably shielded anti-Mubarak demonstrators from the accusation of "for-

---

54. "Tahat she'ar "kifayya" harb al-modhahrat tashta'el bi misr" [Under the rubric of kifayya, the demonstration wars fire up in Egypt], *Islamonline.net*, April 2, 2005, www.islamonline.net/arabic/news/2005-04/02/article08.shtml.

55. "Ma wara' al-khabbar—azmat kifaya al-dakhiliyya."

56. For a recent example of such attacks by progovernment commentators, see Mohamed Ali Ibrahim, "Kifaya Al-Misriyya wa shaqiqatiha Kmara al-amrikiyya" [Egyptian Kifaya and its American sister Kmara], *Al-Ghumoriya*, May 27, 2010, www.eltahrir.net/chairman/theeel_31.html.

eign agency" and from the nationalist rhetoric that the NDP had used to undermine Kifaya years earlier.

Conclusion

The U.S.-sponsored nation-building experiment in Iraq may have fallen short of delivering the promise of democratic change to the rest of the Middle East that supporters of the U.S. invasion had anticipated. However, it certainly shaped patterns of political activism in the rest of the region, sometimes in surprising and contradictory ways. Sectarian violence in the new Iraq, as well as the political dominance of Iran-friendly Shiite groups in the post-2003 political order, colored public perceptions of the efforts advanced by Shiite activists in nearby states to gain greater political rights and representation. By reinforcing sectarian divides in other countries, the new Iraq in some ways undermined cross-sectarian opposition cooperation, as the case of Bahrain illustrates. Ultimately Arab autocrats emerged victorious in that particular battle, as fears of chaos, sectarian violence, and foreign meddling enhanced support for the political status quo in countries with significant Shiite populations.

This analysis shows that the Bush administration was correct about one thing, that the new Iraq would galvanize political activism in the rest of the region. Yet ironically, as the case of Kifaya shows, much of this activism was not aimed at celebrating or supporting the U.S. democracy promotion agenda, but rather at resisting and protesting Washington's policies. The story of Kifaya shows how the war paved the way for cross-ideological cooperation within the Egyptian opposition. The "Iraq cause" and its resonance with ideologically diverse actors in the Egyptian political arena justified an unusual partnership between Islamist and secular actors. It also rationalized their call for transformative political change, on grounds that resisting the so-called American schemes in the region demands serious democratic reforms. Even in this confrontation, however, Arab authoritarianism carried the day—at least until the challenge of the Arab Spring came to surface. While widespread dissatisfaction with American policies in Iraq helped Kifaya maintain its unity and mobilize supporters, this same dissatisfaction ultimately became a weapon for the Mubarak regime. The regime used the Iraq cause to draw parallels between its challengers, including Kifaya, and members of the Iraqi opposition who collaborated with the U.S. occupation of their country. As a result, despite the anti-imperialist credentials that Kifaya built through its opposition to U.S. policies in Iraq, Mubarak's supporters often labeled Kifaya members as stooges for Washington's plots to control the region. It was only when Mubarak's challengers picked a different battle that had little to do with Iraq or foreign policy—namely, the failure of the state to address the widespread socio-economic grievances and imbalances in Egyptian society—that the opposition was able to mount an effective antiauthoritarian challenge that proved immune to the regime's traditional accusations of foreign agency.

The stories told in this chapter, whether Iraq's troubled democratic experiment or struggles for political change in the Arab region, are evolving and (one would hope) are anything but over. There is a strong temptation to project a happier ending, one in which Iraqi democracy succeeds in a way that offers the rest of the Arab world a successful model that could encourage meaningful democratic change in nearby countries that continue to resist pressures for reform. There are a number of considerations, however, that call into question the likelihood of such a scenario.

It is important to note that, notwithstanding the relative improvements in the security situation that Iraq has seen in the past few years, the Iraqi nation-building experience is yet to yield a stable democratic model that could plausibility inspire democratic change in the rest of the region. The long conflicts that surrounded the outcome of the 2010 election is one of many examples illustrating that the stability of democracy in Iraq is at best in development, and at worst tenuous. Moreover, it will take more than just free and fair elections and seamless power transitions for democratization in Iraq to succeed and, equally importantly, for democracy to endure.[57] While a full assessment of the Iraqi political system is beyond the scope of this discussion, it takes a great deal of diligence to overlook the fact that the Iraqi political system continues to suffer from major deficiencies in its protection of fundamental civil liberties, including freedom of expression and religion, the rule of law, and judicial independence.[58] In sum, for those who ask whether democracy in Iraq can inspire positive change in the rest of the region, the short answer is no, because democratization in Iraq, by most optimistic standards, is far from complete.

For those who wonder whether successful democratization in Iraq, along the lines of the third scenario that Phebe Marr and Sam Parker outline in their chapter, could someday inspire a regionwide yearning for democracy, the answer is less certain. Although many scholars take seriously the notion that successful democratization in one country could inspire a similar process in nearby countries,[59] the unpleasant history of post-2003 Iraq

---

57. Larry Diamond articulates this perspective eloquently in Larry Diamond, *The Spirit of Democracy: The Struggle to Build Free Societies throughout the World* (New York: Times Books and Henry Holt and Company, 2008).

58. Freedom House summarizes these challenges in the Iraq section of *Freedom in World* (New York: Freedom House, 2010), www.freedomhouse.org/template.cfm?page=22&year=2010&country=7843.

59. See, for example, Brinks and Coppedge, "Diffusion Is No Illusion," 463–489; and Gleditsch and Ward, "Diffusion and the International Context of Democratization," 911–933.

will likely continue to negatively shape Arab political activists' views of the democratic experiment in Iraq, even if it succeeds. Images of sectarian violence and chaos from earlier stages of Iraq's nation-building experience may continue to uphold the rhetoric of Arab autocrats and their supporters that the road to democracy is too horrific to justify meaningful political change. Such discourse will probably remain a powerful force in shaping Arab public perceptions if the new Iraq fails to prove wrong those who believe that the country's political order is built on the marginalization and persecution of Sunni communities. Iraq will hardly become a force for democratic change in the region if its politics remain stuck in sectarian divisions and identity conflicts.

Finally, as recent developments have shown, the prospects for transformative political change in the Arab world will certainly not hinge upon the outcome of Iraq's democratic experiment, however it ends, though developments inside Iraq can strengthen authoritarian survival strategies in other countries, as this chapter has demonstrated. Even so, as long as Arab autocrats continue to label their challengers as agents of the American (or Iranian) Middle East project, and as long as opposition groups continue to brand their rulers as lackeys of Western imperialism, Iraq as a policy issue may remain an important element in debates on political reform in the rest of the region.

9

Ties that Bind

The United States, Iraq, and the Neighbors

Kenneth M. Pollack

In any conversation about Iraq and its neighbors, the United States is always the proverbial elephant in the living room. For some years to come, the United States will unavoidably play a critical role in Iraq. American troops will remain in Iraq until at least the beginning of 2012, and it is widely expected that a large training and advisory mission (likely with some residual combat capability) will remain for some time thereafter, although that remains to be negotiated. The United States has also pledged itself, by way of a Strategic Framework Agreement signed with Iraq in 2008, to a long-term program of economic, military, and diplomatic assistance to Iraq encompassing virtually every aspect of Iraq's myriad reconstruction and development needs. And Iraqis, and their neighbors, will continue to believe that the United States is pulling all the strings in Iraq long after it has stopped even trying.

Consequently, when Iraq's neighbors look at Baghdad, they often see Washington—gladly or grudgingly. For Iraq's neighbors, their relationship with the new Iraq is inextricably intertwined with their relationship to the United States. They know that actions directed at Iraq will often trigger a response from the United States. Indeed, for some of Iraq's neighbors, the primary aim of their policy toward Iraq is really to influence Washington. For other regional states, their policies are torn between the imperatives of their bilateral relationship with Iraq and their bilateral relationship with the United States—which can potentially push in completely opposite directions. Finally there are those countries whose goals toward Iraq are powerfully reinforced by their policies toward the United States, making it extremely difficult to change their policies if Washington does not like them.

For all of these reasons, and as all of the preceding chapters of this book have made clear, one cannot talk about Iraq's regional role or even its bilateral relations without discussing the United States. But that does not mean that America's interests regarding Iraq's relationships with its neighbors are identical to Iraq's interests in those same relationships. As a new Iraqi government increasingly asserts itself and pursues what it sees to be its own goals, important differences are emerging on a range of critical issues regarding Iraq's internal and external policies. It is no longer the case, as it was from 2003 to 2009, that whatever was best for Iraq was therefore what was best for the United States because the United States had to see Iraq succeed in every way.

Today, Iraq's fate is more and more its own to decide, whether Americans like it or not. This is not to say that the United States no longer has vital interests at stake in Iraq—it does. It is merely to point out that since the signing of the Security Agreement of 2008, which ended the American occupation on January 1, 2009, America's interests in Iraq have changed dramatically and so too, therefore, must American thinking about Iraq's relations with its neighbors.

What's in It for the United States?

America's interests in Iraq begin simply, but become complex as the aperture is expanded. At the most basic level, the United States needs to ensure that Iraq is not a cause of instability in the Persian Gulf that could impede or diminish the irreplaceable flow of oil from the region. This means that Iraq needs to be both stable itself, so that spillover from an Iraqi civil war is not roiling the Gulf region, and that Iraq cannot be an aggressive, expansionist state threatening its neighbors. These constitute the United States' minimal requirements from Iraq in the future. However, it would also be in America's interest to see Iraq emerge as a strong, prosperous, and pluralist (even democratic) state allied with the United States. This represents America's maximal interest in Iraq and should be seen as an aspirational goal rather than an irreducible necessity.

As Phebe Marr and Sam Parker sketched out in their chapter on the view from Baghdad, at present, there seem to be three broad scenarios for Iraq's future: a return to civil war, slow progress toward an imperfect form of stability, and somewhat more rapid progress toward a strong, pluralist state. It should be apparent that the first scenario would fail to meet even

America's minimal interests in Iraq, the second would satisfy only its minimal requirements, while the third offers the possibility of achieving the maximal goals.

Consequently, all U.S. policy toward Iraq, including U.S. policy toward Iraq's neighbors, has to be framed to avoid the reemergence of civil war (or the emergence of a rapacious new Iraq). Beyond this, whatever additional resources and energy the United States chooses to devote to Iraq should be employed to try to help push Iraq from the second scenario into the third. But the former is a requirement, a sine qua non for the United States' vital interests, while the latter is merely a highly desirable bonus.

Although Iraq is making progress, it is hardly out of the woods yet. In particular, the Iraqis need to establish a government that can actually govern. Iraq remains a deeply dysfunctional society: its infrastructure, education, economy, sanitation, water, agriculture, and legal and industrial systems desperately need repair, redefinition, and institutional guidance. Similarly, there are a plethora of outstanding differences remaining from the civil war (the hydrocarbon law, the status of Kirkuk and other disputed territories, and the relationship among the central government, the provinces, and the Kurdistan Regional Government are only the best known). All of these desperately need to be addressed, and they can only be addressed by a new Iraqi government, one with the political strength to strike compromises, build institutions, let contracts, hire and fire personnel, and make laws that previous governments have lacked. Without such a government, at best Iraq will stagger along as the sick man of the Gulf, able to be bullied by its neighbors, unable to defend itself (militarily, economically, or diplomatically), and a constant battleground for its neighbors' proxies— effectively a larger version of Lebanon today. At worst, the failings of the government will allow and enable militias to reemerge, lay claim to territory and population, and reengage in civil war—like Lebanon in 1985 or Iraq in 2006.

In addition to these worrisome signs from Iraq itself, the historical record also demonstrates that the risk of a resumption of civil war remains all too dangerous. Extensive academic work on intercommunal civil wars akin to what Iraq experienced in 2005–7 demonstrates that roughly 50 percent of the time the country falls back into civil war within five years of a cease-fire. Moreover, when the country in question possesses valuable natural resources like diamonds, gold, or oil, the likelihood rises even higher.[1] Thus, Iraq is highly vulnerable to a resurgence of civil war,

---

1. Paul Collier and Anke Hoeffler, *Greed and Grievance in Civil War*, Policy Research Working Paper Series no. 2355 (World Bank, May 2000); T. David Mason, *Sustaining the Peace after Civil War* (Carlisle, PA: Strategic Studies Institute, U.S. Army War College, December 2007); Barbara Walter and Jack Snyder, eds., *Civil Wars, Insecurity, and Intervention* (New York: Columbia University Press,

and the forces that could drag it back down are omnipresent, floating just below the surface of Iraqi politics—and across its borders. The militias and insurgents are down, but not out. The fear and anger remains pervasive. And many Iraqi leaders still seem to believe that they would be better off with a return to violence than a continuation of peace.[2]

If Iraq returns to civil war, it will be disastrous for the security of the Gulf. As history has demonstrated, major intercommunal civil wars inevitably generate large-scale refugee flows, secessionist movements, terrorism, economic disruption, the radicalization of neighboring populations, and foreign military interventions throughout the wider region. Indeed, Iraq in 2005–7 was generating every single one of these manifestations of spillover among its neighbors, and examples of worse abound from Congo to Lebanon to Yugoslavia to Somalia to Afghanistan. In many cases, the spillover from a major intercommunal civil war in one country can cause civil war in another country, and/or spark a regional war over the carcass of that state.[3] All of this would be devastating to the Persian Gulf region and America's vital interests.

As disconcerting as the history of recurrent civil wars and their impact on their neighbors may be, there is an important silver lining. What the academic literature also demonstrates is that when a major, external great power is willing to serve as peacekeeper and mediator in an intercommunal civil war, then the likelihood of a recurrence falls to less than one in three.[4] This, of course, is the crucial role played by the United States in Iraq today. The key is that the United States needs to be able to continue to play that role for some time to come, until Iraq is truly able to handle its own security, diplomacy, economy, and politics. And that is going to be hard because the United States is no longer in charge in Iraq. Which is why it is going to need the help of Iraq's neighbors.

An End in Itself or a Means to an End?

Since 2003, Washington's relationships with Iraq's neighbors regarding Iraq have not been easy. For much of the 1990s, most of the states of the

1999); Barbara Walter, "Does Conflict Beget Conflict? Explaining Recurring Civil War," *Journal of Peace Research* 41, no. 3 (May 2004): 371–388.

2. See, for instance, Kenneth M. Pollack, "The Battle for Baghdad," *National Interest*, no. 103 (September/October 2009), 8–17.

3. On the effects and impact of civil wars on neighboring states, see Daniel L. Byman and Kenneth M. Pollack, *Things Fall Apart: Containing the Spillover from an Iraqi Civil War* (Washington, DC: Brookings Institution Press, 2007).

4. Walter and Snyder, eds., *Civil Wars*; Walter, "Does Conflict Beget Conflict?"

Middle East had consistently told the United States they would support a "decisive" American move that would topple Saddam Hussein from power altogether—but nothing less. In the run-up to the invasion, however, there was considerable discord. Some continued to back the Bush administration in private, while remaining largely quiet in public. Others, including some of the most important leaders in the Arab world, like King Abdullah of Saudi Arabia, opposed an invasion. Many did so because they feared that the Bush administration did not understand Iraq or the Pandora's box it was opening and would create as many problems as it solved. When Washington invaded anyway, few were willing to put their opposition (and their fears) behind them and support the American efforts to rebuild the country. When it did turn out that the Bush administration was woefully unready to deal with the problems of Iraq, and by its failures loosed a host of troubles upon the region, Iraq's neighbors were largely content to sit smugly and suffer the consequences. Few were willing to do much to try to mend the damage, even the damage being done to themselves.

Thus, from March 18, 2003, till January 1, 2009, Iraq was America's problem largely alone. Despite the Bush administration's rhetoric of a "coalition of the willing," few states made meaningful contributions to the reconstruction of Iraq, and virtually none of its neighbors made any constructive contributions at all. And the United States desperately needed their help. Washington needed debt forgiveness (and the neighbors did make some concessions there) for Iraq, money, translators, diplomatic cover, and diplomatic recognition for the new Iraqi government, foreign investment in Iraqi industries other than oil, and support in the United Nations and other international forums. Perhaps more than any of these constructive activities, the United States needed Iraq's neighbors to stop doing destructive things that were helping to propel Iraq into civil war. Washington needed them to stop Salafi terrorists from crossing their territory to get to Iraq (and returning when they needed sanctuary), to stop supplying weapons and money to Iraq's warring militias, to stop dumping cheap manufactured goods on the Iraqi economy, to stop buying smuggled Iraqi oil, and to stop intervening with their military forces (Turkey) or irregular warfare specialists (Iran and possibly Jordan) in Iraq.[5]

Since 2009, however, all of that has changed. First, the United States is no longer in charge in Iraq. Since the signing of the 2008 Security Agreement between Iraq and the United States and the end of American occupation in January 2009, Iraq is now fully in charge. The United States is

---

5. Author's interviews with U.S. military and intelligence officers, Iraq, 2007–9.

no longer responsible for Iraq's fate, except in the macro sense of needing (for our its interests) to prevent a relapse of civil war. Second, as Marr and Parker's chapter in this volume related, Iraq is slowly coming into its own. It has emerged from civil war and, while it may slip back into renewed conflict, at present it seems to be finding its feet and reasserting its own interests. Moreover, the emergence of democratic pressures as powerful factors shaping Iraqi politics means that Iraq's own leaders are increasingly being held accountable by the Iraqi people for the country's welfare. In other words, America is increasingly less responsible for Iraq's fate, and Iraq's own leaders increasingly are.

As a result, America's interests in Iraq have changed, and what the United States needs from Iraq's neighbors is changing too. Indeed, at some level, Washington's approach to Iraq's neighbors can be seen as having gone through a sea change. The United States no longer desperately needs the help of Iraq's neighbors to help it succeed in Iraq. Instead, Iraq's own leaders desperately need American help with Iraq's neighbors in order for them to succeed. That is a very important thing to understand.

This point needs to be considered in light of America's needs in terms of the larger Iraq issue. As noted, for its own interests, the United States needs to ensure that Iraq avoids falling back into civil war. It would also be desirable, but not essential, that Iraq emerge as a strong U.S. ally and a prosperous, pluralist state.

The key to all of these American objectives is Iraq's domestic politics. They are now the "center of gravity" for American policy toward Iraq. If Iraq falls back into civil war it will be the result of some catastrophic failure of Iraq's domestic politics—a rupture between Baghdad and the Kurds, the Sunni tribes deciding that the Shi'a will never give them their fair share of power in Baghdad and so returning to insurgency, violence among rival Shiite factions vying for power, a government unwilling to relinquish power after an electoral (or parliamentary defeat), a military coup that succeeds only in fracturing the army and resuscitating the militias. These are the (unfortunately all-too-plausible) nightmare scenarios that haunt the leadership in Baghdad and Washington, the pathways back to civil war.

The problem for Washington is that while U.S. influence in Iraq remains very great, it is much less than what it once was. The United States is no longer the viceroy of Iraq. While the Iraqis are still very dependent upon it, psychologically as well as materially, that dependence is steadily diminishing. That trend line is also being steepened by the attenuation of U.S. resources committed to Iraq. Everyone knows that America's troop presence declined to 48,000 by August 2011, and may well evaporate altogether on December 31, 2011, when the Security Agreement comes to an end. But America is also cutting provincial reconstruction teams, civilian personnel, aid programs, and everything else it has been providing Iraq.

As a result, it is absolutely critical that the United States learns to prioritize its interests in Iraq. Washington no longer has the influence to do everything it would like to do. Instead, it must focus its remaining influence on those things that are most important to American interests, and at the top of that list is Iraq's domestic politics. It is not that the United States needs to control or even guide Iraqi domestic politics. Instead, it is about ensuring that Iraqis "play by the rules" of their own system: that no one employs violence, that no one subverts the constitution, that disputes are settled by political and legal processes, that corruption does not undermine the economy or the political system, and that Iraqis—both as individuals and groups—develop a sense of trust in their system and in each other. That is the only way out of the civil war trap for a country like Iraq.

The difficulty that the United States faces is that the one area where the Iraqis absolutely do not want its help is with their domestic politics (except, of course, any one who is losing through the legal political process, who then wants the United States to intervene to advance *their* interests). The Iraqis are thrilled to have American help with security, with diplomacy, with their economy, with their legal system, with their educational system, with anything except their domestic politics. Since 2005, whichever group has been in power in Baghdad has increasingly seen the United States as a meddlesome interloper because America has systematically stepped in to prevent it from abusing the powers of government to serve its narrow political interests. If the United States is going to prevent a resumption of civil war, that is exactly what it will have to keep doing for some time to come, and while that is unquestionably in the best interests of Iraq and the Iraqi people, it is not necessarily in the best interests of whoever is in power in Baghdad.

Diplomacy as Leverage

This brings us back to Iraq's relations with its neighbors and the U.S. role. In the past, Washington needed the neighbors to do things to help America's reconstruction efforts in Iraq. But those days are now past. Increasingly, it is Iraq's own policies that could benefit from the help of neighbors, and the Iraqis need U.S. help to get it. That means that Iraq's relationships with its neighbors, and American influence with Iraq's neighbors, need to be seen as sources of *leverage* with the government of Iraq.

Indeed, everything other than Iraq's domestic politics should be seen as sources of leverage. This may seem counterintuitive to Americans accustomed to fighting to rebuild Iraq's economy, security services, educational system, etc. However, this misses the extent to which the U.S.-Iraqi relationship has changed as a result of the implementation of the Security Agreement and the end of the U.S. occupation. Previously, the United States attempted to rebuild those things because Washington needed the American reconstruction of Iraq to succeed. For better or worse, that effort has ended; it is no longer the American reconstruction of Iraq, but the Iraqi reconstruction of Iraq. It is no longer a vital interest of the United States that they succeed, although it is a vital interest that they not fail. All of the scenarios that lead to failure are all about Iraq's domestic politics. For instance, it is certainly true that economic collapse could lead to failure, but given Iraq's enormous (and growing) oil wealth, actual economic collapse could only be the result of outrageous mismanagement of the economy, which would stem from domestic political problems, not pure economic factors. Likewise, Iraq's security forces are strong enough—and the threats weak enough—that absent a catastrophic breakdown in domestic politics, the security forces should now be more than adequate to handle them. Again, all of the scenarios for failure begin with large-scale problems in Iraq's fragile domestic politics. That is why everything that the United States provides Iraq today needs to be treated as sources of leverage to maintain American influence over Iraqi domestic politics, the most important thing going on in Iraq today, the one thing that could threaten America's vital interests in Iraq, and the one thing that the Iraqi government wants to try to keep the United States out of.[6]

A nice example of this in the diplomatic realm, where Iraq has some big needs when it comes to Kuwait. As Judith Yaphe's chapter describes, the Iraqis need Kuwait to forgive Iraq's residual debt from the Iran-Iraq War, they need Kuwait to agree to end the reparations payments resulting from the 1990 invasion, and both the Iraqis and Kuwaitis need to arrive at an equitable arrangement regarding the interstate border that will allow the Iraqis free access to their port at Umm Qasr (described in greater length later in this chapter). The truth is that the Iraqis are probably not going to be able to secure any of these things on their own. It is going to require the United States putting tremendous pressure on Kuwait to make concessions on all of these issues—along with some Iraqi compromises. These are very important problems for Iraq's leadership, but they are not terribly important for American interests in Iraq. Consequently, they should become part of a panoply of assistance that the United States provides to

---

6. Anything in the Strategic Framework Agreement—the pact between Iraq and the United States by which the United States agreed to provide Iraq with long-term military, political, economic, and diplomatic aid—should be considered as leverage by the United States to continue to play an active role in Iraqi domestic politics.

Iraq in return for preserving America's ability to influence Iraq's domestic politics to prevent it from exploding into renewed civil strife.

Diplomatic Geometry

All of Iraq's neighbors are equally important in advancing America's interests in Iraq, but some are more equal than others, to paraphrase Orwell. They are all important because all of them create potential opportunities and risks to Iraq. Iraq has equities with all of them, and to the extent that the United States remains concerned about anything that affects Iraq, all are therefore important. Moreover, in virtually every case, Iraq's equities with each of its neighbors are bound up with issues related to the United States.

Syria is a good place to start. Iraq has critical long-term issues with Syria over water rights, trade, the return and status of Iraqi refugees, and Syria's apparent interest in acquiring nuclear weapons. However, Baghdad's most pressing problem with Damascus is Syria's continued willingness to allow small numbers of Salafi terrorists to cross Syrian territory to Iraq, where they are often the deadliest of the remaining terrorists still plaguing Iraq. The Iraqi regime believes that many of the worst bombings they have experienced since 2008 have been perpetrated by figures who crossed into Iraq from Syria. The Iraqis are furious at Damascus over this and have repeatedly demanded that the Syrians cease and desist.

The problem is that Syria's audience seems to be the United States more than Iraq, as Mona Yacoubian points out elsewhere in this volume. The Syrians continue to want a rapprochement with the United States, a grand bargain in which they would get a peace treaty with Israel that meets all of their needs in Lebanon and the Golan, along with all of the American diplomatic, economic, and perhaps military support they could ever dream of. The Syrians seem to regard the flow of foreign fighters into Iraq (which they have reduced over the years), and the provision of sanctuary for others, to be an important source of leverage in that effort: it is a nagging pain for Washington that Damascus hopes will remind the United States that it cannot afford to ignore Syria, and a chit to be traded to the United States in return for everything that Syria seeks when the deal is finally struck. Thus, Iraq's problem with Syria is ultimately America's problem with Syria.

As noted above, Kuwait is another interesting example. The Iraqis and Kuwaitis still have some very important unfinished business. Although Iraq's per capita GDP in 2009 amounted to only $3,600 (159th in the world) while Kuwait's stood at $54,100 (7th in the world), Kuwait continues to collect a percentage of Iraqi oil revenues as reparations for Saddam's invasion and brutal occupation. This would be ridiculous if it weren't appalling: Saddam is gone, the Iraqi people—who cannot be held complicit for his actions—desperately need every nickel, and the Kuwaitis are rich as Croesus. Similarly, in demarcating the border after the Persian Gulf War, the UN Commission effectively hemmed in Iraq's second port of Umm Qasr (one of only two it possesses), making it impossible for ships to pass up the Khawr Abdallah waterway and disembark there without passing through Kuwaiti territorial waters. This too is a situation requiring obvious remedy, probably in the form of an agreement between Kuwait and Iraq governing transit along the Khawr Abdallah to Umm Qasr.

Like others in the region, the Kuwaitis are deeply concerned about Iraq's future and they have so far refused to negotiate either issue because they see them as leverage over a potentially unfriendly Iraqi government. Of course, their unwillingness to negotiate makes it more likely that they will get an unfriendly Iraqi government. It is obvious to all concerned that the United States will ultimately have to broker a deal between Kuwait and Iraq. Only the United States has the influence with both states to press them to make the necessary concessions and find ways to reward them for those compromises. Indeed, a frequent complaint of senior Iraqi officials and diplomats about the Obama administration is that it has made virtually no effort to address Iraq's disputes with Kuwait.

Iraq's differences with Kuwait and Syria are very important issues for Iraq, and will almost certainly require American intervention to resolve. Thus, they are also important to America's interests in Iraq—and important sources of leverage with Iraq. But as important as these issues are, they pale in comparison with America's interest in Iraq's relationships with Turkey, Saudi Arabia, and Iran. If any of Iraq's relationships with its neighbors can be said to be critical, it is these three dyads that are critical—not only to Iraq's interests but also for securing America's interests in Iraq. Indeed, all of them are really triangular relationships among Iraq, the United States, and the other state in question. To put it bluntly, Washington needs to find ways to keep Turkey doing the right thing, get Saudi Arabia to start doing the right thing, and keep Iran from doing too much of the wrong thing. As always, all of this is easier said than done.

Turkey

As Henri Barkey's chapter in this volume explains, Turkey has been doing all the right things with regard to Iraq. It has managed to play a constructive role with both the central government in Baghdad and the Kurdistan Regional Government (KRG) in Erbil, no small feat. And it has played a constructive role diplomatically, economically, and even militarily. Turkey's efforts have not solved Iraq's problems, but they have been unquestionably salutary. Consequently, the United States has a strong interest in seeing them continue.

It is certainly true that Turkey has been pursuing this course because Ankara sees it in its own interests to do so. This may not always be the case, however, and it would be useful for the United States to provide Turkey with some added incentives to stay this course. Elsewhere, Barkey has described a range of steps that the United States could take to help cement Turkey's positive role in Iraq for the medium or even long term. These are worth summarizing as thoughtful examples of the ways that Washington should be consciously (and conscientiously) working to keep Turkey on the right path in Iraq:

- The United States should press the KRG to extirpate the remnants of the terrorist Kurdistan Worker's Party (PKK) from northern Iraq, a critical security concern of the Turks.
- The United States should open a consulate in Erbil, not only to demonstrate solidarity with the Kurds, but also with Ankara, which has already opened its own consulate there.
- The United States should push Iraq to ensure that its natural gas exports (when these finally come online in several years) flow north through Turkey's Nabucco pipeline.
- The United States should establish qualified industrial zones between Turkey and Iraq (including Turkey and the KRG) to promote trade and create jobs in both countries.[7]
- American diplomats should include Turkish diplomats in their efforts today in hope that doing so will result in Turkish diplomats returning the favor later (when they may have more influence or entrée than their American counterparts).

Saudi Arabia

Since 2003, Saudi Arabia has been a great source of frustration for successive American administrations and Iraqi governments. From Washington and Baghdad's perspectives, Riyadh ought to see its interests best served by what the United States and Iraq most fervently desire as well—a strong, stable new Iraq. Both Americans and Iraqis tend to argue (probably correctly) that strength and stability will require pluralism, the rule of law, and political equality to ensure that all of Iraq's major subelements do not feel discriminated against and thus do not resort to force of arms. This means that a strong, stable Iraq will almost certainly require continued progress on democratization, and a democratic Iraq means an Iraqi electorate

---

7. Henri Barkey, "Turkey's New Engagement in Iraq: Embracing Iraqi Kurdistan," Special Report no. 237 (Washington, DC: United States Institute of Peace Press, May 2010), 14–16.

dominated by Iraq's Shiite majority even if not necessarily by sectarian Shiite political parties.

Of course, as Toby Jones' chapter explains, the Saudis do not see it that way. King Abdullah has steadfastly refused to take actions that could be helpful to Iraq. He has refused it diplomatic recognition, let alone diplomatic support. He has done nothing to encourage Saudi investment in and trade with Iraq, and has committed relatively paltry amounts of aid. Neither have the Saudis made much of an effort to curb the flow of Saudi terrorists traveling to Iraq to make mischief. Indeed, the king has generally treated Iraqi prime minister Nuri al-Maliki like a pariah.

King Abdullah claims that his antipathy is entirely directed at Maliki himself, and that once he is gone (if he is gone), Riyadh will gladly reconcile and aid Iraq regardless of who is in charge. But there is reason to doubt this claim. Many Saudis will openly say that they cannot and will not countenance Shiite dominance of Iraq, whether it is Maliki or someone else. Indeed, Saudi Arabia poured money into Iraq during the 2010 election campaign, backing every Iraqi Sunni group as well as 'Ayad Allawi's secular Iraqqiya Party. Although Allawi is a Shi'a, he has long been considered acceptable by Sunnis in and out of Iraq, and much of his electoral support was drawn from Iraq's Sunni tribal community—the Iraqi groups closest to Saudi Arabia.

None of this is helpful to Iraq or to American interests in Iraq. The problem is that Saudi policy toward Iraq is not just unhelpful, it is positively dangerous and is exacerbating the flaws in Iraq's domestic politics that could bring about a resurgence of civil war. At one level, Saudi financial support for the Sunnis can be seen as a counterweight to Iran's financial support to various Shiite groups. However, this backing—coupled with Riyadh's unwillingness to countenance continued Shiite dominance of the government in Baghdad—risks reinforcing those voices in the Iraqi Sunni community who argue that the Shi'a will never give them equal power in the central government and therefore Iraq's Sunni-dominated provinces should either cease cooperation with the central government or actively oppose it through a return to insurgency. Both would lead to the resumption of civil war, the latter merely quicker than the former.

Moreover, as the de facto leader of the Arab world, Saudi Arabia's unwillingness to accept Iraq back into the Arab fold will force Baghdad into the arms of Tehran as its only alternative. This is not inevitable: the vast majority of Iraq's Shi'a, including all of the current major leaders, are nationalists who would prefer to keep the Iranians at arms length, and ultimately see themselves first and foremost as Arab Iraqis, not Shi'a. It is important to always remember that the Iraqi Shi'a did not rise up in revolt against Saddam during the Iran-Iraq War as Khomeini expected; they fought for Iraq because they hated the Persians more than Saddam. Similarly, since 2003, Shiite leaders in Iraq have been consistently forced to demonstrate to the Iraqi electorate that they are not beholden to Iran, and conspiracy theories to the contrary notwithstanding, all of the available evidence suggests Maliki himself sees Iran as more of a threat than an ally. Yet if Iraq is left with no alternative, it will turn to Tehran by default, and that is not in anyone's interest—not Iraq's, not America's, and not Saudi Arabia's.

Consequently, Washington needs to make a major push to bring Riyadh around on the issue of Iraq. Certainly this is going to require a lot of long, patient conversations with the Saudis in which American diplomats will have to work to convince their Saudi counterparts that their fears about Iraq are unfounded—and that the best way to avoid the resumption of civil war that is Riyadh's worst nightmare is to buttress the new Iraqi government, and not to keep undermining it. However, it is going to require more than that. Part of reassuring the Saudis is going to mean bringing them into American and Iraqi counsels so that they can become comfortable with Iraq's leaders and their plans. A good vehicle for this, ultimately, would be the regional security structures discussed later in this chapter, but those are somewhat longer-term projects. In the near term, it might be helpful for Washington to broker a series of meetings among U.S., Iraqi, and Saudi officials to discuss Iraq's future course. Over time, this might even be expanded to a standing commission that could bring in other Gulf Cooperation Council (GCC) countries as well, and expand its scope to address collective economic and political matters. What should be clear though is that Washington cannot simply throw up its hands in frustration with the Saudis as an answer.

Iran

And then there's Iran. Early on after the invasion, Iran's forbearance was an important element in the sluggishness of Iraq's descent into civil war. However, since early 2006, Iran has played a largely unhelpful role in Iraq. Iran suffered some critical setbacks in the ousting of Muqtada al-Sadr's Jaish al-Mahdi from Basra and Sadr City in 2008, the defeat of their partisans in the 2009 provincial elections, and their inability to forge a Shiite alliance before the 2010 national elections, but they have not given up the fight. To a great extent, they have simply changed their methods, and retain considerable influence in Iraq. They continue to fund many Iraqi political parties, militias, and terrorist groups. They dominate Iraqi trade and its lucrative religious pilgrimage industry. They remain influential in Iraqi religious circles, and they have reminded Iraq that when the Americans finally leave, they can pose a serious military threat to Iraq too.

As Mohsen Milani's chapter lays out, most of Iran's leadership abhors a civil war in Iraq, but others might welcome it. Moreover, Iran's leadership has a very complicated skein of goals and interests in Iraq, and throughout history such complexity can often lead a state to take actions that result in outcomes it never sought and may actually have tried to prevent. Iran's support of armed Iraqi groups and heavy-handed interference in Iraqi politics is not meant to cause the resumption of civil war, but especially in light of the historic propensities in this direction, that could well be the result.

Even if Iran's efforts do not help propel Iran back into civil war, if they succeed, they will likely produce a weak and divided Iraq subject to Iranian manipulation and domination. That is, after all, Iran's principal positive objective in Iraq. At least until the Iranian regime is ready to make peace with the United States and its allies in the Middle East and refrain from undermining regional stability by support to all manner of violent rejectionist groups across the region, such an outcome would be a very significant threat to American interests. It is also not something that the Iraqis or its Arab allies would find desirable or even palatable. Indeed, it would greatly exacerbate fears of a new "Shiite crescent" among many of the Sunni Arab states, and could well prompt them to take a range of precipitous and belligerent moves toward Iran that would be equally destabilizing for the region and deleterious to American interests.

The problem is that the United States has little ability to affect Iranian behavior directly. It is worth noting that Washington is struggling to find a way to convince Tehran to stop its nuclear program, even though the United States nominally has the support of all of the great powers and most of the rest of the world to do so. It is not that Iran is very powerful, it is that Iran is willing to endure great hardship to persist in its current policies and the United States and the rest of the world is reluctant to take the kind of steps that would be necessary to change Tehran's calculus. Americans, Europeans, and Arabs alike may all hope that UN or multilateral sanctions will cause the Iranian regime to change its mind, but few expect they will, at least not in the near term.

If that is the bad news about America's ability to influence Iranian activities, in the specific case of Iranian influence in Iraq, the United States has a critically important trump card it lacks on every other policy issue with Iran: Iraqi nationalism. As noted earlier, Iraqis generally do not like Persians and staunchly resist Iranian efforts to interfere in their affairs, let alone dominate Iraqi politics, security, and economics. As former U.S. ambassador to Iraq Ryan Crocker used to explain, Iraqi nationalism provides a "natural limit" on Iranian influence in Iraq. The problem right now is that Iraq is weak and divided (although much less so than a few years ago). The stronger and more unified Iraq becomes, the more that Iraqis—Sunni, Shi'a, and Kurd—will feel confident enough to push back on Iran. And the Iraqis can push back on Iranian activities in Iraq far better than the United States can, as witnessed by the stunning reversal of Iranian fortunes after the Iraqi moves against Basra and Sadr City in 2008. Thus, the best way to deal with Iranian meddling in Iraq is to continue to build up an Iraq strong enough to stand up to Iran, something that could be greatly aided by continuing Turkish and new Saudi assistance.

Protecting the Neighbors from Iraq

Forging a strong Iraq is a good answer to some of Iraq's problems and to some of the problems of Iraq's neighbors. Unfortunately, it could also be the cause of other problems for Iraq's neighbors, and those problems will also require the attention of the United States. Of course, it is unlikely that Iraq will grow into a strong state within the next five years, but it has the potential to do so at some point thereafter, and could certainly be a much *stronger* state by then. For these reasons, another element of American policy regarding the relationship between the United States, Iraq, and the Gulf region must be to establish conditions now that will mollify the risks inherent in the reemergence of a strong Iraq at a later point.

Even a strong Iraq will still have security concerns because Iraq lives in a dangerous neighborhood. Indeed, the Iraqi military leadership and elements of its political leadership are already looking beyond the lingering vestiges of the insurgency and the last embers of the civil war to think once again about Iraq's external security considerations. The trick will be finding ways for a strong Iraq to address its security concerns in such a way that does not threaten its neighbors.

Inevitably, Iran looms large in this strand of Iraqi thinking. The Iran-Iraq War was a ghastly conflict and one of the worst experiences that many living Iraqis had to live through (exceeded for some only by the horrors of the civil war of 2005–8). Its memory remains fresh, and the fear that a weak Iraq will be an enticing target for a malevolent Iran is widespread even among Shiite Iraqis. Moreover, many of Iraq's generals want to return to what they see as their glory days, when the Iraqi military reached its pinnacle, at the end of the Iran-Iraq War, when the Iraqi Army smashed Iran's ground forces and forced Tehran to make peace. Not surprisingly, Iraqi generals speak openly and regularly about their desire to rebuild something like that military, with thirty or more ground divisions and hundreds of combat aircraft, able to defeat any Iranian aggression—and even coerce Tehran if the need ever arose.

Since 2009, Iraqi generals have also begun privately to voice their concerns about the Iranian nuclear program. Because of Iraq's weakness so far and the extent of Iranian influence in the country, this topic has largely been off-limits, but as Iraqi self-confidence has grown, so too has their willingness to discuss it. Not surprisingly, Iraqis are extremely discomfited by the idea of living next door to a nuclear-armed Tehran. They know that they will never be allowed to match this capability, and know that they must find some other way to deal with it.

Unfortunately, as the world learned in 1990, any Iraq strong enough to balance against Iran is also plenty strong enough to overrun Kuwait and northern Saudi Arabia—if not more. Consequently, a critical challenge for the United States over the next five years will be to help Iraq continue to strengthen and grow, putting in place mechanisms that will allow Iraq to defend itself against legitimate threats while also simultaneously limiting its ability to act aggressively. This will be no small feat and a crucial requirement of stabilizing the Gulf region over the long term. An Iraq that is capable of balancing Iran (and Syria) *without* threatening its neighbors would do wonders for the region and the world.

There are at least three broad strategies the United States should pursue to try to accomplish this goal: we should try to cement the strong defense relationship between Washington and Baghdad, maintain a U.S. military presence in Iraq, and develop a new regional security architecture.

Sustaining the U.S.-Iraqi Defense Relationship

The more that the United States remains Iraq's paramount military partner, the stronger the Iraqi Armed Forces will be and the less likely (or even able) they will be to threaten neighboring states. The modern military history of the Arab states makes crystal clear that Arab allies of the United States become completely dependent on the United States and lose the capacity to project power without American support (and therefore approval).[8] Today, Jordan, Egypt, and all of the GCC states coordinate military operations with the United States. They rarely try to project power beyond their borders because they are effectively unable to do so without American support—a situation deepened by their tendency to buy weapons platforms at the expense of logistics and other support functions.

Egypt is perhaps the best example of this phenomenon. Since realigning itself with the United States in the late 1970s and reequipping its armed forces with American weaponry, Egypt went from a country able to support 70,000 troops in combat in distant Yemen during 1962–67, to one that could

---

8. On this see Kenneth M. Pollack, *Arabs at War: Military Effectiveness, 1948–1991* (Lincoln: University of Nebraska Press, 2002).

not move or sustain 40,000 troops in Saudi Arabia in 1990–91. During the Persian Gulf War, the United States had to provide all of the transport and all of the logistical support for the two Egyptian divisions that deployed for Operations Desert Shield and Desert Storm. The Egyptian attack during Desert Storm was a virtual spoof of Egypt's remarkable assault across Suez in 1973. It was heavily dependent on U.S. logistics, command and control, and intelligence support, and made virtually no progress despite the collapse of the Iraqi Army at the outset of the coalition offensive. Moreover, in 1995, Egypt attempted to mount air strikes against Khartoum in retaliation for the failed assassination attempt on Hosni Mubarak in Addis Ababa, which Cairo blamed on Sudan and Iran. No such air strikes ever took place because the Egyptian Air Force was incapable of mounting the operation without extensive U.S. logistical support, which Washington declined to provide. Even before Egypt had rearmed its military with American equipment, Anwar Sadat launched an invasion of Libya meant to end Muammar Qadhafi's regime in 1977, only to cancel it at American insistence.[9]

Such dependence was certainly not the experience of Arab states that relied on the Soviet Union for their military support. Soviet weaponry was often less capable than American equipment, but the Soviets were glad to provide their Arab clients with whatever they needed to go on the warpath—as Syria, Egypt, Libya, and Iraq did on numerous occasions in the 1960s, 1970s, and 1980s. Iran is not an Arab state, but during the Iran-Iraq War it increasingly relied on Chinese military hardware and its relationship with Beijing proved no impediment to its willingness and ability to mount invasion after invasion of Iraq. (The Chinese also sold quite a bit of hardware to the Iraqis during the same war.) The evidence is less definitive with the European countries—the British-backed Arab Legion did reasonably well in Palestine in 1948, but since then European countries have not been the dominant supplier of any Arab countries.

Thus, there is tremendous evidence that a strong defense relationship (including large-scale arms sales and an emphasis on weapons platforms over logistical support) with the United States has limited, if not eliminated, the ability of even the most powerful Arab states to project power without Washington's consent. The evidence with other countries—including the two most likely alternatives in China and Russia—demonstrates the opposite.

For this reason, the United States should welcome Iraq's desire to develop a long-term military-to-military relationship with it and to buy masses of American weaponry (while eschewing logistics capabilities). Iraq's generals would like to return to the glory days of 1988–90, but one

---

9. Pollack, *Arabs at War*, 131–147.

thing that they do not want to recreate if they can avoid it is their reliance on Soviet military hardware. Iraqis have long recognized that Western (particularly American) weaponry is superior to that of all else, and they have always coveted it. Since the fall of Saddam and their intimate exposure to the U.S. military, that desire has only grown. Today, Iraqi generals make clear that they want American weaponry: they know it is the best in the world, and they want the best in the world. There is *zero* perception on the part of Iraqi generals and their political counterparts that the United States is forcing them to buy American as payback for America's efforts to rebuild the country. The Iraqis *want* American equipment. However, they are quick to point out that if the United States won't sell them what they want, they will go elsewhere, and with their oil money, they will find Russian, Chinese, European, or other sellers if they can't buy American.

Interestingly, the GCC perspective on handling the military threat from a strong, stable Iraq is identical. GCC officials unanimously aver that they want to see a close military-to-military relationship continue between the United States and Iraq, coupled with large-scale arms sales. More than anyone else, the GCC states recognize that a military's reliance on American arms and American training and assistance makes that military *dependent* on the United States for logistical support, intelligence, command and control, and a variety of other requirements. GCC officials say quite openly, albeit only in private, that an extensive Iraqi-American arms and security relationship is the best insurance they can get that Iraq will never threaten their countries with its conventional might again.

Continuing a U.S. Military Presence

Building the kind of strong defense relationship between the United States and Iraq envisioned by both sides is going to require a lot of Americans in Iraq. It is only possible with the kind of significant American military presence that the United States has in the GCC and Egypt, and the kind it had in places like Iran before the fall of the Shah. There will need to be hundreds, if not thousands, of American trainers, technicians, and other support personnel. Moreover, given the state of the Iraqi military, they will doubtless need thousands more American advisers for some period of time.

Moreover, it would be highly desirable from the strategic perspective of Washington, Baghdad, Riyadh, and the other GCC capitals to maintain American combat forces of some kind in Iraq for some years to come. There are at least four very compelling reasons to do so. First, because Iraq is still at risk of sliding back into civil war, American combat forces are essential for peacekeeping and providing the last, best line of defense against such a calamity. Maintaining a residual combat capability in Iraq—even if it is merely a continuation of the currently envisioned 35,000 to 50,000-man residual force whose personnel nominally serve primarily as advisers and trainers—would preserve that vital firebreak. Second, Third World militaries that have been trained to perform counterinsurgency campaigns like Iraq's have a distressing tendency to overthrow their civilian governments except when foreign combat forces are present to prevent it.[10] Given Iraq's own long history of military coups, this is a very real threat. Third, because Iraq's security forces are still developing and remain focused on internal security, Baghdad feels itself vulnerable to military pressure from Tehran. Iran's move to seize an Iraqi oil well along their border in 2010 was a not-so-subtle Iranian reminder of this. Maintaining American combat forces in Iraq will reassure Baghdad that Iran cannot do much more than seize single oil wells lest they find themselves tussling with the American military. Last, it will greatly reassure the GCC states to retain U.S. combat forces in Iraq because as long as they remain, Iraqi aggression against America's regional allies is unthinkable.

All of this creates the need for a new status-of-forces agreement for American military personnel in Iraq when the current Security Agreeement runs out at the end of 2011. From a strategic perspective, this is a no-brainer. Both countries, and all of Iraq's neighbors (in some ways, even Iran), will be much better off with a continuation of the U.S.-Iraqi military relationship and the American military presence that is its manifestation. The problem is domestic politics in both countries. In Iraq, Iran and its Iraqi allies have successfully misled many Iraqis into believing that the Security Agreement—and any follow-on agreement—is a concession by Iraq to American overlordship, perpetuating a neocolonialist relationship. For that reason, many Iraqi politicians have avoided even discussing a follow-on agreement. The situation is little better in the United States, where many on the political Left react hysterically to any discussion of retaining troops in Iraq, as if doing so will somehow mean the perpetuation of the strategic situation of 2006, not 2012. So far, the Obama administration has been equally silent about the need for a follow-on agreement. Certainly a new document could be drafted quickly in theory, but the United States' experience with the 2008 Security Agreement, which took nearly a year, ought to make us err on the side of caution—a good rule to follow in Iraq on all things.

---

10. On this historical propensity, see Kenneth M. Pollack and Irena L. Sargsyan, "The Other Side of the COIN: The Perils of Premature Evacuation from Iraq," *Washington Quarterly* 33, no. 2 (April 2010): 17–32.

Forging a New Regional Security Architecture

Lord Ismay famously said of NATO that its purpose was to keep the Russians out, the Americans in, and the Germans down. The United States may need a new arrangement that does something similar in the Gulf: keeps the Iranians out, the Americans in, and the Iraqis down. Of course, in this instance, there will be some important differences. First, none of the neighbors wants a militarized containment system against Iran like that employed against the USSR. Second, in the case of NATO the fear was that America would leave after World War II and return to its wonted state of isolation. In the Gulf, the hurdle will be making an American military presence (even at much lesser levels than in Cold War Europe) palatable to local populations that tend to be decidedly anti-American. Finally, it will not be possible or desirable to limit Iraqi rearmament as NATO did with Germany, but a new security architecture could help channel Iraqi military development and reassure the Gulf states that they won't have to endure a repeat of 1990.

This is not the place for a full exposition of what a new security architecture for the Gulf region could or should entail.[11] However, because it could be an extremely important vehicle for the United States to secure its interests by routinizing and institutionalizing the strategic interactions of Iraq and its neighbors, it does deserve more than passing mention here.

The United States should work with Iraq and its GCC allies along two parallel tracks. The first would be a revised alliance system that would bring Iraq and the United States into a new multilateral security relationship with the GCC states, and possibly with Egypt and Jordan as well. The goal here would be to create some sort of security structure that would create standing military-to-military relationships including regular training and exercises, officer exchanges, joint planning, and command and control networking. Ideally, it would provide for mutual defense and even include provisions for the stationing of troops on one another's soil (albeit only at the request of the host nation). The intent of this would be to establish a more formal military arrangement (even a pseudo alliance) that included both Iraq and the United States, thereby helping to legitimate the U.S. military presence, grounding Iraq more formally in diplomatic and security ties with the GCC states, and bolstering the likelihood that a potential aggressor would not be able to divide and conquer.

---

11. See, instead, Joseph McMillan, "The United States and a Gulf Security Architecture: Policy Considerations," *Strategic Insights* 3, no. 3 (March 2004); Kenneth M. Pollack, "Securing the Gulf," *Foreign Affairs* 82, no. 4 (July–August 2003): 2–16; James A. Russell, "Searching for a Post-Saddam Regional Security Architecture," *Middle East Review of International Affairs* 7, no. 1 (March 2003).

The other would be a broader security organization for the region that would include not only Iraq, the United States, and the GCC, but also Iran and potentially the other four permanent members of the UN Security Council. The purpose of this grouping would be to try to find ways to decrease tensions and defuse crises in the region. The organization should probably begin with a regular forum in which all member states would send representatives to discuss various security issues—both immediate and long-standing. The hope would be that over time, these conversations could lead to confidence-building measures, followed by security agreements, and eventually arms control and reduction treaties. One possible analogy is to how the Organization for Security and Co-operation in Europe (OSCE) evolved in similar fashion during the last decades of the Cold War.

Since the early 1970s, when the United States first took over from Great Britain the responsibility of serving as the "Guardian of the Gulf," in Michael Palmer's phrase, Washington has tried a wide variety of methods to keep the region stable and secure. It has tried using regional proxies, balance of power, offshore balancing, onshore balancing, and finally invasion and occupation. None of them has worked very well. Each one led (or contributed) to long periods of painful commitment, typically followed by a catastrophe of one kind or another—the Iranian Revolution, the Iran-Iraq War, the Iraqi invasion of Kuwait, the American invasion of Iraq. As Iraq continues to emerge from civil war and begins to refocus on its external security and regional relationships (and while the entire region frets over the changes that will be wrought by Iran's likely achievement of a nuclear capability), the United States will have the opportunity to try a completely different approach to securing this vital region. As demonstrated in Europe and East Asia, cooperative security organizations backed by strong military alliances can produce peace and stability in parts of the world that have only known endemic warfare and revolution for centuries. It is never a quick or easy process, nor is it guaranteed to succeed, but there is no reason that such an effort cannot succeed in the Middle East, and every reason to try.

The Wider Aperture

In the Middle East, every silver cloud has a dark lining and every miracle brings with it a host of new problems from hell. So too may it be with Iraq. If somehow the United States gets its fondest wish and Iraq slowly transforms into a stable, strong, prosperous, and democratic state, it will bring a raft of new issues to be managed in its wake. Managing the security needs of such a new Iraq will be only part of the task.

A problem of potentially much greater and farther reaching impact will be managing the impact of a democratic Iraq on the rest of the region, as Hesham Sallam's chapter has suggested. Contrary to popular (and academic) mythology, the vast majority of Arabs want democracy, even if they may not always fully understand what it means. But in survey after survey, substantiated by anecdote after anecdote, and demonstrated further in what they ask from their governments, the Arabs have demanded more democracy in the form of greater representation, accountability, transparency, equality (including equality of the sexes), justice, and the rule of law.[12]

To the extent that Arabs resist democratization, they tend to rebuff the imposition of "made in the USA" brands of democracy. A great part of the problem they face is that many Arabs are wary of the democratic models they see because they feel "foreign." Democracy, of course, is a system of government that can be adapted to mesh with the culture, history, traditions, values, and collective aspirations of any society. But so far, the world has never seen a true Arab democracy, so those that the Arabs can look to as models—whether North American, Latin American, European, South Asian, East Asian, or even African—do not look or feel right to Arabs because they all have been shaped by the unique culture, history, traditions, values, and aspirations of *those* societies.[13]

If Iraq actually succeeds and emerges as a functional democracy, it will change all of that. For the first time, Arabs will be able to observe a democratic system adapted to Arab sensibilities, and that is likely to galvanize

12. See, for instance, Asad AbuKhalil, "A Viable Partnership: Islam, Democracy and the Arab World," *Harvard International Review* 15, no. 2 (Winter 1992/93): 22; John L. Esposito and Dalia Mogahed, *Who Speaks for Islam: What a Billion Muslims Really Think* (New York: Gallup Press, 2008), 31–32, 47–48, 57–58; Amaney A. Jamal, "Reassessing Support for Islam and Democracy in the Arab World? Evidence from Egypt and Jordan," *World Affairs* 169, no. 2 (Fall 2006): 51–64; Thomas Carothers and Marina Ottaway, "The New Democracy Imperative," in *Uncharted Journey: Promoting Democracy in the Middle East*, ed. Thomas Carothers and Marina Ottaway (Washington, DC: Carnegie Endowment for International Peace, 2005), 8; Abdou Filali-Ansary, "Muslims and Democracy," in *Islam and Democracy in the Middle East*, ed. Larry Diamond, Marc F. Plattner, and Daniel Brumberg (Baltimore, MD: Johns Hopkins University Press, 2003), 199–201; Ronald Inglehart, "How Solid Is Mass Support for Democracy: And How Can We Measure It?" *PS: Political Science and Politics* 36, no. 1 (January 2003), 52; Radwan A. Masmoudi, "The Silenced Majority," in *Islam and Democracy in the Middle East*, ed. Larry Diamond, Marc F. Plattner, and Daniel Brumberg (Baltimore, MD: Johns Hopkins University Press, 2003), 260–262; Dalia Mogahed, "Understanding Islamic Democracy," *Europe's World*, no. 2 (Spring 2006): 163–165; Pew Global Attitudes Project, "Support for Terror Wanes among Muslim Publics: 17-Nation Pew Global Attitudes Survey," Pew Research Center, July 14, 2005, 2; Kenneth M. Pollack, *A Path Out of the Desert: A Grand Strategy for America in the Middle East* (New York: Random House, 2008), esp. 239–245; Mark Tessler, "Public Opinion in the Arab and Muslim World: Informing U.S. Public Diplomacy," in *"In The Same Light as Slavery": Building a Global Antiterrorist Consensus*, ed. Joseph McMillan (Washington, DC: National Defense University Press, 2006), 15–16; United Nations Development Program, Arab Fund for Economic and Social Development, *Arab Human Development Report, 2003* (New York: United Nations Publications, 2003), esp. 151–157.
13. Pollack, *A Path Out of the Desert*, 224–237.

demands for greater democracy elsewhere in the Arab world in a way that nothing else has. The impact of Japan on East Asia is a useful historical antecedent. Before Japan democratized (as a result of American occupation and reconstruction), East Asians had never seen an Asian democracy and so democracy had great difficulty taking hold there. Indeed, many Westerners, including sympathetic Westerners, insisted that the Asian countries were culturally incapable of sustaining democracy and did not want democratic forms of government. This was always nonsense, and has since been proven as such as every country in East Asia except North Korea has moved in a democratic direction, some faster than others. None of this was possible until Japan democratized and then East Asians could see a democratic system shaped by culture, tradition, history, and values similar to their own. It was then that they began to imagine and desire a similar system for themselves. The result was the wave of East Asian democratization that began in the 1980s and has continued to this day.

Of course, it took roughly forty years for Japan to have this impact on East Asia. The pace of change has unquestionably accelerated, and perhaps a democratic Iraq would have its own impact much quicker, but it is still likely to be measured in decades, not years.

Nevertheless, such a transformation, when and if it comes, would still be profound and many countries and many of their elites will oppose it. Few of the Arab autocracies, even the most progressive, are ready for wholesale democratization. Few Arab autocrats are ready to play the role of Lee Kuan Yew or the Queen of England in fostering democracy and then stepping aside. Some, perhaps many, will resist ferociously and in so doing court civil and foreign war to try to hold power and retain their prerogatives.

This then will become a new challenge for the United States. Because of its power and role in the region, and because large-scale war—inter- or intrastate—is likely to be dangerous to its vital interests in the region, it will need to try to help manage this transformation.

To some extent, the need has already arisen because the clamor for democracy is already several decades old and all of the Arab states are responding, more or less, with some elements of reform. But many of the Middle East autocracies have found ways to resist these demands, while those that have acceded have often done so halfheartedly and far more incrementally than may be viable if Iraq is seen as a great success.[14] In that case, if Iraq does emerge as a functional democracy, kindling similar desires elsewhere in the region, all of these states will face much fiercer pressures to change,

---

14. Steven Heydemann, *Upgrading Authoritarianism in the Arab World*, Analysis Paper 13 (Washington, DC: Saban Center for Middle East Policy, Brookings Institution, October 2007).

possibly resulting in the kind of popular upheavals that shook East Asia and Southeast Asia in the 1980s and 1990s.

Because of America's interests in the stability of the Middle East and the promotion of democracy—as well as its experience in helping other states make similar transitions—it will doubtless find itself called upon to help manage this transition. Succeeding in that task will be as important as helping Iraq to reach stability in the first place. To circle back to the starting point of this essay, it is the region and its oil supplies that make Iraq so important to American interests. The upheaval unleashed on neighbors by a democratizing Iraq might be as tumultuous and potentially threatening to those interests as that of an Iraq in the throes of civil war.

It would be the ultimate irony if the United States saved its own interests by barely preventing Iraq from descending into a civil war resulting from America's utter unpreparedness to deal with the threat of civil war, only to find those same interests threatened by Iraq's ascent to democracy and America's utter unpreparedness to deal with that equally revolutionary development.

Index

Contributors

Editors

Henri J. Barkey is the Bernard L. and Bertha F. Cohen Professor of International Relations at Lehigh University and a visiting scholar at the Carnegie Endowment for International Peace. He served as a member of the U.S. State Department Policy Planning Staff in 1998–2000, working primarily on issues related to the Middle East, the Eastern Mediterranean, and intelligence from 1998 to 2000. He has taught at Princeton, Columbia, the State University of New York, and the University of Pennsylvania. His past books include *Turkey's Kurdish Question*, with Graham Fuller, *Reluctant Neighbor: Turkey's Role in the Middle East*, which he edited, and, most recently, *European Responses to Globalization: Resistance, Adaptation and Alternatives*, which he coedited with Janet Laible.

Scott B. Lasensky directed the United States Institute of Peace's "Iraq and Its Neighbors" initiative from 2004 to 2009. The project combined focused research and dialogue efforts in the region and involved participants from Iraq, the United States, and all of Iraq's neighbors. A senior program officer at the Institute's Center for Conflict Management, Lasensky was an adviser on Middle East policy to both the Gore-Lieberman and Obama-Biden presidential campaigns. He is the coauthor, with Daniel C. Kurtzer, of *Negotiating Arab-Israeli Peace: American Leadership in the Middle East* and the forthcoming *The Peace Puzzle: America's Quest for Arab-Israeli Peace*.

Phebe Marr has been a scholar and analyst of southwest Asia for more than forty years and is a leading U.S. specialist on Iraq. From 2004 to 2006 she was a senior fellow at the United States Institute of Peace, where she researched and published work on Iraq's post-2003 leadership, and in 1998–99 she was a senior scholar at the Woodrow Wilson Center for International Scholars, where she worked on recent Iraqi history. From 1985 to 1998, she was a senior fellow at the Institute for National Strategic Studies at the National Defense University, where she was responsible for long-range studies on U.S. security policy. Prior to 1985, she served as an associate professor of Middle East history at the University of Tennessee in Knoxville (1975–85) and California State University Stanislaus (1970–75). Dr. Marr has advised high-level U.S. officials, written op-ed pieces in national journals, and testified before the U.S. Senate on Iraq and Gulf affairs. An Arabist, she is the author of numerous books and journal articles. The third edition of her book, *The Modern History of Iraq*, was published by Westview Press in 2011.

Contributing Authors

Toby C. Jones is assistant professor of history at Rutgers University. His scholarship focuses primarily on the political history of the Persian Gulf. Jones has also taught at Swarthmore College and served as political analyst of the Persian Gulf at the International Crisis Group, where he wrote about political reform and sectarianism. Jones is author of *Desert Kingdom: How Oil and Water Forged Modern Saudi Arabia*. He is currently working on a new book project titled *America's Oil Wars*, to be published by Harvard University Press. His articles have appeared in the *International Journal of Middle East Studies*, *Middle East Report*, *Foreign Affairs*, and elsewhere.

Mohsen M. Milani is professor of politics and chair of the Department of Government and International Affairs at the University of South Florida in Tampa. He has written extensively about the Persian Gulf, the Iranian Revolution, and Iran's foreign and security policies. He served as a research fellow at Harvard University, Oxford University's St. Antony's College, and Foscari University in Venice, Italy. He is a frequent speaker at international and national conferences on Iran and the Persian Gulf.

Sam Parker is an Iraq adviser at the Office of the Secretary of Defense. In summer 2010, he served as an adviser to General Raymond Odierno in Baghdad. Prior to that, he was a program officer at the United States Institute of Peace, where he did research on Iraq in addition to assisting in the development of the Institute's peacebuilding programs on the ground in Iraq. He holds an MA in Arab Studies from Georgetown University.

Kenneth M. Pollack is the director of the Saban Center for Middle East Policy and a senior fellow at the Brookings Institution in Washington, D.C. One of America's leading experts on national security, military affairs, and the Persian Gulf, he served as director for Persian Gulf affairs at the National Security Council. Pollack also spent seven years in the CIA as a Persian Gulf military analyst. He is the author most recently of *A Path Out of the Desert: A Grand Strategy for America in the Middle East.*

Hesham Sallam is a doctoral candidate in government at Georgetown University and coeditor of *Jadaliyya* e-zine. He is a former program specialist at the United States Institute of Peace. His research, which has received the support of the Social Science Research Council and the United States Institute of Peace, focuses on Islamist movements and the politics of economic reform in the Arab World.

Mona Yacoubian is a senior program officer for the Middle East at the United States Institute of Peace, where she provides analysis and policy advice on the Middle East and North Africa. She currently directs the Institute's Lebanon Working Group and also contributes to the Institute's ongoing work on Syria. She has worked on a broad range of issues in the region, including democratization and civil society promotion, as well as counterterrorism strategy. Yacoubian has consulted for a number of organizations, including the World Bank, the U.S. Department of State, the RAND Corporation, and Freedom House. A member of the Council on Foreign Relations (CFR), she is a frequent commentator on leading U.S. and international news outlets. She was a Fulbright scholar in Syria and an international affairs fellow at CFR. Yacoubian earned a BA in public policy from Duke University and a master's degree in public administration from the Kennedy School of Government at Harvard University.

Judith S. Yaphe is Distinguished Research Fellow at the Institute for National Strategic Studies (INSS) at the National Defense University, Ft. McNair, Washington, D.C. She specializes in Iraq, Iran, and the strategic environment in the Persian Gulf region. Before joining INSS in 1995, she served for twenty years as a senior analyst on Near East Persian Gulf issues in the Office of Near Eastern and South Asian Analysis, Directorate of Intelligence, CIA. Among her accomplishments in government was her role as senior political analyst on Iraq and the Gulf, for which she received the Intelligence Medal of Commendation and other awards. She received a BA with honors in History from Moravian College, Bethlehem, Pennsylvania, and a PhD in Middle Eastern History from the University of Illinois, Champaign-Urbana. She served as an adviser to the Iraq Study Group headed by former secretary of state James Baker and the Hon. Lee Hamilton.

United States Institute of Peace Press

Since its inception, the United States Institute of Peace Press has published over 150 books on the prevention, management, and peaceful resolution of international conflicts—among them such venerable titles as Raymond Cohen's *Negotiating across Cultures*; John Paul Lederach's *Building Peace*; *Leashing the Dogs of War* by Chester A. Crocker, Fen Osler Hampson, and Pamela Aall; and *American Negotiating Behavior* by Richard H. Solomon and Nigel Quinney. All our books arise from research and fieldwork sponsored by the Institute's many programs. In keeping with the best traditions of scholarly publishing, each volume undergoes both thorough internal review and blind peer review by external subject experts to ensure that the research, scholarship, and conclusions are balanced, relevant, and sound. With the Institute's move to its new headquarters on the National Mall in Washington, D.C., the Press is committed to extending the reach of the Institute's work by continuing to publish significant and sustainable works for practitioners, scholars, diplomats, and students.

Valerie Norville
Director

About the United States Institute of Peace

The United States Institute of Peace is an independent, nonpartisan institution established and funded by Congress. The Institute provides analysis, training, and tools to help prevent, manage, and end violent international conflicts, promote stability, and professionalize the field of peacebuilding.

Chairman of the Board: J. Robinson West
Vice Chairman: George E. Moose
President: Richard H. Solomon
Executive Vice President: Tara Sonenshine
Chief Financial Officer: Michael Graham